ENCYCLOPEDIA OF SPORTS

Volume - 5

SPORTS JOURNALISM

ENCYCLOPEDIA OF SPORTS

Volume - 5

SPORTS JOURNALISM

Edited By:

Y.K.REDDY

SURESH PADMANAVIA

SRISHTI BOOK DISTRIBUTORS

NEW DELHI (INDIA)

ISBN - 81-89948-22-9 Vol-5
ISBN 978-81-89948-20-7 Set

Published by :
SRISHTI BOOK DISTRIBUTORS
4378/4-B-202, 2nd floor,
J.M.D. House, Ansari Road,
Daryaganj, New Delhi-110002
E-mail : srishtibookdistributors@yahoo.co.in
Ph. 011-23284904

***Edition* : 2009**

Rs.1000 (Each Volume)

Printed at
Suman Printers
Delhi-110093

Preface

Sports journalism is an essential element of any news media organization. It is a form of journalism that reports on sports topics and events. While the sports department within some newspapers has been mockingly called the toy department, because sports journalists do not concern themselves with the 'serious' topics covered by the news desk, sports coverage has grown in importance as sport has grown in wealth, power and influence.

Sports journalism includes organizations devoted entirely to sports reporting — newspapers such as L'Equipe in France, La Gazzetta dello Sport in Italy, Marca in Spain, and the now defunct Sporting Life in Britain, American magazines such as Sports Illustrated and the Sporting News, all-sports talk radio stations, and television networks like ESPN.

Sports journalists are like any other reporters, and they must find the story rather than simply relying on information given to them by the sports team, institution or coaching staff. Sports journalists must verify facts given to them by the teams and organizations they are covering. Often, coaches, players or sports organization management rescind sports journalists' access credentials in retaliation for printing accurate yet disparaging information about a team, player, coach or coaches, or organization.

Access for sports journalists is usually easier for professional and intercollegiate sports such as American football, ice hockey, basketball, baseball and football.

Sports stories often transcend the games themselves and take on socio-political significance; Jackie Robinson breaking the colour barrier in baseball is an example of this. Modern controversies regarding the compensation of top athletes, the use of anabolic steroids and other, banned performance-enhancing drugs, and the cost to local and national governments to build sports venues and related infrastructure, especially for the Olympic Games, show that sports still can intrude on to the news pages.

Sportswriters face much more deadline pressure than most other reporters, because sporting events tend to occur late in the day and closer to the deadlines many organizations must observe. Yet they are expected to use the same tools as news journalists, and to uphold the same professional and ethical standards. They must take care not to show bias for any team. Sports journalists usually must also gather and use voluminous performance statistics for teams and individual athletes in most sports.

Many of the most talented and respected print journalists have been sportswriters. Increasingly, sports journalists have turned to long-form writing, producing popular books on a range of sporting topics, including biographies, history and investigations.

It is in this context this present fresh approach on this powerful genre has been dealt with. In this book starting from the basic requirements of a sports journalist to different aspects of sports journalism are described with ease and comfort. The editors are hopeful the book will serve the basic need of the students, Journalists and researchers working in this field.

CONTENTS

CONTENTS

CHAPTER

1

Growth and Significance of Sports Journalism

Sports journalism is highly specialised and requires specialist knowledge, but the disciplines and practices employed by a sports journalist do not differ greatly from those of a standard journalist. It is hardly surprising that the route into working in sports journalism is the same as that of any other form of journalism: training takes place either on site (most usually on a local newspaper) or through a formal course.

Sports journalism is a form of journalism that reports on sports topics and events. While the sports department within some newspapers has been mockingly called the *toy department*, because sports journalists do not concern themselves with the 'serious' topics covered by the news desk, sports coverage has grown in importance as Sports has grown in wealth, power and influence.

Sports journalism is an essential element of any news media organization. It includes organizations devoted entirely to sports reporting — newspapers such as L'Equipe in France, La Gazzetta dello Sports in Italy and the now defunct Sporting Life in Britain, American magazines such as *Sports Illustrated* and the *Sporting News*, all-sports talk radio stations, and television networks like ESPN.

SPORTS JOURNALISTS' ACCESS

Sports teams are not always very accommodating to journalists: in the United States, while they allow reporters into locker rooms for interviews and some extra information, sports teams provide extensive information support, even if reporting it is unfavourable to them. Elsewhere in the world, particularly in the coverage of soccer, the journalist's role is often barely tolerated by the clubs and players. Sports journalists are like any other reporters, and they must find the story rather than simply relying on information given to them by the sports team, institution or coaching staff. Sports journalists must verify facts given to them by the teams and organizations they are covering.

Often, coaches, players or sports organization management rescind sports journalists' access credentials in retaliation for printing accurate yet disparaging information about a team, player, coach or coaches, or organization. Access for sports journalists is usually easier for professional and intercollegiate sports such as American football, ice hockey, basketball, baseball and football.

SOCIO-POLITICAL SIGNIFICANCE

Major League Baseball gave print journalists a special role in its games: They were named official scorers and kept statistics that were considered part of the official record of the league. Active sportswriters were removed from this role in 1980. Although their statistical judgment calls could not affect the outcome of a game, there was still the perception of a conflict of interest.

Sports stories often transcend the games themselves and take on socio-political significance; Jackie Robinson breaking the colour barrier in baseball is an example of this. Modern controversies regarding the compensation of top athletes, the use of anabolic steroids and other, banned performance-enhancing drugs, and the cost to local and national governments to build sports venues and related infrastructure, especially for the Olympic Games, show that sports still can intrude on to the news pages.

Sportswriters face much more deadline pressure than most other reporters, because sporting events tend to occur late in the day and closer to the deadlines many organizations must observe. Yet they are expected to use the same tools as news journalists, and to uphold the same professional and ethical standards. They must take care not to show bias for any team. Sports journalists usually must also gather and use voluminous performance statistics for teams and individual athletes in most sports. Many of the most talented and respected print journalists have been sportswriters.

THE GROWTH OF SPORTS JOURNALISM

The tradition of sports reporting attracting some of the finest writers in journalism can be traced to the coverage of Sports in Victorian England, where several modern sports - such as association football, cricket, athletics and rugby - were first organized and codified into something resembling what we would recognize today. Cricket, somewhat like baseball in the United States, possibly because of its esteemed place in society, has regularly attracted the most elegant of writers. The *Manchester Guardian*, in the first half of the 20th Century, employed Neville Cardus as its cricket correspondent as well as its music critic. Cardus was later knighted for his services to journalism. One of his successors, John Arlott, who became a worldwide favourite because of his radio commentaries on the BBC, and was also known for his poetry.

The first London Olympic Games in 1908 attracted such widespread public interest that many newspapers assigned their very best-known writers to the event. The *Daily Mail* even had Sir Arthur Conan Doyle at the White City Stadium to cover the finish of the first ever 26-mile, 385-yard Marathon. Such was the drama of that race, in which Dorando Pietri collapsed within sight of the finishing line when leading, that Conan Doyle led a public subscription campaign to see the gallant Italian, having been denied the gold medal through his disqualification, awarded a special silver cup, which was presented by Queen Alexandra. And the public imagination was so well caught by the event that annual races in Boston, Ma, and London, and at future Olympics, were henceforward staged over exactly the same, 26-mile, 385-yard distance, the official length of the event worldwide to this day.

The London race, called the Polytechnic Marathon and originally staged over the 1908 Olympic route from outside the royal residence at Windsor Castle to White City, was first sponsored by the *Sporting Life,* which in those Edwardian times was a daily newspaper which sought to cover all sporting events, rather than just a betting paper for horse racing and greyhounds that it became in the years after the Second World War.

In France, *L'Auto*, the predecessor of *L'Equipe,* had already played an equally influential part in the sporting fabric of society when it announced in 1903 that it would stage an annual bicycle race around the country. The Tour de France was born, and sports journalism's role in its foundation is still reflected today in the leading rider wearing a yellow jersey - the colour of the paper on which L'Auto was published (in Italy, the Giro d'Italia established a similar tradition, with the leading rider wearing a jersey the same pink colour as the sponsoring newspaper, La Gazzetta).

SPORTS STARS IN THE PRESS BOX

After the Second World War, the sports sections of British national daily and Sunday newspapers continued to expand, to the point where many papers now have separate standalone sports sections; some Sunday tabloids even have sections, additional to the sports pages, devoted solely to the previous day's football reports. In some respects, this has replaced the earlier practice of many regional newspapers which - until overtaken by the pace of modern electronic media - would produce special results editions rushed out on Saturday evenings. Some newspapers, such as the, The Sunday Times, with 1924 Olympic 100 m champion Harold Abrahams, or the London Evening News using former England cricket captain Sir Leonard Hutton, began to adopt the policy of hiring former sports stars to pen columns, which were often ghost written. Some such ghosted columns, however, did little to further the reputation of sports journalism, which is increasingly becoming the subject of academic scrutiny of its standards.

But sportswriting in Britain has continued to attract some of the finest journalistic talents. The *Daily Mirror*'s Peter Wilson, Hugh McIlvanney, first at *The Observer* and lately at the *Sunday Times*, Ian Wooldridge of the *Daily Mail* and soccer writer Brian Glanville, best known at the *Sunday Times*, became household names in the late 20th Century through their trenchant reporting of often earth-shattering events that have transcended the back pages and been reported on the front pages: the Massacre at the Munich Olympics in 1972; Muhammad Ali's fight career, including his 1974 title bout against George Foreman; the Heysel Stadium disaster; and the career highs and lows of the likes of George Best and Lester Piggott and other high profile stars.

Specialist Sports Agencies

The 1950s and 1960s saw a rapid growth in sports coverage, both in print and on broadcast media. It also saw the development of specialist sports news and photographic agencies. For example, photographer Tony Duffy founded the picture agency AllSport in south London shortly after the 1964 Tokyo Olympics, and, through some outstanding photography (such as Duffy's iconic image of the American long jumper Bob Beamon flying through the air towards his world record at the 1968 Mexico City Olympics) and the astute marketing of its images, saw the business grow into a multi-million pound, worldwide concern that ultimately would be bought and re-named Getty Images.

McIlvanney and Wooldridge, who died in March 2007, aged 75, both enjoyed careers that saw them frequently work in television. During his career, Wooldridge became so famous that, like the sports stars he reported upon, he hired the services of IMG, the agency founded by the American businessman, Mark McCormack, to manage his affairs. And Glanville wrote several books, including novels, as well as scripting the memorable official film to the 1966 World Cup staged in England.

Sports Books

Increasingly, sports journalists have turned to long-form writing, producing popular books on a range of sporting topics, including biographies, history and investigations. In London, through the 1980s and 1990s, one shop on Charing Cross Road - the area known for its book shops - was entirely devoted to Sports, although the growth of online book sales through websites such as Amazon eventually led to the closure of Sports Books. This was not before, though, the establishment, through sponsorship from William Hill, the bookmakers, of an annual prize for the sports book of the year. This was first held in 1989, when Dan Topolski's book about one of the most controversial University Boat Races was declared the winner.

The status of the awards, and of sports books generally, were enhanced greatly in 1992 when Nick Hornby's first novel, *Fever Pitch*, took first prize. Both *Fever Pitch* and *True*

Blue have subsequently been adapted into feature-length motion pictures. Only one author, Donald McRae, in 1996 and 2002, has won the William Hill award more than once.

Unsurprisingly, given cricket writers' often literary aspirations and the appetite for books on cricket, the summer game has four times been the subject of the prize-winning book, the same number as football. The award has not been without controversy in recent years. In 2000, the award went for the first time to a "ghosted" book, Lance Armstrong's *It's Not About the Bike*. At the time, some also observed the irony of the award going to the American Tour de France winner, when, in 1990, Paul Kimmage's stern critique of doping in cycling, *Rough Ride*, had been declared the winner.

The judges - the same panel is used each year - were also criticised in 2006 when they chose Geoffrey Ward's *Unforgivable Blackness*, because it had been first published in 2004. The 2007 winner of the award, announced at a ceremony staged at Waterstones, Piccadilly, on November 27, was *Provided You Don't Kiss Me*, the account of local newspaper reporter Duncan Hamilton working with the controversial Nottingham Forest manager, Brian Clough.

INVESTIGATIVE JOURNALISM AND SPORTS

Since the 1990s, the growing importance of Sports, its impact as a global business and the huge amounts of money involved from sponsorship and in the staging of the Olympic Games and football World Cups, has also attracted the attention of well-known investigative journalists. The sensitive nature of the relationships between sports journalists and the subjects of their reporting, as well as declining budgets experienced by most Fleet Street newspapers, has meant that such long-term projects have often emanated from television documentary makers.

Tom Bower, with his 2003 sports book of the year *Broken Dreams*, which analyzed British football, followed in the tradition established a decade earlier by Andrew Jennings and Vyv Simson with their controversial investigation of corruption within the International Olympic Committee. Jennings and Simson's *The Lords of the Rings* in many ways predicted the scandals that were to emerge around the staging of the 2002 Winter Olympics in Salt Lake City; Jennings would follow-up with two further books on the Olympics and one on FIFA, the world football body.

Likewise, award-winning writers Duncan Mackay, of *The Guardian*, and Steven Downes unravelled many scandals involving doping, fixed races and bribery in international athletics in their 1996 book, *Running Scared*, which offered an account of the threats by a senior track official that led to the suicide of their sports journalist colleague,.Cliff Temple.

But the writing of such exposes - referred to as "spitting in the soup" by Paul Kimmage, the former Tour de France professional cyclist, who now writes for the *Sunday Times* - often requires the view of an outsider who is not compromised by the need of day-to-day dealings with sportsmen and officials, as required by "beat" correspondents. The stakes can be high when upsetting sport's powers: when in 2007, the English FA opted to switch its multi-million pound contract for UK coverage rights of the FA Cup and England international matches from the BBC to rival broadcasters ITV, one of the reasons cited was that the BBC had been too critical of the performances of the England football team.

SPORTS JOURNALISM ORGANIZATIONS

Most countries have their own national association of sports journalists. Many sports also have their own clubs and associations for specialist journalists. These organizations tend not to operate as trades unions, but do attempt to maintain the standard of press provision at sports venues, oversee fair accreditation procedures and to celebrate high standards of sports journalism.

The International Sports Press Association, AIPS, was founded in 1924 during the Olympic Games in Paris, at the headquarters of the Sporting Club de France, by Frantz Reichel, the press chief of the Paris Games, and the Belgian, Victor Boin.

The first statutes of AIPS mentioned these objectives:

- To enhance the cooperation between its member associations in defending Sports and the professional interest of their members.
- To strengthen the friendship, solidarity and common interests between sports journalists of all countries.
- To assure the best possible working conditions for the members.

AIPS operates through a system of continental sub-associations and national associations, and liaises closely with some of the world's biggest sports federations, including the International Olympic Committee, FIFA, football's world governing body and the IAAF, the international track and field body. In Britain, the Sports Journalists' Association stages two prestigious awards events, an annual Sports Awards ceremony which recognises outstanding performances by British sportsmen and women during the previous year, and the British Sports Journalism Awards, the industry's "Oscars", sponsored by UK Sports and presented each March.

Founded as the Sports Writers' Association in 1948, following a merger with the Professional Sports Photographers' Association the organization changed its title to the more inclusive SJA in 2002. Its President is the veteran broadcaster and columnist, Sir Michael Parkinson. The SJA represents the British sports media on the British Olympic Association's press advisory committee and acts as a consultant to organizers of major events who need guidance on media requirements as well as seeking to represent its members' interests in a range of activities.

In March 2008, Martin Samuel, chief football correspondent of *The Times*, was named British Sportswriter of the Year, the first time any journalist had managed to win the award three years in succession.

THE INDIAN SCENE

The role of Mass Media is central to the popularization of Sports amongst the people at large. The Electronic Media, including the National Broadcasters, the Private Channels and the Print Media would be suitable mobilized for strengthening a Sports Culture in the country. As a resurgent India confidently enters the New Millenium, Sports (and related activities) will be increasingly utilized as a medium for promoting cooperation and friendship in the Region, as also globally. Sports Exchange Programmes will be pursued with all friendly Nations, with emphasis, on the one hand on Advance Training for Sports persons and Coaches, Scientific Support, the latest Research Aids and Development of Infrastructure, and earning laurels for the country, in Sports and Games, on the other.

The National Sports Policy, 2001 would be reviewed, periodically, in order, inter-alia, to incorporate changes/ modifications which may be necessitated by technological and other advancements in the field of Sports.

CHAPTER

2

Creating Feature Stories and Sports Television Journalism

Here we will be discussing how to create feature stories with video. Your role is that of a journalist, and your job is to write a story for the event. The story you write will make the footage come alive for the viewer. The story will be the emphasis, which may help your team or a specific player become great. You may be having your own cameraperson and/or you may be using the footage from the game camera. You as a reporter should remember this about your game-camera or sideline videographer.

Their job is to capture the action, and during the game the framing of the shots and keeping up with the action will be what they are thinking about. Oftentimes they will not be able to tell you what the game was actually like. Shooting the game is a specialized and difficult process, it is telling the story visually, and this person is continuously working and keeping a good picture for the entire event. They only see through the viewfinder, and miss much of the story, Do not rely on them to write your story - rather your story and their visual story is one which you will work together on in editing and create your feature.

However if you are going to create feature stories about sports you will have to know how to put together a good story. There is not much of a leap from a print story to a video story. But to make that leap you are going to have to learn to write. You have the regular Television News story that is 30 seconds or less and you have a feature story, which may be any length. We will discuss the longer feature here rather than the short clip. While you are in the reporter mode try and forget that you are making a video feature, pretend that your words alone will have to tell the entire story. In this way the addition of the video will make your story stand out.

You are used to going to the games and talking about them afterwards, you can expand your short versions to a real story. We are going to put together a plan here.

Introduce yourself, as a reporter you need to identify your self to everyone you will need to speak with. Have a nice card printed, (with the computer available you can print your own card) preferably one that has your picture on it. Few people have their photo on a card, this alone will help you stand out in the mind of the people you will be working with. Introductions are important for the remainder of the season, the first introduction will be the one remembered so make the best impression you can - even dress up and wear a tie for a change – *Laughing*.

1. Going to the game is the first thing, your job starts well before the game because there is a lot of information you need to have. Before the game is time you will have to get it. You will need the rosters for both teams and the statistics for both teams. You want the coach's names. You want the schedules.

   The statistics are important but they are not the entire

story, you use them to make the story more interesting. Do not rely on statistics to write the story for you.

Get all the newspapers the next day and clip (cut out) the stories that were written, add these to the information which you gather during the game. Reading these stories will often add to the story which you write. If you do use any of this material - give the reporter and the paper credit - the last thing you want is to make an enemy of a fellow reporter or the paper they work for. Other reporters are excellent sources of information and a comradrary and friend ship exists between all of the reporters and photographers of the different media.

Be free with what you know and share, help the other members of the working press as much as possible. This is really the spirit of reporting. A simple thing is to have a multiple power connector to plug in your electronics, and share the extra plugs with other reporters. Duplicate mikes, headsets, and other cords are good for you but will allow you to be a good person to know at the games, pencils, papers, scotch-tape and duct-tape, extra copies of the rosters and the statistics are good to have to share.

2. Get all of the background interviews before the game, after the game you will get the reactions to the outcome. If you are doing an unbiased version you will have interviews from both teams, if your doing a piece for your team and being supportive you will only interview your players.
3. You don't get to just watch the game - you have to keep the statistics and write the story as you go, make notes and be creative.
4. After the game you get your final interviews with the heroes and coaches, or any other special interest story you are working on.

5. Now the real work takes place you have to set down and write your story. Write as much as you possibly can, the big stores and the little ones. You have your heroes but you have the other heroes who seldom get recognized - the player's assists are what make heroes. The way the team works together is what results in a winning team. Your viewpoint will be special and the more comprehensive and complete you are the better the story. Your stories can help make a team and can definitely make a player.
6. Think you're done - nope - now go back and re-read it and revise it. Clean it up
7. Done yet - nope - now read the story OUTLOUD - with PACEING AND EMOTION - how does it sound - is the sentence structure clear - now you need to go back and make it HEARABLE AND UNDERSTANDABLE for the viewers.
8. The final step is the voice over itself - and - as you read it for the recording you will undoubtedly want to change a word or two - but try to keep this to a minimum, writing the story over as you record it will take you forever and you really don't have that much time.
9. You will have a mix of audio for the final programme: (a) natural sound from the game; (b) the interviews; (c) your commentary; (d) music and or sound effects. A feature programme is not simply the reading of your story it is the compilation of all the parts of the documentation process.

THE BEGINNING OF YOUR VIDEO SCRIPT

We are not finished with the discussion of writing yet. How we will expand your story into a video programme will come later. You story is going to be viewed well after the event is over, and this can be a real plus for you. You have reported the story and you have the writing and the revision done, now you can go back once more and get the inside story. Expand the story into a timeless piece.

The coverage of the team will be a long-term project and over the course of the season you are going to gather many unrelated facts and stores, a good notebook or system of files is going to be indispensable for you now. As you write the story your research and will come together and you can tie things which you did not believe you would use into an interesting and complete story.

Now back to the beginning again, before the event. You need to know the rules, if you are going to understand the calls of the referees. And if you know the rules you can comment on the game in a more complete manner. A knowledge of the rules of a game and the knowledge of the game itself is not static - the game changes - the rules change - the style of playing changes. You as a sports writer/ videographer will need to know and keep up with the Sports, and not just one Sports but all of the ones you cover.

There are a number of people that you need to know, the principal, and the athletic director, all of the coaches, players, managers, and business manager. All of these people are sources of information for you, and you will need to speak with them all at one time or the other.

Quotes - get used to making the quotes in context, and are absolutely accurate. The video camera is going to be indispensable for you here, because you don't have to transcribe the words. Your questions will determine how freely the person talks, you will want to spend a few minutes with each person you interview and discuss what you are going to ask them, so they can get the topics in their mind. If you have prepared before the game you can have the questions written out and give the list to them before the game, when you ask them if you may come to them after the game for the interview.

Example

In editing you will cut some of the comments, and cover them with action or still shots. Don't hurry the person you are interviewing - and don't cut them short so you can get to the next question. Sometimes the person will ramble and take a while to get to the point, its alright. You will be able to have more material to edit (choose from). Hopefully the interview will be so smooth that you will be able to use all of it.

Player Interviews: You will want to make these interviews - and get the responses and feelings of the player - their history - Practice sessions and after the game -are the best times - If you are going to do pre-game interviews do them well before the game starts, a couple of hours if possible.

Team Group Shots: Is there a sports expert - (student) (parent) (fan) who you can interview?

INFORMATION DURING THE GAME

You will need to learn to organize your self and have the method for saving all of your information. Things you will need:

1. A clipboard and plenty of paper. If you are doing play by play have two clip boards (or a stiff cardboard which you can have two papers side by side) and tape so you can secure the rosters.
2. Blank the statistics sheets
3. Extra pencils and a small sharpener
4. A steno pad
5. A couple of large zip lock plastic bags to store materials, you can use these to put notes into as you compete sections - the programme - and other materials which you will gather. We recommend large zip-lock bags because they are waterproof - and can be the file folder for the information later on - these bags will keep the pages from becoming scattered.

A waterproof marker will be handy to write on the outside of the bag for later identification. Conference games - may have the managers print the statistics and distribute them to the reporters at half-time and following the game - be sure to pick up these copies. The school paper is a good source of information - if one is available put one of them in the bag also.

You don't have to set in the press box that little table may end up being more of a problem than an asset. Place yourself where you have another point of view, such as behind the players bench, or in the crowd. You will see and hear the game differently from another point. The attitude of the crowd and what they say may give you a better story. If your are behind the scorers table you will be able to follow the discussions, which always happen during a game. These are little vignettes, which can be good for your story.

If you are doubling as a cameraperson, while writing these stories you will not be shooting continuously. Instead you will only shoot when some particular event occurs. Also if you are responsible for the interviews after the game - your nearness to the court will place you in a position to reach the Players - Coaches - or Officials faster. After the game there is always a press of people trying to speak with all of them. Being there first will give you the best chance of having your questions answered. In this situation the camera will be hand held or preferably on a monopod - Stable shots are important.

The reporter & photographer team — this is the best way to get the interviews. Now from the start remember you are a team - and you help each other - setting up and carrying equipment - contacting people and gathering information. If you observe the professional television news teams, you will see this is not the case, rather the reporter (on camera personality) will more likely have an elitist attitude. If you are the Reporter don't start you career as a prima-donna, you will make your photographer hate you, and the other media personnel will laugh at you. Again we are stressing the importance of the team attitude, you may be the star but you won't be for long unless you strive to be helpful and share the workload.

Using the camera as both a way of recording the action and reporting the game makes an interesting technique. You can shoot the action and following or during the shot make a comment on the tape. Your on camera mike will pick up your voice well - if the game is loud - speak up - a little experimentation will give you the knowledge of how loud you need to be. You can have a headset mike plugged into the camera for this purpose.

You have four options when recording into the camera:

1. The on camera microphone
2. A hard-wired mike - Be sure to have a good insulated cable to connect between the mike and the camera. (here you have the option of a hand held mike or a lavaliere (clip-on) mike
3. A wireless (hand held or clip on) mike and receiver
4. The facility may have an audio breakout box

Each one of these options will require you to have a different technique when you shoot, and interview.

1. You will need to be close to the subject and have your camera zoomed out wide;
2. Being hardwired, you can be further away - the mike may be placed on a podium or clipped on the subject.
3. Wireless - you are going to be subject to many variables, it is a good thing to have a receiver which you can tune to the house frequency- your own mike frequency may be interfered with by - cell phones - short wave - CB- am/fm radio - television station - other wireless mikes- transformers - electrical cabling - microwave transmitters - or the battery may just die - The wireless mikes are the most subject to problems of all - be ready to change to another system.

4. The Breakout box, is a box, which the house will provide to the video crews, to keep the podiums from being filled with microphones, and the floor covered with cabling. These boxes have XLR connections and you may have a MINI PLUG on your camera. Be ready to adapt. Have a long XLR cable for this connection. An adapter to go from XLR to MINI.

The choice of HAND-HOLDING - MONO-POD - TRIPOD holding of the camera will depend on the circumstances. If you are using a new lightweight camera you need some kind of support, or the camera will be shaking all over the place. You can use your tripod as a monopod by extending just one leg, have the head loose and support and direct it with both hands. A monopod is better than shoulder holding the camera but not as good as using the tripod for stability.

Refer to the page on field and look at the list of possible shots which your photographer will be finding from the sideline positions. These shots are all elements of your story, and you need to be aware of what is going on every where as a reporter - not just the action on the field. We have gotten all the way to here, and have not talked about the editing of the video. The question now, do you have to fit into a time frame or can this feature be of any length. It will be best to work in 10 min, 15-min -30-min - one hour time frames. Now depending on the nature of the story and the material you have available you will pick one of those time frames. We are not locking the time in stone its just a guide line.

The times you will add up to determine the programme length will be:

1. Your Story as a voice over, covered with video
2. Your interviews - a mix of subject and illustrative video
3. The Cutaways with crowd sideline comments
4. Game footage - with or without play by play - and or natural sound

5. The time for the title and introduction
6. The time for the close and the credits.

Your story is going to determine how the video footage is used, and so you will record your story piece by piece - remember - the phrases, sentences and paragraphs will have footage to illustrate both covering the speaker and \ between the speeches.

List all of the shots/scenes in categories, shots for the-open - interviews - game camera footage - floor camera game footage - cutaways - close footage. In vision - your video starts with an open - a set of scenes and title screens, you will have either music or natural sounds over this section. How do you introduce the video, your choice - a voice over or shot of the narrator from your introduction you assemble your programme with all of the narrative sections, you will go back and insert video to cover the black. If you have your voice over sections with a black screen as the video or the narrator as a talking head. It will be clear where your inserts belong. The inserting of the footage is a creative process, and you will probably make changes as you insert edit. Commonly you will shorten up the existing cutaways and add more shots, to pick up the pacing of the programme. As you look at the project, most likely you will have a stack of tapes and a lot of sheets of paper.

Your Editing script will have the tape number and the time code or control track number listed. Remember to log the tape well - have the tape clearly labelled and the accompanying log labelled and keep them close. If there is time-code on your tape finding a specific clip will be much easier, because they are always present. If you are relying on control track numbers the tape will have to be rewound each time and the counter zeroed for you to find the clip. The digital format has the time code numbers - usually the VHS, SVHS, 8mm, and Hi8, do not have them.

After you have edited a few programmes you will develop your own system and style. However you list and mark your tapes and information makes it consistent and clear. You will find yourself making last minute changes, correcting and improving the programme. In spite of your best effort to be accurate, you will find many times the information you were given is wrong, or has changed, you will want to correct all of the mistakes, and if you cannot find the clips you need you will have to spend a lot of extra time.

Sports News is going to focus on sports journalism for several issues. There are fewer available jobs in sports journalism than in management or retailing, but the topic should still be of interest to anyone who has wondered how people become sports reporters or commentators. Rather than lump all journalism jobs together, we are going to take a look at the different media (print, radio, television) separately. All sports journalism jobs require the ability to communicate to an audience, but often the different media require different skills and training. We will start with television jobs since those usually attract the most attention.

CAREERS IN TELEVISION

Television jobs fall into three basic categories: on-camera, off-camera, and technical. Of the three, on-camera work is the area most athletes think about getting into. It's the glamorous side of the business (e.g.,reporter, analyst, commentator, talk-show host). Off-camera work involves all the behind-the-scenes activities that are necessary to get a show on the air (e.g., writing, researching, producing). Technical jobs have more to do with running the equipment (e.g., camera operator, lighting director, audio technician).

There are so many different job options within the television industry that to cover them all in detail is beyond the scope of this newsletter. It would take a book to explain who does what to create a nightly news show or a televised sporting event. However, since there are often misconceptions concerning the hiring of television personnel, we will discuss some factors (including sports experience, sports knowledge, educational background, and on-the-job training), which play a role in landing a job in sports television journalism.

There are two primary routes to sports television jobs today: a high-visibility sports background and/or formal communications training. There are, of course, people who break into television sports journalism without either, but they are the exception.

Does being an Athlete help you get a Job in Television?

Being an athlete, especially a famous athlete, will open some doors. But if you don't have the right skills, you won't get very far. Many athletes naively think that when they finish competing, well-paying jobs in television will be waiting for them. But the industry doesn't work like that. Only a few athletes are ever offered the chance to work in television and even fewer of them will last in the business very long. A small number of athletes and coaches are naturally gifted communicators and can easily move into broadcasting jobs. But most are awkward at the beginning and will have to polish their television skills if they want to do more than occasional guest appearances. Television sports directors are open to using former athletes and coaches in hopes that they will be knowledgeable about their sports, provide insightful commentary, and attract viewers.

Examples:

- Marcus Allen decided to retire from the Kansas City Chiefs (after 16 years as a top running back in the National Football League) when CBS offered him a job as a studio analyst. Said CBS Sports president Sean McManus, "Ninety seconds into Marcus' audition, you could see that he had all five of the qualities we were looking for: high credibility, deep understanding of the game, ability to express that understanding, star quality and personality."

- NBA star Reggie Miller (a member of the Indiana Pacers) was hired to be a WNBA analyst for Lifetime because of his own playing experience and because he is the brother of Cheryl Miller (who has been a star basketball player, a television commentator, and now a WNBA coach). Said Brian Donlon, an executive at Lifetime, "We wanted someone with a perspective on women's basketball while having a pro career - someone who would be appealing to both women and men. Obviously Reggie fits that bill. In addition to being a Pacer, the fact that he and Cheryl were a fiery brother-sister team on the playgrounds is pretty well known".

But if sports celebrities can't do the job, producers will turn to those who may not have a competitive sports background themselves but who are better on-camera. Often it is easier to teach a skilled television reporter the ins-and-outs of sports than it is to teach a skilled athlete the ins-and-outs of television reporting.

According to Fox sportscaster James Brown "... the influx of ex-athletes and coaches (to television) can be a plus. Some of these fellows have just a wonderful way of telling riveting football stories, and they, more than anyone, understand what the guys on the field are going through. But unquestionably, the successful ones are those who know they have to put in the time, that they have to work as hard in television as they did in football, that they have to learn to track a story and how to talk around sound bites."

Chris Berman (who works with former NFL players on ESPN's "NFL Sundays") said, "Our team members are celebrities, but they're not celebrities first, not the way we do it here. ... ESPN has hired those people so they could tell you what they are looking at. If their (celebrity) status helps, fine, but they are on the air because they know more football than most."

Celebrity athletes are most often hired for commentator or analyst jobs. For example, among 15 analysts hired by CBS Sports to cover the 1998 Nagano Winter Olympics, only one wasn't an ex-athlete or former Olympian. Celebrity athletes are less likely to be hired as play-by-play announcers or news reporters unless they have also had formal journalism training.

As for off-camera and technical jobs, most of these go to people with the appropriate professional training. But sometimes athletes have an inside edge in terms of having access to television producers and their staffs. They may have a chance to talk to and observe crews working on location. In addition, if those crews need extra help, an athlete who volunteers to assist them can pick up skills which may pay off in entry-level jobs later on.

FIELD VIDEO TAPING TECHNIQUES

In video, a field is one of the many still images which are displayed sequentially to create the impression of motion on the screen. Two fields comprise one video frame. When the fields are displayed on a video monitor they are "interlaced" so that the content of one field will be used on all of the odd-numbered lines on the screen and the other field will be displayed on the even lines. Converting fields to a still frame image requires a process called deinterlacing, in which the missing lines are duplicated or interpolated to recreate the information that would have been contained in the discarded field. Since each field contains only half of the information of a full frame, however, deinterlaced images do not have the resolution of a full frame.

In order to increase the resolution of video images, therefore, new schemes have been created that capture full-frame images for each frame. Video composed of such frames is called progressive scan video.

Video shot with a standard video camera format such as S-VHS or Mini-DV is often interlaced when created, whereas video shot with a film-based camera is almost always progressive. Free-to-air analog TV was mostly broadcast as interlaced material because the trade-off of spatial resolution for frame-rate reduced flickering on Cathode ray tube (CRT) televisions. High-definition digital television today can be broadcast terrestrially or distributed through cable system in either interlaced (1080i) or progressive scan formats (720p or 1080p). There are now some prosumer HDV camcorders that can shoot in progressive scan (720p) formats.

In video editing, it is crucial to know which of the two (odd or even) fields is "dominant." Selecting edit points on the wrong field can result in a "flash" at each edit point and playing the video fields in reverse order creates a flickering image.

Shooting Additional Scenes for Insertion in the Editing Process

To make an interesting video of these events have this shot list:

1. *Introduction - and title area*
2. Wide shot of location
3. Interior shot of groups before the event
4. Wide shot which pans the room and centres on the podium at the end - you will dissolve to the event speakers from there.

Body of the Video

5. There will be more than one speaker. The Camera will make a series of shot changes using the zoom function.
   (a) Start with a wide shot that slowly zooms in to the first speaker
   (b) Hold on one shot and both follow and lead the speaker if he moves - do not go closer than a head and shoulder shot, and wider if the speaker is a walker.

(c) When the speaker changes - you will get the cue from the introduction - Widen out to pick up the new speaker - then zoom back in to a good shot of that speaker.

(d) You will not change the shot often - but - when you do let the camera stay on that shot for a while. You are not trying to make an interesting video with lots of camera movement - you are documenting a speaker and the message.

(e) Lighting - seldom will you have the ability to set lights, and you will have to deal with the existing light set ups.

5. If you have a second camera - have it at the front of the room and shoot cutaways of the crowd reacting to insert for interest. (you will have an assistant shoot them).

You will want to take a few shots of the main speaker talking with the groups after the event and you will run the final credits over this section. You may be asked to make one of these event videos into a complete programme. You will build that programme by listening to the speaker and shooting video, which illustrates the speaker's message. This video will be inserted over the delivery. If you are requested to perform this type of work remember it will be very time consuming, and will be difficult to project the finish time or the expense required.

Some considerations for these projects:

1. Transcribe the speaker's delivery.
2. Make a shot list - from the speaker's clues
3. The inserts may interrupt the delivery and have its own sound
4. Shoot many more scenes than you think you will need. You will want them.
5. Ask for photos that you can copy to insert into the video.

6. Video Documents for interest.
7. Books displayed attractively - close up on the titles

Bands

A Band, is as a difficult a process as you will ever encounter. You will find there are no harder clients to please than these are. The audio will seldom please them, and editing one of these projects can be a forever project. Lighting will usually be difficult to deal with and to compensate for.

Before you begin one of these projects - determine how the video will be used. The most time consuming project will be the song which you illustrate. You may have to shoot the band and singers in many locations, they may change costumes, you may have many close ups. You may have to stage an entire story with Actors. The cameras may be moving, be located at strange angles and tilts. The list of variables may go on and on. You will have countless hours in pre-production planning, Actual taping, and postproduction re-shooting and editing. Its easy for the band to dream up their perfect video, but this video may be so time consuming that it will not be cost effective. If its a labour of love - well of course thats different. You will absolutely need to learn Non-lineal editing (computer editing).

A band Demo can be one of the easiest projects. For a Demo use one camera, set on a tripod, place the tripod at the "sweet spot" for the sound in the room. This tape is supposed to show the band the way the audience will see and hear them. One to three songs are recorded.

1. Have the camera high enough to see all the band members
2. Find the spot where the sound is the best, when picked up by the on camera mikes or place a set of crossed microphones and feed them into the camera.
3. If there is an audience, speak to them and make sure they realize you are making a DEMO. No yelling,

during the piece, don't block the shots, don't bump the camera position, no loud talking.

4. In editing Title each song, you will have many options.
5. Use smooth pans, tilts, and zooms and show each member during their leads.
6. Be sure that you are in a place where you can see the drummer - of all the band members the drummer is most often neglected on videos.

The next situation when you are shooting bands is the on line edit. You will have one or more cameras, more the better. You can both live switch the songs and record tape in the camera for later editing. The more cameras you have and use in this situation the better. Music videos are fast pace and you may be superimposing one picture over another, the piece will determine the style of shooting.

1. Leave the camera on for a complete song.
2. Shoot lots of cut away of the crowd.
3. Watch MTV - country music - in general all the variations, and see the way the cameras move for the various shots.
4. Shoot lots of hands and instruments close up.
5. Have a number of wide shots to default to - from different angles - these will be so far back that they can fit almost anywhere in the song.

Last is the produced music video, this will be the most edit intensive of all. You may shoot the same song over and over and will have to sync the lips and movements to a studio produced music track. The band may wish many of the shots produced which illustrate the lyrics. This type of production will be subject to many revisions. These are a lot of work but will make you proud when you finish them.

Music and Voice Recitals

A recital will take place in an auditorium or hall normally, It is best to find a spot in the room and set up a tripod where you can see the performer enter and exit. Natural Sound will be the most usual way to record the audio - but - you may patch into the house or mike a loudspeaker, depending on the circumstances.

1. Make all the zooms, pans and tilts smooth.
2. Place the camera so you can frame a number of pretty pictures of the performer
3. The camera moves very little

Press Conferences

The two types of press conferences are formal and informal. Formal Press conferences will have a podium, occasionally audio breakout boxes are supplied, seats for reporters and areas for the camera crews determined. Informal Press conferences will be totally different experience, with every reporter, photographer, and videographer trying to get in the best position. You may have to handhold the camera just to get the shot. For most press conferences the footage will be used as a sound bite if you are shooting for a television news programme. To learn more about press conferences, attend a few, and observe the working press.

Fairs and Outdoor Celebrations

These events are really fun, shoot everything - get lots of strange angles - shoot from the rides - get close ups. Before you take your camera out of the bag and with nothing in your hands walk around the area and look, get a complete idea of what is going on. A story of the event may come to your mind. With that story in mind then start shooting. Keep in mind you are telling a story, you could start the video with a picture of the main entrance or a poster. It will help a lot to have a reporter with you - someone who will speak and talk about the event in this way you can put together the final video as a much more exciting presentation.

Products and Demonstrations

Here we are entering commercial videography, this is a very interesting and profitable aspect of the business. All of the production skills you can apply should be used here, before you attempt this study every aspect of camera operation, equipment use, lighting, audio, and scripting.

Your assignment with these projects will be to help the client produce a video, which - is clear and understandable - is convincing - is attractive - and especially people remember the product. When you demonstrate the use of the product, the viewer should be thinking, "I can use that", and hopefully "I want that!". This manual will help you on your way to becoming a professional, keep reading and studying.

Training and Safety Videos

There is a very simple way to do these videos, and avoid the entire scripting phase. Business which need these videos, need them because, they have a large turnover of personnel and need consistent training materials. These tapes save money for the business by protecting the employs and customers. There is less unit cost for training the new employ, plus that employ is better trained by the tape. You can produce this tape, by attending the training of one or more new employs and taping the sessions. You can then edit them together. You view this tape with the client, and discuss every part of it. Producing these videos it really helps to have a small crew. One person to handle a boom mike and another to take care of the light. Or just one person to do both. You will be making shots/scenes of opportunity, every location at the business potentially may be the area you are taping. The extra expense of these two helpers will be more than made up in the final quality of the tape.

The extra freedom for the trainers and will allow them to be more natural. Have a work jacket or the same outfit for them to wear every time you tape. Then you will have continuity throughout the tape.

Sports

Sports are one of the best areas for the cameraman to begin learning. You will learn to be an intuitive cameraman with experience in this field.

Promotional Videos and PSAs

The need of Non-Profit organizations for Public Service Announcements and Promotional Videos is never met. Your organization is in constant need of funds and you have many obligations. Videos are the perfect medium for outreach. Your projects can be shown rather than simply being described to prospective donors. Your services can be shown and the message widely known. Your group can gain so much with a well thought out and prepared video.

The average PSA will be from 15 to 60 seconds in length. Informational videos may be of any length. Although they may be as long as you want them you should keep in mind the attention span of the average television viewer is roughly 10 minutes. This may be conditioning, by the networks, who insert their commericals. The shorter PSA, is much easier to produce, because a simple message is being presented. The date of an event, and appeal for help would be the normal PSA content. These may be as simple as writing a script, and choosing a location, setting up your equipment and shooting it. Or as complicated as rehearsing performers, building sets, with elaborate lighting, or having many locations to travel and shoot in. Of course you see the variability possible.

You are story telling in both the short and long PSA. If you will view commericals and record them you can break down the number of cuts in editing and count the scene setups, analize the use of music and sound effects. You can turn the sound off and see how the storys are told visually, and you can listen with your eyes closed and learn the use of the audio.

A PSA is an important promotional tool for any orginaziation, if you do it well you will achieve results. But your problem is compounded or relieved because of the rule of committee, which represents your group. If you utilize the group, for the preparation of the script, and engage the group in all of the pre-planning and organization, then you will start with a brainstorming session. You will accept every idea the group presents and attempt to integrate them into a tentative script. This script will then be rewritten eliminating portions, which simply don't work. You finalize the script, and detail all of the needs.

You then delegate your members to the various needs described in the script: 1. Locations; 2. Make-up; 3. Costuming; 4. Performing; 5. Audio; 6. Camera; 7. Lighing; 8. Set design; 9. Posters or titles, — this list of assignments can go on and on. The point of this is to emphasize how important the team function can be. A non-profit The worse individual in the group is the critic, who will find problems, prompt arguements and discord, and will be unable to supply solutions for their perceived problems. Sorry to say there are too many groups that fit this description. If yours is one of them - and its going to be left to a tiny group to accomplish this big project - don't start. Do the work of your organization and let this idea go. But if you have a cohesive group try it.

Trips and Travel Documentary Video

For this type of footage, you will have only a simple list of the type of shots that you will take. If you have been to these locations, you will have an idea and can list those shots in advance, these shots will form the beginning of your documentary and you should look for the other interesting scenes, details which you may not remember yet will add body and interest to your final video.

Talk about what you are shooting, with your companion while you tour the site. Dont just start shooting, walk around and see what scenes you want to record. The reason for this is so you can plan the story of the site you are visiting. If you are shooting for personal use this will allow you to do in-camera editing saving you from having to edit later.

If this is for professional use you will be shooting scenes in a different manner, you will hold on any given scene for a longer period, and you will shoot many more detail/cut-away shots. When the day is over review your footage and make more notes on the shot sheet. You may decide you need more footage, if this is so try to shoot at the same time of day trying to duplicate the lighting conditions of your first set of shots. Of course you may see that the lighting was all wrong and be replacing those original shots. Remember If you do your job you will save yourself much time when it comes to the editing process. On site narration, can be as easy or difficult as you want to make it. If you are taping yourself or another as the speaker, knowing what the speech/delivery will be is all important. Don't just try to wing it and be cute and glib, instead be friendly and informative. Practice the delivery and know what you are talking about, you dont have to have an exact script, you do have to know what you mean. You or your talent even after practicing may change the delivery as you are doing it. This is ok. It doesn't hurt a thing to do the scene over, but dont erase the first one.

You remember the movies, where you see a movie being made, and the little guy runs infront of the camera with a clap board and shows it to the camera and "Clacks" it. That is an easy way to keep track of the scenes, and if you will work out a way of doing it yourself, you will help yourself or the editor save time. When you are recording narration, use a clap board or a paper with enough information to help you in editing to find the shot you want.

Historical Documentaries

You may not consider current events as historical, yet in truth they are. After all by the time you view any tape, it is a historical document. You can consider every orgainized event historical, but on the other hand unplanned circumstances may be of historical significance. Disasters always fit this description, many unplanned things happen every day. These are opportunities, and you may have little or no time to prepare for them, you may have to be there already to capture them. Life in general has more unexpected events than planned ones. Sports videography will give you the ability to capture the unplanned opportunity. You may also include unplanned opportunities as a sub-set of the orgainized event. By being alert, you may see and shoot or be positioned to capture the speech of someone, and that footage will be far more significant than the planned event.

The visits of famous individuals are all historical events, and every thing they do may have significance in the future. The events which take place in a community are also important. You may believe with so many cameras around that everything is well covered, just the opposite is true. At best one small portion of the event will receive through or adequate coverage, and the rest will go unremarked.

Few individuals will think of telling the whole story. You can with just a little study and planning produce a wonderful tape of any event you attend. The event will have spokes-persons which will be happy to be interviewed. You should have done your homework and have questions prepared, but if you didn't, tell them so before the interview, and discuss what you will talk about. Let the spokes-person help you with the details, and tell you the important questions to ask.

A common complaint of people who have been interviewed is: (1) everyone asks the same questions; (2) no one asks what is important. You will be unique if you remember this, and the interviews will become much more informative. You will receive a lot of help as a result of your consideration. Tips on what to shoot and when. You may receive advice on other people to interview. A wealth of possibilities will open up for you with an approach such as this.

SPORTS VIDEOGRAPHY

There are various books on writing sports stories for the news. Study how to write and organize a print story and apply the knowledge to video. The average parent has little or no experience with the video camera, and quite possibly purchased the camera specifically to record their children.

Getting over Embarrassment

First of all, when you are video taping, you have the right as well as the duty to place yourself in a position where you can actually capture the event you are shooting. Insecurity, is natural when you first begin, but all sports events expect the camera people to be where they need to be. You will be told if you have placed yourself in an area which is forbidden. Then simply ask which of usually many areas you may shoot from.

Many of you take your camera to an event and then sit in the bleachers and handhold the camera. This is so wrong, its wrong for three reasons.

1. You are interfering with the sight lines of the other spectators.
2. Hand holding the camera never produces really good video, it is shaky and usually poorly framed. The only place handholding is at all appropriate is on the floor close to the court, or on the sidelines of a field game. In fact using a tripod in these situations is forbidden, because the tripod represents a danger to the players.
3. In the bleachers you will have to stand and sit - stand and sit - and someone will obscure the very shot you want most in front of you.

At indoor events, look around and observe the professional camera crews, and behave as they do. There are rules of behaviour,

1. Be polite,
2. Do not get in front of another cameraman and block his shot,

3. Give way to the professional crews, their living relies on their work, they often show up well in advance of the event and set up their location.

Indoor Court Events: You can watch any professional event, the actual game play itself will be from one camera, and this camera is normally high above the court at the centreline. This camera position allows you to see the entire court, and game well. You need to use a tripod from this position.

A Check List for Your Equipment

1. Your camera
2. Your power supply and battery charger
3. Three batteries minimum - charge your batteries as soon as you get home
4. Two brand new tapes
5. Tripod and the plate to attach the camera to the tripod (if one).

   The number of people who think all tripods are the same, and buy the least expensive one is amazing. They end up with a tripod that is no good at all and actually defeat the purpose of using a tripod.
6. Headphones - Wal-Mart 5$
7. Handheld mike - Wal-Mart 5$
8. Roll of Duct tape
9. Extension cord - have an adapter to fit a two prong plug in - incase you are somewhere with older ungrounded wiring.
10. Two large garbage bags (one for a rain coat - one to put all your equipment in).
11. A couple of small plastic bags to make a waterproof camera cover in case you need to shoot in the rain.
12. A 15 or 20 foot long extension cord.
13. Large diaper bag is one of the best camera bags there is, they usually have lots of pockets - and they are waterproof.

14. Battery tester (one with leads) - small screwdriver set, pair of pliers.- small flashlight (with extra flashlight batteries)

Technique for Taping the Event

You should instead include the player as part of the game and only make a close-up when he or she becomes the central person in a play. By making the tape tell the story of the game and focusing on your player, only when they are doing something exceptional you will produce a video which will be interesting and have a lasting appeal to the family.

When you are shooting a game there are two alternatives; 1. only shoot the plays, or 2. Shoot the entire game. Remember no matter how good you are - some time you will make a bad shot or loose the ball - or the camera will shake or jiggle — accept it - and try not to let it happen again that game.

The game tape style - for volleyball and soccer - never ever lose the ball. These two events are similar, in that you will have a wide shot most of the time. There are only a few moments that will allow you to zoom in for one or two people' shots.

Volleyball zoom in shots:

1. Before the serve you can do a portrait shot of the server, watch the referee and with his hand motion start zooming out to your wide shot.
2. Who ever scores - zoom for a hero shot. - catch the hi 5's
3. The time out periods - zoom in to the group
4. Zoom in for substitutions
5. Zoom in to the refs and line judges when appropriate.
6. Zoom in to the coaches when they show emotion - happy - sad - or mad
7. Zoom in to the score board at every time out.
8. Zoom in to the net and frame a nice shot showing the final pass of the teams.

In Soccer - you seldom zoom in close - you want to show as many players as possible all the time. This Sports really needs a camera on the sidelines, which you will edit onto your main tape. If you have one camera concentrate on your team and your goal - you will move from the centreline to the goal area shooting. Here you can try for really tight hero shots. You will loose the ball at times. If you get behind the goal and shoot through the net - manual focus your camera-at infinity - so you don't show just the net. Remember you are telling a story with both cameras.

Soccer zoom in shots - game camera

1. The starting kick off zoom in to show the ref and the kicker and zoom back wide before the kick off for the action.
2. In soccer the ball is really travelling fast, and it is easy to lose, so always lead the action (put the empty part of the screen in front of the player, so if they kick the ball you wont lose it.
3. Zoom in for the throw in - again back wide to catch the reception
4. Corner Kicks - zoom in while they set the ball - the wide showing the kicker and the goal —other wise you will lose the score if there is one
5. Dribbling contests - where the player with the ball is head up with another player, go in to a two shot at the most — and be ready to zoom wide when they pass the ball.
6. Injuries - zoom in for the story

All sports camera operators should know the game, because you can develop an intuitive style - you will know that when the person with the ball pulls their foot back they are going to pass it. The cameraperson who will second-guess the action on the field will tell the story of the game in a more interesting way.

The Game Tape Style - for Football

This technique produces a fast pace tape, by leaving out everything but the plays. A camera operator and one play-by-play announcer, will be able to co-ordinate their taping and narration, if the cam-op will simply make the same hand signal for starting and stopping each time. He starts just before he makes the signal and stops just after, giving the announcer an opportunity to wind up the phrase. The announcer keeps in mind the last statement, and attempts a continuity each time he speaks. The announcer does not say "Well We Are Back", Or Any Variation, Ever. If the announcer starts saying "we're back", that will become the main comment on the tape.

I recommend this style for different reasons: You will have a one-hour or less tape for the game.The coaches can use it for training better three. The shorter tape will be easier to programme on cable four. Your gross expenses will be less in material costs and time investment five. You and your announcer can be anywhere on the field or court and you can move between plays. The second elaboration of this technique, requires the announcer to keep in mind the shot list below, by using this list -pointing out to the cam-op - one shot can cut to the next and make sense. The announcer can announce the shot, or simply pick up the narrative thought on the tape. If the "Band", (for example) was the shot cut to, the announcer may not have said anything, and could choose to comment on that shot or simply go on with the game play. This technique works because there is a time lapse between plays, and you can observe if the team is slow or fast to the line, or if there are a lot of flags and time-out periods.

When you shoot the plays by themselves you are creating a 'Game Tape', this is the type video the coaches use. The camera starts recording as team leaves the huddle, and stops with the end of action, when the referee blows his whistle. This is repeated for every play of the game.

Continuous Coverage

The continuous coverage, means you turn the camera on before the game starts and turn it off at half time, or for long time out periods. Getting the play is the hard part, if you are looking through the viewfinder at the quarterback and have a wide enough shot you will be able to see if he is passing-off, running or throwing the ball. If the ball is passed-off you can zoom-in to a closer shot. If running widen out to see the play - will the tackle catch him. If passing widen out watching for a 'sack' and be ready to follow the ball wide—zooming in on the receiver when appropriate.

Your announcer can tell the story of the receiver on the kick off, and you can have a wide shot of the line up, which has found and zoomed tight on the receiver for the catch. As soon as the catch is made widen out so you can see the run and the play - defence and offences players. If you are shooting for a coaching tape, you show the entire line including the ends and then zoom in loosing the ends and show the primary line, all the players on both sides. You will not zoom in any further than this, the coaches want to see how all the players performed.

Pass plays — you can see if the quarterback hands the ball off or if he steps back and sets for a throw. Follow the person carrying the ball and try to keep him centred in the frame. On a pass play - put the quarterback on the side of the picture so he will throw into the empty frame. Try to keep the ball in the frame at all times, and as the ball is reaching the receiver, try to have the receiver centred in the frame. The rule of the thumb for zooming in, zoom in just enough to be able to read the numbers on all the jersey's, while at the same time keeping the largest number of players in the picture as you can.

Tennis: Tennis is a simple coverage - place your camera high at one end of the court - looking at your player- most of the coverage will be wide so you can see the entire court. If you are going to zoom in for close up shots, you will do it between serves. This Sports can use a second camera low and on the sideline for close ups and cutaways- Close up shots

1. Parents - spouses
2. Coaches
3. Judges
4. Ball boys
5. Serves and returns - don't try to follow the ball when down low. Rather frame the shot and shoot with a fast shutter speed - you can slow motion the shot later or freeze frame the shot.
6. Stay on your player at the end for the winning shot - the play and especially the reaction to the win.
7. Post game ceremonies and awards. Shoot from a low angle and make the player seem bigger than life.

Swimming and Diving

Swimming: This Sports is problematic - the pools are crowded and close even with only a few people at the event. The air is wet and steamy, which can cause your camera to stop working. With approval and co-operation from the event I have a simple track set designed which you could use to follow the leaders of the even up and down the pool - One camera at the start finish end of the pool can catch the dives and the finish and do a reasonable job of following the action. This camera will also be good for the close up of the hero of the event.

Diving

You will need to practice shooting diving if you are to follow the dive well. Go to as many practice sessions as possible to learn to be in close enough and yet wide enough for you to follow the diver and not lose them. Shooting this event would be best done with multiple cameras.

1. Wide and 90 degrees to the side
2. Wide and at a 45 degree angle to the side
3. High and behind the diver
4. Follow camera - for the close up. - preferably on the same side as the diver will exit the pool.

Your tape of this event will be one, which you will want to edit - cutting in as many different cameras as possible. If you can have a play by play - announcer - for the commentary it will really help in the editing. The commentary will take much longer than the action of the event and you can cut in all of the other cameras and do slow motion and still shots over the top of the continuous talking.

Cross Country and Track and Field

You will want to get the wide establishing shots of the entry to the location and the sign-up areas - hands signing-papers filled out - numbers accepted. The cross-country events really need a series of cameras - Locations:

1. Start line
2. Finish line
3. Place where you have the longest fields of views - places where you can track the runners for a long time.
4. Good views of the downhill runs.
6. Get the warming up shots
7. Shots in the finish shoot where the runners are queing to be listed
8. Shots in the final rest area
9. Shots of the medic tents
10. Drink and lunch bars

These are heavily edited tapes if you have a number of cameras to work with. You will want your camera operators to make clear distinctions on the tapes - showing the programme or race list between each event is a good way.

If you only have one camera you will want to plan out all of your moves from one position to another - you will move from the start area to a series of locations so you catch the runners over and over - you will try to be at the finish line in time. You will need to walk your route before the race so you know where you are to be — In a real sense you are going to be running your own race doing this type of event. The play by play for this event will be a really hard one- it will probably be best to do a voice over following the editing of the tape, and report the event as it is seen on the tape.

Track and Field

Everything is going on at the same time, how many cameras can you put together here, if you want to cover every event you will have to have many camera operators. If you can have a coach or some one for your play by play, for each one of the events the tape will come out better - all of these events will be start and stop shooting. You will need to have many batteries for each of the cameras for all of these track events. It is really disappointing to shoot and shoot only to have you battery die at the finish line, or before the event has finished.

Baseball - Fast pitch – Softball

Single camera coverage of these games is really hard, because all of the action is happening all over the field at the same time. Multiple cameras live switched are the best solution. Three cameras all at the same centre location behind the home plate are a simple solution. Use three cameras mounted on tripods one a wide shot showing the entire field a second camera zoomed in to show home - the pitchers mound - and second base the third camera - is operated and follows the ball or catches the play. It will be a judgement call on the photographer's part.

With this minimum of cameras you can make an acceptable continuous game. The announcer for this event is all-important - Ball games have as many cameras as possible to keep the pace going. A good announcer will make or break these programmes. One of the simplest things to do is a feature on the game- shooting and editing out the best shots into a programme. With this type of programme you and your announcer will have to become real journalists. Well as a matter of fact for any feature where you have to edit this is true.

Continuous Shooting

You are a storyteller when you shoot in this manner. Ask yourself first

— How many stories are there to tell

— Lets make a check list

The National Anthem and School Songs are always good places to begin the video, but is not strictly required

1. The game itself
   - *(a)* The warm up period
   - *(b)* The entry to the field
   - *(c)* The coin tosses
   - *(d)* All of the plays
   - *(e)* The score board and the clock and the play clock
2. The referees
   - *(a)* The ball boys
3. The coaches
   - *(a)* Assistant coaches
   - *(b)* Trainers
   - *(c)* Doctors and nurses
4. The benches
   - *(a)* The whole bench
   - *(b)* Individual players
   - *(c)* Injured player
   - *(d)* The water boys
   - *(e)* The trainers and medics
5. The cheerleaders and spirit group
6. The stands
   - *(a)* Parents
   - *(b)* Students
   - *(c)* Band

7. Band
   (a) Marching in
   (b) Half time ceremonies
   (c) In the stands
8. Security
9. The ticket booth
10. The booster club and other groups selling
11. The snack bar
    (a) The servers
    (b) The customers
12. Close up shots of balls and equipment
13. Close up shots of ankles wrapped, or hands doing something
14. Any unusual activity - by anyone - but tell the story from where you find it to its end.
15. Document illegal activities, and tell the officials you have the footage — offer copies these tapes to them.
15. The press box, and all of the individuals and the activities there.
16 The Stadium Announcer and Score Keepers. You have noticed all ready many of the shots on the list cannot be made from the game camera position.

Field Camera Techniques

There are video and audio transmission technology under development at present, which will enable any field camera to transmit A/V to a switcher, these will be lightweight and easy to operate. We will only consider the camera is free and without direction, you are calling your own shots. Accept the fact that you cannot shoot everything at the same time, pick the shot you are trying to get and don't be distracted. You might even miss a touchdown but you will get the reaction to the touchdown. The reaction is just as important as the play itself, when you are preparing a hi-lite tape or participating in a project where your footage will be edited into the programme later.

The list includes all of the shots you could ask for. But others will appear to you when your shooting, try and capture them. It will be almost impossible for you to use a tripod for the field camera, but a monopod can be used. Try for DRAMATIC SHOTS - the camera on the ground as the players run past, the extreme close up shots of action and faces. The field camera should try to capture the face of every single player - at least on your own team - sometime during the game. This will not take long and these shots can be frozen as still pictures:

Play by Play and Colour Announcing: If you have never been an announcer, remember you job is to keep the tape interesting. You do this by always having something to say, and by being excited about what you say, also by making what your statements sound important. Before the game collect information to include during the action and, where there are breaks in the action of the game.

1. The rosters of both teams, and hi-lite the starters
2. Get the programme if any and read it quickly - announce the schedule for upcoming games and any other significant information.
3. Ask for histories and biographies of the players and coaches
4. Get the statistics for the team

Dont Do This

1. Dont say you are sorry when you make a mistake - just correct yourself and go on
2. Dont say 'we'll be right back" or "we are back", instead talk about what is going on — if your camera is breaking at time out periods - the camera man will give you a hand signal - finish your sentence and stop. The cameraperson will give you a hand signal to start talking again.
3. Dont try and be funny - you will sound stupid - have fun and be happy - but jokes will almost always hurt someone' feelings.

Here is where the handheld microphone comes in - the simplest way of recording play by play is to have some one do it live for you. Just plug in the mike to the camera, hand it to the announcer and listen with the headset. Below we will investigate other solutions. The addition of an announcer on your tape will raise the quality of the programme you produce, the play by play will make your tape one which people will really watch and enjoy. Again there are two ways, One 1. Use a radio and, Two 2. Have your own people capturing it live. If you are using a radio again there are two ways to record it.

1. Have a small portable radio, with fresh batteries
2. Have a cable with a male plug on both ends
3. Plug the cable into the headset of the radio and the microphone input of the camera
4. Use headphones and monitor the audio for volume
5. a common mistake is having the volume on your radio too high, being too high it will distort and sound awful-turn it down
6. The second method - A fail-safe is to have someone at home record the game on cassette
   (a) You will copy this tape to videotape
   (b) You will edit the video tape copy of the audio - onto the video of the game
7. This technique Works you need:
   (a) A telephone splitter - to plug into the back of the radio play by play converter. One line will go to the radio station the other to you.
   (b) 50 to 100 feet of telephone cable - you will have a telephone inline connector, which goes to your.
   (c) Converter from telephone to mike level - this is a simple 'Radio Shack' item used to tape record phone calls.
   (d) If you are limited to the amount of equipment you want to carry, just feeding the signal direct to the camera.

(e) A good set of head phones.

(f) The next level is to have an audio mixer and feed the signal from the announcers in one channel and have a crowd mike in another channel. You can then fade from one channel to the other and keep the audio interesting.

If you use two mikes, the complexity increases, you need an audio mixer, two mikes, perhaps three (the third for the crowd sounds). If you have this level you will really need an audio operator to maintain the levels, and while he is doing this you can include a cassette with pre-recorded sponsors messages - and announcements - you may have an audio open and close with music.

Uses and Applications for Your Tape

Getting back to the original premise, that you are a parent shooting for your own home record. If you follow the above script, your player will enjoy it because you will have captured a story showing many of the important people in the life of your child.

The school or the team itself my wish to use your tapes for seasonal hi-lite tapes. If you are shooting a game camera - your tape may be used for coaching. If you shoot in the digital format - your footage will be acceptable to the news media. Both for still shots and video. You may live in an area with a Public Access Television Station, these stations will play your entire tape in their programming.

Cities, which only have cable but no access stations - will often have a channel that will play your tapes. It will simply be a matter of calling them and asking. Many cities have low-power television stations - many of them are Christian stations, often they will offer low cost air time - or provide air time for free. This type of programming benefits them and can increase their rateings, even enabling them to gain cable slots.

Towns and cities, which do not have 'Public Access Television' often, have a channel which only plays a slate with the time and weather — sometimes the cable company will play your tapes on that channel - ask them.

Multiple Camera Productions

This is a description of a professional production unit. Multiple camera productions will come to age soon for the small Production Company when wireless transmission becomes a practical solution. At present, these setups are very complicated. Now we have reached the professional level of production. Be ready for a full day of setup and testing. You may have a chance to work on one of these crews on one of the most basic levels, if possible take the job. This is one of the more interesting and educational jobs you can have as a beginner.

The production trailer is pulled to the site, by the semi truck and is waiting the next morning for the staff member and the crews to arrive. Your first job will in all probability pulling cables, operating a directional microphone, or a runner (passing notes and delivering messages). The day begins with the set-up of the arena or stadium. Cables both audio and video are unloaded from the truck and you will string them out to each of the camera locations. No you won't be alone, and the staff technicians will check everything you do. Each Camera operator will be in charge of setting up his camera position, you may be assisting him in this.

The Game and Chase cameras will be high and centred on the game area. They will have large professional tripods, and the cameras are in many sections, the camera body, the monitor, and the lens. The lens itself will weigh 20 to 40 pounds, just the front glass lens will be 6 or more inches across. The camera body will have a control cable which attach it to one arm on the tripod and the lens will have a focus cable to the other arm. The cable, which you ran from the truck, will be attached to the camera. A headset with a microphone will be connected to the camera also.

These cameras, allow the camera operator to do many different things. He can view the actual broadcast signal, or view just his own cameras out put, the head set allows him to talk within his circuit, hearing the camera director and the other camera operators. If you are assigned to the audio crew, again your first job will be running audio cables to all of the locations, The announcers will have sets of cables the field or the court will have cables, the monitor locations and so on.

There is no set rule for how many audio locations will exist. Each one will have a cable a mike and usually many connections and cable joining's between their position and the Production Van. The audio crew will always encounter more problems than any other of the crews will, cables will fail, or microphones, they will be patched to the wrong locations and so on. You will be running everywhere, doing, redoing, testing and so on, until the job is set for the game. All of the above will take hours, sometimes the entire day just to be ready for the event that evening.

A few hours before the event is to begin, staff meetings will be held and everyone will be told their exact duties for the event. The camera operators will be told what is expected, and portions of the script for the event explained where necessary. A camera crew will have been taping interviews, and getting shots of players to be stored in the "still store" for on air reference when one of them deserves special mention, for example a star or the line up. These stills will have - names and statistics superimposed over them. The interviews will be used in the pre-game show.

The person operating the Character Generator will have typed in the names of all the players, coaches, all of the statistics for both teams. The pages indexed and ready for the event. In the truck will be a tapes position, this position will have a stack of tape players where the interviews are played from. Also each camera position will have a deck recording their output. These tapes will be used for "instant replay". The tape operator will, monitor the cameras and re cue all the decks that captured the significant plays, and the director will call for that deck and the operator will play it, by direction form the producer/director.

The control room for the game will have 50 or more monitors, a bunch of computers, at least two video switchers. One end or side of the production van will be full of monitors. The two largest will be the preview and programme monitor. There will be a monitor for each camera, and tape deck input, the still store, and the character generators, and a monitor of the network or television station playing the programme.

CHAPTER 3

News Writing Techniques

Journalistic style or news writing is the particular prose style used for news reporting (i.e. in newspapers) as well as in news items that air on radio and television. News style encompasses not only vocabulary and sentence structure, but also the way in which stories present the information in terms of relative importance, tone, and intended audience.

News writing attempts to answer all the basic questions about any particular event in the first two or three paragraphs: Who? What? When? Where? and Why? and occasionally How? (i.e. "5 W's"). This form of structure is sometimes called the "inverted pyramid," to refer to decreased importance of information as it progresses.

News stories also contain at least one of the following important characteristics: proximity, prominence, timeliness, human interest, oddity, or consequence. While newspapers, like encyclopedias, generally adhere to an expository writing mode and style, this has changed over time as journalism ethics and standards have (debatably) increased to become more objective and less sensationalistic. There are debated degrees of professionalism among particular news agencies, and their reputability or public value, according to professional standards of idealism and depending on what the reader wants from a news story, may be tied to their ability to be objective. In its most ideal form, news writing strives to be intelligible to the vast majority of potential readers, as well as to be engaging and succinct. Within the limits created by these goals, news stories also aim for a kind of comprehensiveness. However other factors are involved, some of which are practical and derived from the media form, and others stylistic.

Among the larger and more respected newspapers, fairness and balance is a major factor for the presentation of information. Commentary is usually confined to a separate section, though each paper may have a different overall slant. Editorial policy dictates the use of adjectives, euphemisms, and idioms. Papers with an international audience for example, usually use a more formal style of writing. The specific choices made by a news outlet's editor or editorial board are often collected in a style guide or stylebook; common commercial stylebooks are the "AP Style Manual" and the "US News Style Book". The main goals of news writing can be summarized by the ABCs of journalism: accuracy, brevity, and clarity.

TERMS AND STRUCTURE

Journalistic prose is explicit and precise, and tries not to rely on jargon. As a rule, journalists will not use a long word when a short one will do. They use subject-verb-object construction and vivid, active prose. They offer anecdotes, examples and metaphors, and they rarely depend on colourless generalizations or abstract ideas. News writers try to avoid using the same word more than once in a paragraph (sometimes called an "echo" or "word mirror").

Lede or Lead

The most important structural element of a story is the lede or lead—the story's first, or leading, sentence. Charnley (1966) stated that "an effective lead is a "brief, sharp statement of the story's essential facts" (p. 166.). The lede/ lead is usually the first sentence, or in some cases the first two sentences, and is ideally 20-25 words in length. The top-loading principle applies especially to ledes, but the unreadability of long sentences constrains its size. This makes writing a lede an optimization problem, in which the goal is to articulate the most encompassing and interesting statement that a writer can make in one sentence, given the material with which he or she has to work. While a rule of thumb says the lede should answer most or all of the 5 Ws, few ledes can fit all of these.

Article ledes are sometimes categorized into hard ledes and soft ledes. A hard lede aims to provide a comprehensive thesis which tells the reader what the article will cover. A soft lede introduces the topic in a more creative, attention-seeking fashion, and is usually followed by a nut graf (a brief summary of facts). Media critics often note that the lede can be the most polarizing subject in the article. Often critics find bias based on an editor's choice in headline and lede.

Example Lede-and-Summary Design

Humans will be going to the moon again. The NASA announcement came as the agency requested ten gazillion dollars of appropriations for the project.

Example Soft-Lede Design

NASA is proposing another space project. The agency's budget request, announced today, included a plan to send another person to the moon. This time the agency hopes to establish a long-term facility as a jumping-off point for other space adventures. The budget requests approximately ten gazillion dollars for the project. Two other terms common in editing are hed and dek or deck. Hed is used to denote an article's headline or heading. Dek refers to a quick blurb or article teaser.

INVERTED PYRAMID

Journalism instructors usually describe the organization or structure of a news story as an inverted pyramid. The journalist top-loads the essential and most interesting elements of his or her story, with supporting information following in order of diminishing importance. This structure enables readers to quit reading at any point and still come away with the essence of a story. It allows people to enter a topic to the depth that their curiosity takes them, and without the imposition of details or nuances that they would consider irrelevant.

Newsroom practicalities represent another rationale. The inverted pyramid structure enables sub-editors and other news staff to quickly create space for ads and late-breaking news simply by cutting items (*"throw-aways"*) from the bottom ("cutting", literally, at the papers that still use traditional paste up techniques). The structure frees sub-editors to truncate stories at almost any length that suits their needs for space. Poor structure typically begins with a faulty lede. Steeped in the raw material of their interviews and research, apprentice news writers often fail to anticipate what readers will find most interesting or to sum up the information quickly. These elements of their story they present only after their lede and in an article's later paragraphs. This is the reason for the popular newsroom admonition: *"Don't bury the lede!"*

Some writers start their stories with the "1-2-3 lede". This format invariably starts with a 5W opening paragraph (as described above), followed by an indirect quote that serves to support a major element of the first paragraph, and then a direct quote to support the indirect quote..

Feature Style

News stories aren't the only type of material that appear in newspapers and magazines. Longer articles, such as magazine cover articles and the pieces that lead the inside sections of a newspaper, are known as *features*. Feature stories differ from *straight* news in several ways. Foremost is the absence of a straight-news lede, most of the time. Instead of offering the essence of a story up front, feature writers may attempt to lure readers in. While straight news stories always stay in third person point of view, it's not uncommon for a feature magazine article to slip into first person. The journalist will often detail his or her interactions with interview subjects, making the piece more personal. A feature's first paragraphs often relate an intriguing moment or event, as in an "anecdotal lede". From the particulars of a person or episode, its view quickly broadens to generalities about the story's subject.

The section that signals what a feature is about is called the *nut graf* or *billboard*. Billboards appear as the third or fourth paragraph from the top, and may be up to two paragraphs long. Unlike a lede, a billboard rarely gives everything away. This reflects the fact that feature writers aim to hold their readers' attention to the end, which requires engendering curiosity and offering a "payoff." Feature paragraphs tend to be longer than those of news stories, with smoother transitions between them. Feature writers use the active-verb construction and concrete explanations of straight news, but often put more personality in their prose. Feature stories often close with a "kicker" rather than simply petering out.

The ABCs of news writing are Accuracy, Brevity and Clarity. The first and most important is accuracy – a story can be creative and compelling, but if it contains errors, it is worthless. Actually, it is worse than worthless; a false news story undercuts the public trust necessary for the survival of a free press. Keep in mind that the First Amendment specifically protects the press from government control so that the public can receive accurate and unbiased information.

The public needs unbiased information to make intelligent choices in the voting booth. This is critical to the process of democracy in our country. If the public loses faith in the accuracy and fairness of the press, loss of faith in democracy will soon follow. Always check numbers, spellings of names, who said what, and the other basic facts of any story. A reporter's job is to find out what is going on, then write a story that's interesting and informative.

Accuracy always comes first. Second is brevity. Each word in your story should do a job. If not, take it out. Get to the point. Say it just once. Don't be redundant. Don't say "8 a.m. in the morning," since 8 a.m. is in the morning. Just say 8 a.m. Or say 8 in the morning. Remember the inverted pyramid style of writing. Put the most important fact in the lead. Hook the reader's attention. Explain the lead and then go on to the next most important fact in the second inverted pyramid. And then the next. Lead up to an interesting finish. Don't just stop writing when you run out of information. Clarity starts before you write.

Clarity starts with complete, competent reporting. You should understand your subject so completely that your story leaves it crystal-clear in the reader's mind. Your story should leave no questions unanswered. Avoid jargon. Explain anything that wouldn't be obvious to the average person. The more information you gather, the more you have to sift through to determine what belongs in the lead. The more you know, the harder it is to tell it quick and make it simple. It's only easy if you don't know what you're talking about. No one said good reporting is easy.

The Gatekeeper

Who decides what stories will be printed in the Monitor? Who picks the stories for the 10 O'Clock News on Channel

2? Journalists make those decisions, and when they do, they are performing their "gatekeeper" function. They decide which stories to let through the "gate" and which to toss into the trash.

Journalists decide which stories are important enough to run on page one, and which ones run inside. But the gatekeeper function also affects the way we write our stories. The reader looks to the journalist to make sense out of a confusing world. It is the journalist's job to find out what's going on, then choose from a notebook full of scribbles only those facts necessary to give the reader a clear, concise picture of the most important events. Obviously, this process leaves some facts out of the story. You must be sure that your story includes the most important information. But for you to make that judgment, you have to learn everything possible about your subject, and that means you will end up knowing a lot of less-important facts that will never make it into a news story. A good reporter loves to dig into a story. The rule is: "Write 10 percent of what you know."

The Five 'W's

Every news story must cover the "Five W's:" Who, What, When, Where, Why and sometimes How and So What? You don't have to cover all these in the lead, obviously, but usually you will address one or two in the first graph. The rest should come soon. Make sure they are all covered somewhere in your story.

NEWS VALUES

What is news? The cliche is, when dog bites man, it's not news. When man bites dog, that's news. Critics say, why is the newspaper always full of bad news? Because bad news is unusual, and no one wants to read about ordinary events. "The Monitor adviser arrived on campus this morning and found things much as he left them the night before." Who cares? If the adviser finds a mountain lion waiting for the elevator in Building 5, then there's a story. With photos.

News usually has at least one of these elements:

Impact: Impact is determined by the number of people affected, the number of boats that sink, the number of cars wrecked, etc. The more people affected, the more boats sunk, the bigger the impact of the story.

Proximity: The closer your audience is to the event, the greater its news value. If a train hits a bus in Bangladesh, it may receive three column inches behind the sports section. If a train hits a bus on Niles Canyon Road, the Argus will play it on page one.

Timeliness: "New" is a big part of news. If it happened just before deadline, it's bigger news than if it happened last week. Even "big" stories last only a week or so. News, like fish, is better fresh.

Prominence: If it happens to the mayor, it is bigger news than if it happens to the Monitor adviser. The public cares more about celebrities than they do about people they don't know. If President Clinton goes jogging, reporters take pictures. If the Monitor adviser goes jogging, dogs bark, but no one else notices. (This is fine with the adviser.)

Novelty: If an event is unusual, bizarre, the first, the last, or once-in-a-lifetime, it is has more news value than if it is something that happens all the time.

Conflict: War, politics and crime are the most common news events of all. If everyone got along, there wouldn't be much news.

Relevance: How does the story affect the reader? If there's no effect at all, maybe there's no news.

Usefulness: How can I use this information? Home, business and leisure news sections have sprouted in newspapers in an attempt to give readers news they can really use.

Human Interest: A story may be weak on the other news values, but be interesting anyway. It can be as simple as an interview with a fascinating person who does unusual things.

If people are talking about it, it's news, even if it doesn't meet the criteria of our other news values.

Objectivity/Fairness

The reporter's job is to find out the truth and tell it, regardless of who might be made uncomfortable. The reporter's responsibility, as implied by the First Amendment, is to serve only the reader. The public needs unbiased information in order for democracy to succeed. That means that your stories must be unbiased. Most reporters believe pure objectivity is impossible. When you select one word over another, your judgments enter the story.

But fairness *is* possible, and fairness should be every reporter's goal. Fairness requires the reporter to recognize his or her own biases in the story, and then consciously include all relevant points of view — even ones that the reporter doesn't like, personally. Always look for the "other side" in any story. If someone or some institution is accused of something by a source in your story, you have an absolute obligation to contact the accused party and give them the opportunity to respond. This should be done in the first story, not in some later "response" story.

Use neutral language. Avoid exclamation points. Don't say "our college" when referring to Ohlone. Say Ohlone. Our tone should be one of the disinterested, but honest observer. A reporter's credibility is the only guarantee the reader has of the story's accuracy. There are no policemen in the newsroom forcing reporters to be accurate. The First Amendment wouldn't allow that. If we write inaccurate or biased stories, the readers will stop trusting us. And if that happens, we all might as well go into some other field.

The Lead

The lead is usually the toughest part of writing a story. The lead is the first word, sentence or paragraph of the story. Sometimes it can be two or three paragraphs.

Whatever its length, the lead has several important jobs to do. First, it must interest the reader in the rest of the story. Imagine the reader as impatient, with lots of other things he or she could be doing instead of reading your story. Imagine the reader saying, "Get to the POINT! Don't waste my time! Tell me the STORY!" If your reader were stranded on a desert island with nothing to read but your story, you could probably get away with a vague, rambling lead. But today's reader has a BART train to catch, the kids are fighting again and the TV never stops blaring. Your story has tough competition.

Surveys have shown that most people say they get their news from TV, but many then turn to newspapers for the details behind the headlines. Your job is to write a short, punchy, informative lead to attract readers who have grown accustomed to TV's "sound bite" journalism. But then you must supply the details, the insights, the context that TV doesn't have time for.

What are the rules for a good lead?

- *Keep it Short:* News writing is always tight, but the lead calls for special care. Condense your story into one sentence, then one phrase, then one word. Make sure that word is near the beginning of the lead. As a general rule, no lead sentence should be longer than 10 words.
- *Get to the Point:* What is the story about? Tell the reader in the lead. Don't say, "The city council met last night." Tell the reader what the met last night." Tell the reader what the city council did. "Business taxes were raised a whopping 30 percent on a 6-1 vote of the city council last night." What's the story about? Taxes. So get taxes in the lead.
- *Focus on the Action:* Use the "active voice." Instead of saying something happened, say who did what to who. Use the action word. If nobody did anything, it may not be a news story.

- *Hook the Reader:* Put the most important, the most interesting, the most exciting thing in the lead. A novel may take 100 pages to lead up to the climax of the story; a news story puts the climax first and then explains what led up to it. These rules are sometimes thrown out for feature leads, or "anecdotal leads" that start with a little story that sets the scene for the point you are trying to make. But the lean, punchy news lead will work best on most stories.

The Nut Graph

Every story needs a "nut graph" that answers the question: Why am I writing this, and why do I think the reader should read it? The best way to make sure your story has a point is to state it, simply, somewhere near the top of the story. It doesn't have to say, "The point of this story is..." But if the story is about a budget shortfall, a good nut graph might quote a district official on whether the shortfall would force an increase in tuition. How does the story affect the reader? That's what should be in the nut graph. If it doesn't affect the reader, maybe it shouldn't be a news story.

Quotes

Quotes bring a story to life. Let your sources tell the story. The reporter's voice in the story should outline the main points and set the stage for the quotes. Quotes let your sources "talk" to the reader, giving a personal impact that you can't get any other way in print. But quotes should be special. Don't use quotes for information that can be more clearly explained in your own words. Only direct quotes are contained inside of quotation marks. Information inside quotation marks must be the source's exact words. But another step is needed to achieve accuracy: The words inside the quotation marks must also convey the intent of the speaker. To use the speaker's exact words to say something he or she did not mean is to take the quote *out of context.* It is a serious complaint often made by sources. At the end of the interview, always check quotes that you intend to use, and if you are unsure what the speaker meant, ask.

The proper form for using a direct quote is: "I won't run for president," Dan Quayle said Thursday. "But I may walk a little." Notice that punctuation is inside the quote marks. The quote is attributed after the first sentence. Try to minimize the use of partial quotes:

When asked about his presidential plans, Quayle said he "won't run." The first example, using the full quote, is both more interesting and more accurate. The partial quote leaves a false impression. Indirect quotes don't have to use the speaker's exact words, but they must convey what the speaker meant. For example:

> Brett Favre Thursday denied reports that he would retire from football at the end of the season, but he said he is feeling his age. Indirect quotes can be used to introduce direct quotes. For instance, the next sentence in the Favre story could be: "I feel every tackle of my career when I wake up in the morning," he said. Make sure that the reader knows who is talking. If you've quoted one person for several paragraphs, and then plan to quote someone else, use a graph of transition between the two quotes. For instance: Meanwhile, another city councilman had opposite views. "I think the planned development stinks," said Councilman Joe Smith.
>
> If you end one quote and start another without tipping off the reader, confusion will result. Remember, you may accurately report what a person said, but that person may be wrong. Verify any questionable statement by calling other sources. It's not enough to say later, "But that's what he said." Keep in mind that your goal is to inform your readers. Never rely on only one source. If you find that one

of your sources doesn't have the information you need, switch sources.

Transitions

Each paragraph in your story should flow naturally from the one before it. If you have gathered enough information, and if your lead is strong enough, you may find that your story seems to "write itself," flowing naturally from beginning to end. But other stories seem "choppy," with the narrative taking jags and loops that could lose or confuse the reader.

Transitions smooth out those jags and make the story easier to read. Here are some guidelines:

- Make sure your story elements are presented in a logical order. The most common order is the chronological order. This happened, then this happened, then this happened. For the sake of variety, you want to use the word "then" no more than once.
- Use introductions as transitions between speakers. For example: Ed Smith, professor of biology at Ohlone, disagrees with the idea that frozen yogurt causes split ends. "That's the craziest idea I've ever heard," he said.
- Set the scene for a new area of discussion. Don't just start in a new direction without notifying the reader. For example: Meanwhile, a group of Ohlone instructors have been developing another theory, one based on experiments with bananas. "We think we're on to something," said Professor Harold Foote.

Endings

Although the news writing style tries to put the most important information in the beginning, in order to draw in readers, it is also important to save something for a good ending. A good ending gives a "rounded out" feeling to a story, especially if the end makes reference to information in the lead.

For instance, in a story by a Monitor staff member about a young man trying to quit gang crime and turn his life around, the ending was: Valle gave a convincing "yes" when asked if he is going to graduate from college. This means that he will have to see his mother cry again, although this time he will see her from a stage while he is wearing a cap and gown, holding a diploma in his hand. The lead had talked about how his mother cried when he received a scholarship to attend college, shortly after he had been released from jail. The ending made a smooth reference to the lead, tying the story together.

Other Stuff

Avoid one-source stories. Talk to as many people as possible in the time you have for reporting. Make sure you leave enough time for the writing portion of the story. How do you know when you've done "enough" reporting, talked to enough sources, read enough reports? Experience will teach you the answer, and it will be a lot more than you thought at the beginning. The news reporter's job has three parts: Reporting, writing and meeting deadlines. All three are important, but news reporting couldn't exist without deadlines. The deadline is your discipline. Learn to meet deadlines, learn how to gather information, and the writing style will come eventually. There is a broad, clear distinction between news writing and advertising. Use your normal objectivity and fairness when writing about advertisers, even if they push you for a "positive" story, and threaten to pull their advertising if they don't get it. Our focus is on the reader. Our job is to write truthful, fair stories, and sensible advertisers will respect that.

The same applies to our college administration. We must always give all sides of a story, and we must ask for reaction from all interested parties, but our job is to report the news objectively, regardless of who is involved. Make sense out of numbers. A number is meaningless without a comparison.

If enrolment grew 5 percent this fall, how does that compare to last fall? How does it compare to the average fall semester? Story-telling is part of being human. We try to understand experience by turning it into a story. We use the story to remember the experience, and to share the experience with others. We learn through stories. News is a special type of story, one that presents facts without the storyteller's judgment.

How to Write a News Lead?

1. Condense story into one or two words. Put those words as close to the beginning of the first sentence as possible without destroying the flow of the lead sentence.
2. Keep leads short — 20 to 30 words for the first sentence. Or fewer.
3. The news lead should tell the reader what the story is about and be interesting enough to draw the reader into the rest of the story. Remember that the readers won't know what the story is about until you tell them.
4. Find the action in the story. Put the action in the lead.
5. Always double-check names and numbers. Check spelling, style and grammar. Put everything in order.
6. Attribute opinions. Stick with the facts.
7. Details, description. Report first, then write. Learn all, tell 10 percent.
8. Decide which of the news values best applies to the lead of the story. Write a lead that emphasizes that news value.
9. Write in the active voice.
10. Don't lead with a name, time or place unless that is the most interesting/important thing in the story.

What Not to Do in Leads?

1. Don't make the lead too complicated. Don't load it down with too many names, figures or details. Keep the lead sentence short – never more than 35 words.

2. Don't begin with the time, day or date, or place. Better to focus on the action, the who or what.
3. Don't begin with an empty, say-nothing expression or a generality that fails to distinguish this news from other news: There were... In a report released today... According to...
4. Don't begin with a question if the question is answered in the story. Question leads are cliché leads.
5. Don't begin with a direct quote if it is a full sentence. Don't start with a quote unless it is an exceptional quote.
6. Don't use a form of the verb to be in the lead, if you can avoid it. Use an action verb.
7. Don't overstate the news in the lead, making it more dramatic than it really is. Watch "disaster" words.

Elements of Good Writing

1. *Precision:* Use the right word. Say exactly what you mean. Be specific. Avoid sexism in your writing. Use generic terms: firefighters instead of firemen, letter carriers instead of mailmen.
2. Clarity: Use simple sentences. Noun, verb. Think clearly, then write. Watch grammar and punctuation.
3. *Pacing:* Movement of sentences create a tone, mood for the story. Long sentences convey relaxed, slow mood. Short declarative sentences convey action, tension, movement. Use variety of sentence lengths. Use shorter sentences when writing about the more active, tense part of the story.
4. *Transitions:* Progress logically from point to point. Put everything in order.
5. *Sensory Appeal:* Appeal to one or more of our five senses: sight, hearing, smell, taste and touch. What does it sound like? Was the room too hot? Could you smell the cooking outside on the walkway? Did the

person speak slowly and carefully, or rapidly, with confidence?

6. *Using Analogies:* Describe it as being "like" or "as" something that is familiar to readers.

Ten-Point Checkoff List

1. Accuracy
2. Brevity
3. Clarity
4. Be specific
5. Get to the point
6. Put things in order
7. Get quotes right
8. Write smooth/active voice
9. Grammar/spelling/AP style
10. Five Ws/answer all the questions

Story Organization

What do I want to say? Where do I put it?

1. The lead
2. Material that explains and amplifies the lead
3. Necessary background material
4. Secondary or less important material
5. Descending pyramids
6. Narrative
7. Transitions
8. Quotes
9. Ending

Form Versus Content

Form becomes part of content. Without form, content can be lost. Know what you want to say. Then say it. Don't begin by saying something else which you think will lead up to what you want to say. (The city council met last night.) Never start writing without a plan in mind. Even long, complicated stories can be stated in a sentence or two.

Avoid Logical Fallacies

Hasty generalization — a conclusion based on insufficient or unrepresentative evidence. Deaths from drug overdoses in Fremont have doubled in the past three years. Therefore, more Americans than ever are dying from drug abuse. Many hasty generalizations contain words like all, every, always and never, when qualifiers such as most, many, usually and seldom would be more accurate. Either have enough data to verify your statements or use qualifiers. Non Sequitur (Latin for "does not follow") — a conclusion that does not follow logically from preceding statements or that is based on irrelevant data.

False Analogy — falsely assumes that because two things are alike in one respect, they must be alike in others. *If we can put a man on the moon, we should be able to find a cure for the common cold.* Both are scientific challenges, but quite different.

Either... Or Fallacy — the suggestion that only two alternatives exist when if fact there are more. *Either the 49ers find a new running back, or they will never make it to the Super Bowl. Actually,* the team could make it to the Super Bowl without a new running back.

Faulty Cause-And-Effect Reasoning — assuming that because one event follows another, the first is the cause of the second. Like a non sequitur, it is a leap to an unjustified conclusion. *Since Gov. Smith took office, unemployment in the state has decreased by 7 percent. Gov. Smith should be applauded for reducing unemployment.* We must show Gov. Smith's policies caused the decrease.

Circular Reasoning — instead of supporting the conclusion with evidence, the writer simply restates the conclusion in different language. *Faculty and administrators should not be permitted to come to student council meetings because student council meetings should be for students only.* The writer has not explained the position, but has merely repeated the point.

Active Voice, Passive Voice

Voice is that inflection of a verb that shows whether its subject is the doer of the action indicated or is acted upon. If the subject performs the action, the verb is in the active voice. If the subject is acted upon, the verb is in the passive voice. Active voice is dynamic. Passive voice is static. Active voice is vigorous and emphasizes the actor. Passive voice is evasive about naming the actor.

News writing should almost always be in the active voice because news is about action and actors. To test for the active voice, find the subject and verb in the sentence. Put the subject before the verb so that the subject takes action: *Jill hit the ball,* not: *The ball was hit by Jill.*

CHAPTER 4

Sports Interview

Being an exceptional sports writer simply means being an exceptional interviewer— the writing pales if the interviewing skills are mediocre. You can't use in print what you don't get during an interview. Some techniques are simply timeless. Consider the following three quotations, the first from William Zinsser (1985) book, *On Writing Well, An Informal Guide to Writing Nonfiction*; the second is from John Brady (1976) The Craft of Interviewing; and the last is from DeWitt Reddick (1949) Modern Feature Writing.

Interviewing is one of those skills that you only get better at. You will never again feel so ill at ease as when you try for the first time, and probably you will never feel entirely comfortable prodding another person for answers that he or she may be too shy to reveal, or too inarticulate. But at least half of the skill is purely mechanical. The rest is instinct— knowing how to make the other person relax, when to push, when to listen, when to stop. And this can be learned with experience (Zinsser, 1985, p. 79).

Interviewing is the modest, immediate science of gaining trust, then gaining information. Both ends must be balanced if the interview is to be balanced and incisive. Yet they are often fumbled in the anxious heat of an interview. The interviewer will either yearn too desperately for his subject's trust and evoke flatulence, or he will restrain his sympathies, demand data—and get like in return (Brady, 1976, p. 68).

The writer should prepare in advance many of the questions he plans to ask. These questions should not be haphazard and unrelated, but should spring from the central idea of the story, as he sees it. Preferably he should visualize two or three possible lines of development for the story, and think out questions along each line; thus he will be prepared to adjust himself to the line which seems most promising during the interview. The beginner will find it helpful to write out his leading questions; most experienced writers may prefer to think clearly through the story as it may develop along three or four angles, and to carry these lines of thought in mind (Reddick, 1949, p. 94).

There are a variety of techniques and tricks of the trade regarding the *art* and *craft* of interviewing. Many can simply be summarized. Some rules and guidelines for interviewing may easily be recognized by novice writers—others, however, are matters of psychology and perception that may require some experience. Understanding these advanced principles and ideas may help the novice or intermediate interviewer obtain much more valuable interviews. (The techniques and guidelines in this section refer largely to the person-to-person interview. On occasion, however, the telephone interview or the mail response may be used.) In this section, suggestions and guidelines are offered, generally in order from the basic to the most advanced and in the most logical order.

Read all you can about your subject before the interview. If you work for a newspaper, ask your newspaper librarian to dig up back files for you. Read everything in newspaper or magazine form that has been published about your subject. This will allow you to *Prepare in advance*. Write down likely questions. Both DeWitt Reddick and John Brady refer to the Boy Scout motto: *Be prepared*. There is no substitute for preparation.

If you prepare for two or three or four avenues of interview development, the more information you will obtain and the less likely you will be to be caught off guard mentally during an interview. Time the interview to fit your subject's schedule. Change your own schedule first, if possible. Don't inconvenience the subject's time for your own schedule. If you have a deadline for the story, however, mention that. The subject will usually be willing to meet with you at a time that will allow you to complete the article prior to the deadline. Be patient. If you are interviewing someone on the edges of the sports world, this might be the first time they have been interviewed. Many people are unacquainted with reporters or interviewers. In "The Interview or The Only Wheel in Town," the Journalism Monographs' Eugene J. Webb and Jerry Salancik (1966) suggested that there may be problems regarding your subject's answers:

1. The potential source may not know the information (the reporter seeks).
2. The source may be aware and want to tell but lacks the verbal skills to do so.
3. The source may be willing but not want to tell.
4. The source may be willing but unable to produce the information because it is buried beyond his conscious ability to recall it.

Ask questions in chronological order. If you are interviewing for a personality portrait or profile, proceeding through these five areas may give you comprehensive answers:

1. Birth—location and date—and youth;
2. Education;

3. Military service if any—dates, speciality, and location;
4. Marriage—including spouse's name and age of children, if any;
5. Career—to date.

Ask for dates. Ages, dates of marriage, beginning of career, career achievements—the subject's ages at those times. These dates supply readers with a ready reference to parallel their own life to the life of your subject.

Ask why questions: These demand the subject explain positions, career choices, and beliefs.

Why do you believe such-and-such?

If this is your best season as player, *why*?

Why is this team better than last year?

Why do you believe your coaching techniques are better than your opposition?

In addition to *why* questions, the *how or how did it happen* question may be equally important. Professional athletes may not be articulate enough to explain why something happened—why they have a particularly distinct golf swing or why they have a trademark style, or even why they chose a particular play at a particular time.

It might be more productive to ask: "Show me what you do—demonstrate your swing for me.... Show me what you did at that time.... *How* did you do that?"

In watching the *how's* of their technique, you may also be able to determine the *why's*—why they play the way they do.

Get a telephone number for any additional trivial details you may need to call *back for*. Don't drive across town for two or three additional questions if you can make a telephone call. If the subject has an unlisted telephone, promise you won't disclose it to others, and keep your promise.

Interview All Possible Sources: If you are interviewing Bonnie Blair or Picabo Street, two U.S. winners in the 1994 Olympics, for instance, ask them who else should be interviewed: parents, coaches, teammates, or others. The question often arises: How do I know when I have enough interviews for a major story? The cynical answer is: When is your deadline? How much time do you have, working backward from that time, to get interviews done and the story written?

The ideal answer is to interview until you come full circle. During every interview, you should ask, "Who else should I talk to?" If you are interviewing A for a major story, and A tells you to talk to B, C, and D, you work your way around the subject until persons X, Y, and Z tell you to see B, C, and D. When you have run out of interview subjects around A, it's time to start to write the story; or, when you begin to hear the same anecdotes from a variety of subjects, it's time to begin the writing process. It is seldom-good practice to arbitrarily limit yourself to five interviews or six or seven. How do you know that the eighth or ninth or tenth would not have given you the best material for your story?

Don't be a Cheerleader: Asking a question like, "Sure was a good game, wasn't it coach?" leads to a laconic answer: "Yep." That is a very small crumb to use in your story. Even breaking the ice in a conversation with a comment like that is a lame beginning. *Be aware that many coaches and some players expect you to "be on their side."*

Indiana basketball coach Bobby Knight and many others adopt an "us against the media" attitude. As a sports writer, you have at least four choices when encountering these defensive (no pun intended) individuals:

1. Negotiate with them if they show an aggressive attitude towards you as an interviewer.
2. Interview assistant coaches—or "interview around the subject."
3. Trade notes with a reporter from a non-competing publication.

If you work for a newspaper that covers Bobby Knight's team, trade notes with a news-paper reporter in a noncompeting area.

4. Use the coach's belligerent attitude in the story—as accurately as possible.

If he gets into trouble from the story, that's his problem, not your problem as a reporter.

Don't fail to ask the obvious.

Why did you, coach, go for that field goal instead of a pass? Why did you play for a tie instead of a win?

Why did you call for that particular play on the 37 with a minute and a half left in the game?

Games seldom explain themselves fully. Ask about the key play that won the game—or lost it—for a particular coach or team. *If you are a print reporter, learn as much as you can about tape recorders, modem connections, video cameras, and the like.* Radio and TV reporters, for the most part, are adept at electronic equipment. Print reporters are less so. But there is little reason why, in these days, print reporters should not use quality tape recorders. And there are several good reasons why they *should*. If you are working on a controversial story about, for instance, ticket scalping, or illegal university football payoffs, interviews on tape are a sure source of proof of what exactly was said. This sort of taped proof is a good—although not complete—defence against a charge of libel, or a defence against a slightly less dangerous charge: "I was misquoted."

If you have the luxury to delay completing a story for a few days, or don't have an immediate deadline, the tape will stay fresh. It will be as easy to use several days, months, or years later, as it was the day it was made. One key tip that many reporters do not use: If the first draft of a lengthy story "falls flat" or toneless and if the style is not exactly what the writer intended, or if the story has a lack of focus or is weak in transitions or style, reading the story onto tape and listening to it may help the reporter find dead spots that will have to be rewritten.

The reporter should go into an interview situation with the recorder ready for use. The reporter should proceed with the explanation (if an explanation is needed) that the tape will make the interview much more accurate and reliable. If the interview subject objects to a tape recording, then the reporter should go ahead with the interview without the tape—but should try first to negotiate with the subject that the tape is: (a) important, and (b) more accurate than handwritten notes. Few people these days object to tape recordings. (Hint: The reporter might offer to have a duplicate tape made for the subject—to reassure the subject that quotes used in the article were accurately taken from the tape. The cost is minimal and the good will earned is priceless.)

Avoid the moral problems of using "off the record" remarks. What if, during an interview, someone says to you "I'll tell you what you need to know, but don't quote me." What do you do? First, don't agree to any conditions. Don't use the material you hear. If you use it without citing the source, what could be the result? Your interview subject may simply be lying to you and manipulating you (for his or her own purposes). If you didn't confirm the material and if you didn't use his or her name as the source, who is responsible for any potential libel suit? Whose name is on the by line?

As Leonard Koppett (1981) wrote, in Sports Illusion, Sports Reality: A Reporter's View of Sports, Journalism and Society: People have all sorts of ideas, opinions, judgments and intentions that they don't want to see attributed to them in print or on the air. As a reporter, you want to know as many of these things as you can, to increase your understanding of what goes on around you. So you must follow strictly two self-imposed limitations: Confidentiality and relevance. Some of the varieties of confidentiality are:

1. *Off the Record:* Don't say I told you, but use the information if you can substantiate it some other way.
2. *Know but Don't Use:* Be aware that such-and-such is the situation, but don't make it public until I say O.K.
3. *Not for Attribution:* Go ahead and use the information the way I'm giving it to you, but don't say it came from me.
4. *Private:* Here's what happened, but does it really have to be made public?
5. *Top Secret:* If this gets out, I'm finished; let your conscience be your guide.

The reporter may have to determine which of these guidelines applies to the situation at hand, and then work accordingly. Sometimes an agreement can be worked out with the interview subject in a nonverbal way; the reporter may say, "This is not for attribution to you?" The subject may agree with a wink and a grin.

Koppett (1981) also wrote: In his relationship to news sources, the ideal journalist observes four "don'ts" along with stubborn devotion to the principles of confidentiality and relevance:

1. Don't take cheap shots.
2. Don't form close friendships.
3. Don't be afraid of arousing anger, but don't pick on people just to show you're not afraid.
4. Don't deny an error, or compound it by looking for justification.

Get Your Subject to Confirm or Deny Previously Published Material: If there has been an article published recently that pertains to your story, ask your interview subject to comment on it. You may get powerful quotations to use, or a second breaking story. Asking your subject to confirm or deny previously published material also helps in other ways—it clarifies the record for you and eliminates any confusion you might have about the status of your subject in relation to the story in print. (Your subject may not have been able to tell his or her side of the story.).

Interview in Tranquillity: The best interviews are one on one. If you can, get the subject away from the locker room, or his favourite bar, or away from his cronies. The subject may use the locker room to be "on stage" for his friends. He may *play to them* instead of paying complete attention to you.

Ask for PR material, background material, or other material that the subject or press office may have. Many organizations are extremely helpful when it comes to furnishing an interviewer with background material, clippings, and other material. If you receive valuable or rare material of any kind, promise to make copies of it and return the original material as soon as possible. And keep your promise.

If you work with a PR office, be aware that on occasion, their job is to keep press *away* from an athlete or club owner, or to make sure that the writer receives only the "company line." PR staffers usually—but not always—work to aid the writer. If there is any doubt about their motives, ask yourself *who pays their salary?* You don't. Be sure you use slang terms accurately. There is no easier way for a sports buff or interview subject to spot an error in an article than to see slang misused. If you have doubts about what a slang term means—especially in a Sports you have never covered before—make sure you verify it; and not just the meaning—the spelling, too.

Court records, divorces, lawsuits, and the like are public property. You can and should look up this material if it is germane to your story. If you work for a newspaper and have any doubts about how court records can be obtained, consult with a police reporter, editor, or corporate attorney. If you area freelancer, court clerks and staff members may be able to help you obtain court records. Ask controversial questions at the end of an interview, not at the beginning. Don't begin an interview with a fired college football coach by asking about NCAA rules violations. Don't begin an interview with an athlete accused of steroid use by asking about the drug charges. In all probability, the interview will end just after it began.

If you ask these questions at the end of a 2-hour interview, the subject may relent and answer the question, because you have established a solid professional relationship. If, after 2 hours or x hours, the subject refuses to answer, you have your notes and material from the full interview and you can possibly use the anger or denial in the story itself:

At the end of an interview, ask the subject if he or she has anything to add that hasn't been touched upon. Occasionally, a subject will withhold valuable information on the logical theory that if a writer didn't ask about it, it isn't important. The writer might not know about the valuable anecdote that the subject has on the tip of his tongue.

Don't be awed by your subject. In *The Craft of Interviewing,* John Brady (1976) quoted staff writer John Underwood of Sports Illustrated:

> Remember if you tend to be awed by athletes, you will never allow yourself to see a man's inner sanctum, and that will, in itself, distort the picture. The thing about sports heroes is that they are just a cut away from the friend you play golf with. There's a whole lot of difference between Einstein and the guy who makes A's in his college chemistry class, but the professional athlete and the kid who wins letters in college are only a shade apart.

Be skeptical—or wary—of any athlete, owner, or sports figure who has been interviewed frequently in the past. You may complete an interview that appeared to be completely spontaneous, only to discover later, from reading old files, that you got slight variations of the same interview that the subject has been giving for years. Without a fresh angle, your story is essentially worthless. Or, you may discover during an interview that your subject's mind is on "autopilot," rehashing old answers from months or years ago.

The worst situation as a reporter is having no story at all because you were asked to leave after your first question, a controversial one, which the subject refused to answer. The second worst situation is ending an interview only to discover later, with a heavy sinking feeling, that you have the same material that your interview subject has given in interviews countless times before. Be prepared for an occasional "confessional" or "guilt" interview. Although these are rare, some interviewees perceive an interview as the cheapest psychiatric hour possible, and will tell you stories you could not imagine. As a reporter, you should understand that some people will simply perceive you differently than you expect.

You will go into the interview simply as a reporter, but the interview subject may see you as an authority figure, a parent, almost a member of the clergy, a psychiatrist, a threat, a police figure, a temporary respite from their own world, a foil for their own jokes, or a vehicle to spread malicious rumours about others. If they perceive you in the context of those person as, their answers will be "skewed," as researchers say. Even if the interview subject doesn't specifically indicate that you, as a reporter, are a father figure, psychiatrist, priest, or cop, you may perceive that the thrust of the interview is going in that direction. When that happens, facts or data gathering become secondary in nature. Interview hours may become—for subject and interviewer—intense hours of personality analysis: background, motives, behaviours, and personal history.

Does this happen often? No, but when it does, the reporter must be observant enough to recognize what is taking place, how the interview is progressing, and the significance of how the interview subject is perceiving the reporter and the interview.

Personal interviews are often the keys to exceptional nonfiction writing. By remembering the two Ps: preparation and professionalism, sports writers should be able to turn significant and perceptive interviews into exceptional pieces of nonfiction.

THE ART OF OBSERVATION

Careful observation is absolutely necessary for a nonfiction writer. It is said that some writers have a "tin ear" for dialogue: Their conversation on the page simply doesn't sound real (because they don't really listen to how people talk). Other writers have a similar visual tin ear: They omit significant details or use in appropriate ones. The use of observed details in nonfiction serves several important functions:

- The use of substantial details draws the reader into the scene and thus into the article. You can think of observed details as small brushstrokes that fill in a painting; without these details, the painting, the scene, lies lifeless on the page. Without details, you only half-convince readers of what is happening, where, and when. Without details, readers are left with staticicons—cliché images in their imagination. Details add texture to the word painting you are crafting on the page.

  As a sports writer, you are the eyes of your reader—you witness a scene when the reader can't. You must describe a scene or action the reader has not witnessed.
- Observed details also prove the writer was there, witnessing the action. In the following article, note the seventh paragraph from the beginning: "That would be his first time to ride Bodacious, and other riders had been razzing him about it all afternoon." How would the writer know that the "other riders had been razzing him about it all afternoon?" By being there;

by watching and perhaps staking notes. Stated another way, observed details validate the writer's story.

- Observed details reveal human behaviour. Writers should always look for significance in human behaviour. Otherwise, the use of observation and dialogue are point less.

The following article, "Tough Bucks," was written by Houston Chronicle staff writer Cheryl Laird. This article was published in the "Houston" section of the Houston Chronicle, Saturday, March 5, 1994, during the annual Houston Livestock Show and Rodeo, one of the biggest such events in the country. Notice how physically close Laird gets to the chute where Bodacious, the bull, is ready. Note carefully how she describes the preride seconds, then Cody Custer's ride. Later in the article, she describes Bodacious as an "arm-puller," and shows the reader "a star-shaped spot" (scar) on rider Cody Lambert's chin, the result of one ride on Bodacious. Notice also how Laird's use of quotations supplement the observed details:

- "It's a strain," says Darrell Cholach, a bareback rider from Alberta, Canada. "If you're not riding him good with all parts of your body, you're on the ground. He's magnificent."
- "Bodacious is as rank as any there is in the world", says longtime bullfighter Miles Hare. "He'll turn sideways in the air, but he lands on his feet. He's like a cat."
- "He's electric," Hare says. "You react. He reacts. You jump. He jumps. He's on a natural high in life."
- "Bodacious, when he was a calf, you could tell he was an athlete. He could jump sideways and kick the side of a gate when walkingthrough," says his owner, Sammy Andrews of Addielou in northeast Texas. "He's a MichaelJordan of animals."

Tough Bucks: Cowboys Ride Hard and Earn Every Dollar —By Cheryl Laird

His eyes were those of a professional, calm and focused. His ears were the only sign of what was to come. They flapped back and forth, pivoting at every noise. Suddenly, with the speed and sound of a cannon shot, he slammed his forehead hard into the front of the bucking chute. The cowboys pulling the straps around his white belly watched warily, with respect and, in some eyes, fear.

They were dealing with Skoal Is Bodacious—the baddest bucking bull in the Astrodome. Cody Custer, an even-tempered world champion bull rider from Arizona, squatted in his chaps to stretch out his legs. This would be his first time to ride Bodacious, and other riders had been razzing him about it all day.

He'd stared that afternoon at the oversize, off-white Charolais-Brahman crossbreed. "Hey, Bodacious," he'd called. The bull recognized his name and looked at him with placid eyes. But Custer knew the bull wouldn't act the tame barnyard pet before 57,000 people in the Astrodome. Bodacious, in his mind and a lot of other opinions, was the rankest bull in the world. "My heart's beating, and I'm a little bit butterfly-ish right now," Custer acknowledged before the ride. "This is probably the biggest challenge in my life." The slim cowboy lowered himself carefully on the broad white back, held his hand` high in the air, and nodded curtly. The gate flew open.

The bull jumped sideways once, then lunged forward in an elastic buck that sent his back legs flying above his rider's head. For a moment, it looked as if Custer could with stand the force. Then his body flipped forward and to the side. A horn grazed his cheek as he hit the dirt. His attempt at Bodacious lasted two seconds. "I don't know," Custer said afterward, as if he didn't quite believe what had just happened. "He does something to get your feet behind you."

In the rodeo world, tough bucking stock are admired almost as much as tough cowboys. Riders know bulls and broncs by their names, or at least their brands. They know their records.

Each year, they vote on the best bull, bareback bronc and saddle bronc in their rodeo circuits. Stock contractors whose animals are chosen receive cash awards and, more important, a major kind of parental ego boost. Like baseball players who make it to the major leagues, the best animals end up on the Professional Rodeo Cowboys Association circuit. The best of those go on to the biggest rodeos, like Houston's. Of all the bulls at the Astrodome this year, the unofficial consensus is that Bodacious is the rankest. Of the bareback horses, a big gray from Canada named High Chaparral Copenhagen wins top honours.

High Chaparral was voted PRCA bareback horse of the year in 1989 and 1992. Horses don't usually buck off top-ranked cowboys, but High Chaparral is an exception. He's known as an "arm puller" because the force of his jump makes a rider feel as if his arm is being yanked out of its socket. "He's kinda like standing by a railroad track and a train comes by and you grab onto it," says Marvin Garrett, a world champion bareback rider from South Dakota who has successfully ridden the bronc. "I don't know many guys who want to have him." "It's a strain," says Darrell Cholach, a bareback rider from Alberta, Canada. "If you're not riding him good with all parts of your body, you're on the ground. He's magnificent."

Both Bodacious and High Chaparral are scheduled to be ridden, or at least attempted to be ridden, during Sunday's finals at the Houston Livestock Show and Rodeo. For rodeo fans, that lineup is about equal to a Hakeem Olajuwon-Shaquille O'Neal matchup. Riders are randomly assigned to animals. Half of their possible 100-point score depends solely on how hard their mounts buck. For the most adventure some and talented riders, drawing a Bodacious or a High Chaparral is a plus. If they stay on, they're guaranteed to do well.

But even the best riders don't usually stay on Bodacious. In 1993, he was voted the best bucking bull in Texas. Twenty-nine cowboys attempted to ride him for eight seconds last year. Only two did. The most recent was Tuff Hedemanin November. He scored a nearly perfect 95 points. Behind the bucking chutes in the Astrodome earlier this week, world champion bull rider Cody Lambert leaned back his head and pointed to a star-shaped spot when asked about Bodacious. "He put this scar under my chin at this here rodeo," Lambert said. "For six seconds, I thought I was going to be 90 (points). Then I was out. That's the only time I got on him, and that's the only time I want to ride him."

Despite his big size, Bodacious bucks with as much quick movement as a little bull. He doesn't have a set pattern. He jumps high in the air and twists. His front end drops to the ground, as Lambert says, "like an anvil." "Bodacious is as rank as any there is in the world," says longtime bullfighter Miles Hare. "He'll turn sideways in the air, but he lands on his feet. This bull is like a cat." Hare makes his living facing down bulls, trying to distract them as bruised riders hobble away. He has to be especially quick on his feet to stay ahead of Bodacious' curved horns.

"He's electric," Hare says. "You react. He reacts. You jump. He jumps. He's on a natural high in life." Bodacious was born on a ranch in northwest Oklahoma. He was big, active and stream lined like a greyhound. Like about half of today's bucking stock, he was bred specifically for the rodeo circuit. "Bodacious, when he was a calf, you could tell he was an athlete. He could jump sideways and kick the side of a gate when walking through," says his owner, Sammy Andrews of Addielou in northeast Texas. "He's a Michael Jordan of animals."

The first few times with a rider, Bodacious bucked only half-heartedly, Andrews says. But then a rookie caught his hand in the rigging, scaring both himself and the 3-year-old bull. Bodacious has rarely failed to put on fireworks since. Stock contractors Sammy and Carolyn Andrews buy about 30 yearling bulls every year in hopes of getting a good bucker. They usually look for Brahman crossbreeds with broad faces and tiger-striped coats. According to rodeo lore, these usually buck the best.

They put the chosen animals in a wheat field for one year, and then send them to a dairy farm the next year in a sort of exchange programme. The dairy farmer gets free mates for his heifers, and the Andrewses get free grain for their young bulls. At 3 years, the bulls are big enough for riding. For the first time, the Andrewses usually strap a foam-rubber dummy wearing overalls onto the bull's back. If the bulls don't buck at all, they are either retired as breeding stock or made into hamburger.

If they buck, they are matched with beginner bull riders. Usually the teen-age cowboys fall off, which is what the Andrewses want. There's no way to convince a bull to buck, they say. It has to enjoy seeing its rider hit the ground. Sometimes, if an older bull gets sour, Carolyn Andrews says she lets it "throw some kids off and build up his confidence again." Rusty Bradberry, a wiry man with an easy grin, takes care of the Andrewses' bucking stock. Last year he drove Bodacious more than 40,000 miles around the country. He says the bull is starting to like him, but not so much that he allows petting.

"When we first got him, he didn't like anybody. He'd run away from you. Now when we go to feed him, he's the first one there. He kinda knows hegets special attention." Bradberry says. "Everybody thinks they're just dumb animals, and they're not." When Bodacious is finished with his cowboy here Sunday, Bradberry will drive him home to his shaded 100-acre pasture for a week's rest before his next rodeo. The bull is almost 7 years old, and he'll probably travel for a few more years before being retired as a full-time daddy.

Cody Custer hopes he'll have another shot at him before then. After his ill-fated ride in the Astrodome, he glanced over at the big, white bull. Bodacious was standing passively in a metal corral with the other bulls. The cowboy grinned and gingerly touched his swollen, raw cheek. "I ain't a scared of him now," he said, almost convincingly.

In the following article, "KO'ed by His Demons" (Putnam, 1985), notice how much of the "detail" of the article is observed behaviour. Sports Illustrated senior writer Pat Putnam not only captured Aaron Pryor's speech—slurred and in coherent as it was—but also his behaviour, and added summary to buttress his observations, as in this passage: "Pryor, who had been on the verge of tears, now laughs, a tick of joy which passes swiftly. His moods alter from moment to moment, switching bewilderingly from dark storm clouds to bright sunlight." And: "Pryor's eyelids become heavy. His head nods forward. He seems asleep. Then his eyes pop open, blinking, and he rubs them furiously."

Putnam's observed details of Pryor's behaviour and Pryor' statements are buttressed by police records and previous statements to the press (cited towards the end of the article). It seems clear that "the visitor" mentioned early in the article and then again four paragraphs from the end of the article is Putnam the writer, a sophisticated method of "appearing" in the narrative without using the "I" form: "I asked him about such-and-such and he said _____."

Here is the complete article. What do you think of Aaron Pryor?

—KO'ED BY HIS DEMONS

Unbeaten and still a champion, Aaron Pryor is angry, despondent and confused. And he's in no condition to fight, either in or out of the ring.

—By Pat Putnam

The spirit that helped make Aaron Pryor a great boxer seems burned out now. His eyes, half shut against Miami's summer sun, are dying embers in a face left gaunt by too many nights without sleep, too many parties, too many fears. He is surrounded by people with their hands in his pockets, but he drifts alone in a dark world of self-created demons, ever-changing suspicions that taunt and torment him.

He is the reigning and undefeated IBF junior welter weight champion, this gifted and exciting fighter, and each day he pledges that tomorrow he will go back into training. But for Pryor, a fatherless child of almost 30, such a tomorrow dances continually beyond his grasp. His life, always turbulent, has veered almost totally out of control.

He is suing to collect $300,000 that he claims promoter Richard Mangone refused to pay him for a June 22, 1984 decision over Gary Hinton in Atlantic City that left his professional record at 36-0. Pryor's second wife, Theresa, divorced him. A Cincinnati court awarded her more than $200,000 and Pryor's 1983 Cadillac. By June, rumours intensified that Pryor was wedded to another wife: cocaine. His mother, Sarah, signed papers in an attempt to have him committed to a Miami drug rehabilitation centre. He refused to go. On June 30, Pryor told Miami police he had been abducted. The police, after investigating, discounted his story. He says that two of his cars—a 1985 Ford van and an '85 Saab turbo, distinguishable by bullet scars on their bodies, were stolen. He also claims someone made off with his M16 rifle.

Life has lain heavy on Pryor's psyche. He was born out of wedlock and left his home in Cincinnati at 14. "I was a kid nobody paid any attention to," he says. "Some nights I just said to hell with it and slept in a doorway. Wasn't anything at home for me anyway."? From such a beginning, it's not hard to understand why Pryor has always hungered for love and respect; why he has never quite been able to trust anyone.

As a fighter, his strength and skills made him unbeatable. On the street, his suspicious nature and hidden rage left him vulnerable and winless. Still, despite his almost feral lifestyle, Pryor seemed in command of his actions.

Before the first of his two wins over Alexis Arguello, in November 1982, Pryor saw fit to change his image. He replaced his gold front tooth with a white porcelain cap. He abandoned his gaudy wardrobe for conservative suits, white shirts and striped ties. He even carried a briefcase. He was a time bomb in Brooks Brothers wrapping. On this late summer day, Pryor is seated on a gray sofa in the screened-in pool area behind his well-kept home in southwest Miami. He has lived in the area since 1983. His upper body, once thick with muscle, is frail now, covered loosely by a Michael Jackson T shirt. He is holding Norra, whom he introduces as his 10-week-old daughter. "I can trust you," he tells the baby softly. He sighs and looks up. "And my dog, Clyde. I trust him. But nobody else."

Norra (her name is a variation of "Aaron" spelled backward) makes a small sound, and Pryor, who had been on the verge of tears, now laughs, a tick of joy, which passes swiftly. His moods alter from moment to moment, switching be wild eringly from dark storm clouds to bright sunlight. Carefully, he sets the baby beside him on the sofa. "Right now I am confused," Pryor says to a visitor. His voice, barely audible, is sad and wistful. "After my last fight, I felt nobody was concerned about injuries to myself. Nobody was really interested in me, only in what they can find to promote me or find out about me to hurt me. I was made to look the bad guy. Now as I look at you, as I talk to you, I find out even more of my problem. I swear. One of my eyes. I had an eye examination prior to my [last fight]." He switches thoughts without pause or reason. "Made me come across one way, yet at the same time meaning to come across another way to express myself."

Anger strengthens his voice. "Like my left eye here. They don't want me to tell nobody. I've got to tell somebody." Pausing, Pryor covers his right eye with his right hand. "You see that eye here?" he asks, meaning the uncovered left one. He looks down at a small table in front of him. "I can't see nothing on the table. But yet I can open it up," he says, uncovering the right eye, "and see things."

The baby begins to cry, and for a moment the sound washes away Pryor's anguish. "O.K., kid. Shut up," he says laughing. Through an open glass door he calls to his housekeeper. "Hey, Maggie, bring a bottle for the baby."

"Are you blind in the left eye?" the visitor asks Pryor.

"I believe I am," he says. "I don't have enough vision to see. But, yet, nobody wants to talk about the bad part of me, the things that are happening in my life. All they want to talk about is that Pryor has left boxing, he's out doing something else. I'm just doing something about trying to get my eyesight."

"When did you notice the eye?"

Pryor rubs his eyes. "Just after the last fight," he says.

"Was it bothering you before?"

He nods angrily. "It's been about three years now. But nobody was interested in me. Examined in Atlantic City. They told me not to come back there anymore until I can see. That was after my last fight. And, really, you know, my last fight I had a lot of problems."

Pryor's disjointed conversation settles randomly on moments in his career. After stopping Arguello for the second time on Sept. 9, 1983, he abdicated his WBA junior welterweight championship, saying that he was tired, that he didn't want to fight anymore. He was in his prime: just 28 years old and 34-0. Just before that fight, he had been served with divorce papers by Theresa, who once, before they were married, had shot him in the right forearm. But Pryor, who had retained his IBF title, came out of retirement and fought twice, the match against Furlano and the split decision over Hinton. He gave an uninspired imitation of the real Aaron Pryor in both fights.

> "I didn't get paid the first fight, [with] Nicky Furlano," Pryor is saying. "I didn't get one dime. I quit boxing and gave up my title because [they] said I was ... black bottle . . . and preached to me about it."

The black-bottle reference is to his first fight with Arguello, when it was suspected that Pryor had taken stimulants from a bottle wrapped with black tape. The late Artie Curley, who worked Pryor's corner that night, said the bottle contained peppermint schnapps.

> "I said I'll fight Alexis again and there won't be no black bottle," Pryor says. "And then, after I beat him a second time, I thought I had cleared up the black-bottle thing, but I never got no credit for winning straight up. Then I didn't get one dime [for the Furlano fight]. I quit boxing and give up my title.... Then I laid off for a year and a half, and they don't pay me for my first comeback fight. Three hundred thousand. The promoter. Oh, man, why me?"

In fact, Pryor did receive some payment for the Furlano fight—$50,000 in front money and another $50,000 for training expenses. The dispute with Mangone is over whether any more money is due. In June, Pryor and his manager, Buddy LaRosa, were to fly from Miami to Boston to give depositions in their suit against Mangone. LaRosa says that after trying for four days to hook up with Pryor at the Miami airport, he returned home to Cincinnati. Pryor has earned some $4 million in his eight-year career, but friends say he is heading for financial ruin. LaRosa says that if Pryor doesn't get to Boston soon, the court may dismiss his claim against Mangone.

Now Pryor leans forward, his voice a conspirational whisper. "I don't want to elaborate too much because I do hope to fight again, and I don't want to [mess up] my career," he says. "I'm not supposed to mention it. But I'm tired of talking about everything else. Cataracts, cataracts. They told me not to come to Atlantic City or Vegas no more. Because I'm blind in one eye. I want to get my eye fixed and continue to fight."

If Pryor has been banned from fighting for medical reasons, officials in Nevada and New Jersey know nothing about it. "He's not under any suspension here," says Chuck Minker, a Nevada boxing inspector. Bob Lee, the acting commissioner of the New Jersey State Athletic Commission says Pryor is still in good standing in his state. An Atlantic City ophthalmologist, David Smith, did find a cataract in Pryor's left eye before the Hinton fight in March, and the commission warned Pryor to have the problem treated before it hampered his career. But, says Lee, "It wasn't bad enough to prevent him from fighting Hinton. And he's not barred here."

Pryor's eyelids become heavy. His head nods forward. He seems asleep. Then his eyes pop open, blinking, and he rubs them furiously. He calls for Maggie to bring coffee "Cataracts, yeah," he says. "Then my mother. [I hadn't seen] her for at least a year. And she come up here. I didn't know she was coming, but one day she is here. She says what she's heard." What she had heard were rumours of her son's drug problem. In July she told the Cincinnati Post that she had seen Aaron use cocaine.

> "I got the baby and the van and just left home," Pryor says. "Hey, man! Are you giving me a charge or somethin'? You must be giving me a charge or something, in my eye."

"Something wrong?" the visitor asks.

"Need some coffee. Don't you ever get tired? Down in Florida, it's the air. Yeah, my problems. They started when my mother came here. She came to take over. She was handling my checkbook. I feel I'm back where I started because of my mother. She's got a nice house, a Cadillac, she's never worked. And she never introduced me to my father. About nine years ago I put my mother in an institution. I was only 21. She shot her husband. I was driving a school bus and I went home and they say my mama had shot my dad, my stepdad. I put her in a hospital because she had lost her nerves. I think. . . ." He pauses, shakes his head and sighs. "I think she don't like me because she done those things to me."

Mrs. Pryor would make no comment to SI about her involvement in any shooting. She was ordered into silence by William Hardy, her brother-in-law and Pryor's uncle, who is known to family and friends as Uncle Chocolate. "I'm his uncle and his trainer," he says of Pryor, "and this boy is gonna fight better than ever. You are getting that straight from the horse's mouth."

On the patio, Pryor's words continue to tumble forth. "My eye, shocks and everything," he says, casting suspicious glances in all directions. "I think somebody is looking in here and hearing every word we say. I'm a true person. I can feel it." He relaxes after Maggie shuts the patio door. "O.K., I feel better now. Anyway . . . here I am, 36 and oh with 32 knockouts. I went 15 rounds my last fight. I went four days before that fight without eating, I swear. I had to lay in the hallways to lose four extra pounds. I came home, and the only thing I worked on was not Training, because when I train I build up a big appetite. I went on a diet, I lose weight, and people tell me I'm crazy." Pryor gives his weight this day as 138 pounds. He appears to weigh 120 at most.

He puts his face in his hands and gets around to talking about his "abduction." "Oh, it's kind of painful to talk," he says. "I don't have nobody to talk to; nobody comes here; nobody knows me. They all know me, and I don't know them. It hurts so bad. And then I picked a couple of guys up in Miami when I first got here, and we talk: 'Hey, what's going on. All right.' So Linda [Hill, his girlfriend] and the baby [Norra] was at her friend's house, so I go in the house with Linda, and when I come out they had stolen my van. I catch a cab and come home."

Throughout this part of the story there are long, painful pauses. He says that a friend took him to a house where he confronted the men who stole his van. "They said I owed them some money," he says. "Four hundred dollars. I say, 'I don't even know you, man. What do I owe you $400 for? The guy who took me over, they let him go. So he called the police, and the police break in the place and they—these guys—run away, and now my van is gone."

The police released Pryor at 2 a.m. Another young man in the house was arrested for possession of cocaine. Detective Doreen Nash was one of the officers on the scene. "My part was to see if there was an abduction or not," says Nash. "The only means I had was speaking to the witnesses that were in the house with [Pryor]. They all said basically the same thing that he went there on his own to try and get his van back. While in the house, witnesses say he did use cocaine and he wasn't abducted. I talked to Pryor but I couldn't get him to give me anything. He wasn't very coherent." Nash says that Pryor's friend, who gave a false name, told police that the fighter owed $1,000 to the people who took his Ford van.

In selecting friends, Pryor is always zero for whatever the number is at the moment. Not long ago a girl he knew named Candy accompanied Pryor's mother to a grocery store. When they returned, Candy helped carry in the bags, then got into Pryor's '85 Saab. Pryor hasn't seen the girl or the car since.

"Everybody robs me," he says. "I meet a girl and she robs me. I meet some guys and they rob me. People break into my house and steal things. They take my machine gun. I had an M16." The visitor asks about the gun. Pryor shrugs and says, very seriously, "I had planned one day to get on a boat and I don't have no license and I might go to Cuba. I wanted to shoot my way back home. I had plans, like if it is nighttime. They come on your boat and shoot you. I believe I'm getting tired. I'm getting hyper talking, and it's so hot. Oh, man, I feel just like getting into a car and running away."

"Why not go back into training?" he is asked.

Strength returns to his voice. "Oh, I'm ready to go tonight. I'm leaving tonight. I'm going back to Cincinnati. I'm going inside. Ain't you hot? I'm hot? The police come by and mess with me. I had a girl forge checks on me. This is my third checking account. People steal thousands of dollars out of my clothes. I don't even know where the money goes. Ransom. They threaten my kids [he has two besides Norra] that they will kill me if I don't give them money." He pauses, sighing. "Somebody breaks into my house . . . setting little things around, like drugs around my house and in my clothes. I can't take no more. You know, a lot of people lost a lot of money on the Alexis fight. They're a little angry. That's the only thing I can think of."

The champion rises and enters the house, taking his demons with him. He admits to the visitor that he has experimented with drugs. This alone is not necessarily a revelation, since newspaper stories have quoted Pryor as having acknowledged using marijuana. But he is vague, or evasive, about whether he has used any other drugs. On Nov. 23, 1983 he was arrested in Inglewood, Calif. for cocaine possession, a charge that was subsequently dismissed on the grounds that the arresting officers had illegally searched the automobile Pryor was driving. He continues to insist that he doesn't have a drug problem.

"Drugs is a big thing in Florida," he says. "Yes, it is. And I figure just one thing: If you can go to training and you can sacrifice sex and alcohol and go to bed early at night, you can sacrifice drugs. If you want to. There never was any drugs involved in me as far as winning a fight. Why does my eye hurt? You have an electricity charge or something? See my eye cross? That's automatic. I'm tired. I've got to get some sleep."

He starts out of the room, then turns and says, "I can buy anything I want: cars, a house, jewelry. I can buy anything but a friend."

Aaron Pryor didn't go to Cincinnati that night. He hasn't yet. He is still talking about going back into training. And he is still looking for a friend.

CHAPTER

5

Story Leads Writing

THE NEWS LEAD

A good news story, unlike the novel or play, is based on one main idea. That is why it is so important to decide on a focus and stick to it. A well-focused article tells your reader that you worked from a plan. It gives the reader a sense of completeness, a sense that you know what you are doing.

1. In deciding on this focus, you also are working on your lead. By asking yourself about the main theme for your story, you are deciding how to begin, for often the two—a statement of theme and a lead—are one and the same.
2. To help you decide on this theme, sometimes it helps to try the "tell-a-friend" technique. Imagine your friend asking, "What's your story about?" Answer that question in one sentence that captures the essence of the entire story.
3. Now try to refine your answer so it can do two things. It should capture the essence of your story and do so

in a way that encourages the reader to continue. It is your promise to the reader of what is to come. It is your lead.

4. After reading the lead, your reader makes a critical decision: Shall I read on? You have little time, according to Donald Murray, author of *Writing for Readers*. "Three seconds and the reader decides to read or move on to the next story," Murray said. "That's all the time you have to catch the reader's glance and hold it; all the time you have to entice and inform."
5. Think of the lead as a baited hook that lures the reader into the story. Think economy. Imagine you are writing the lead while seated on a hot stove, or carving it into a block of oak. Make each word count and include no extra words. One writer said she writes a lead as if each word cost her $10.
6. There are two main types of leads: direct or delayed. The direct lead reveals immediately what the story is about. It is the summary or statement of the most important events contained in the story. It is the climax, the result of the investigation, the theme. If you told a joke as you wrote a direct lead, you would place the punch line first.
7. The direct lead—also called the summary lead—is usually one sentence, but sometimes two. It answers immediately, in 25 words or less, the main questions of who, what, when and where. It is the workhorse of daily journalism, used at the top of most stories.
8. The best direct leads start with a compelling noun and a strong verb, not with a prepositional phrase. William Caldwell, a Pulitzer Prize-winning reporter, recalled the best lead he ever heard. The year was 1922. "I was on my way home from school and my stint at the local weekly. My little brother came running to meet me at the foot of the street. He was white and crying. A

telegram had come to my mother. 'Pa drowned this morning in Lake George," my brother gasped. I was ashamed to admit my inner response. Before I could begin to sense sorrow, despair, horror, loneliness and anger, before all the desolation of an abandoned child could well up in me, I found myself observing that the sentence my brother had just uttered was the perfect lead. Noun, verb, period, and who-what-when-where to boot."

9. There is a second type of lead that is used mostly on feature stories. It is the delayed or feature lead. It usually sets a scene or evokes a mood with an incident, anecdote or example. The writer may foreshadow events to come or create a sense of foreboding or anticipated surprise. Essential information is temporarily withheld. The writer teases before she pleases.
10. The delayed lead can be short, perhaps two sentences, or it can be longer, up to four paragraphs. The delayed lead still must fulfil the two roles of the lead: It must capture the essence of the story and do it in a way that encourages the reader to continue. Like the direct lead, it leads the reader straight to the heart of the story. Good leads are like good titles: they shine a flashlight down into the story.
11. When the lead is delayed and does not immediately explain the main point of the story, it is important to include the theme statement somewhere high in the story, usually within the first four paragraphs. If you ask the reader to wait before he learns what the story is about, be sure to reward him with a clear statement of purpose, also known as a nut graph.
12. Leads must be honest. They should never promise what does not follow in the story. Don't begin with a startling or sensational anecdote if it is not organically

related to the theme. As writer John McPhee said, "A lead should not be cheap, flashy, meretricious, blaring a great fanfare of trumpets, and then a mouse comes out of its hole."

Types and Techniques of Story Leads

You write your stories like you eat ice cream cones—literally and figuratively, from the top down. Like that first delicious taste of ice cream, the reader savours your story from the top down. The lead is the key to any story. The converse is also true—have you ever tried to read a story with a confusing or inappropriate lead, given up on the lead, and tried to read from the middle of the story to the end? I would assume you rarely do that. Most readers don't. If you don't capture the reader at the top of the story, you lose that reader. The lead of any story—sports articles or any other beginning—attempts to accomplish at least six points:

- The lead draws the reader into the story.
- The lead educates the reader.
- The lead informs the reader about the story.
- The lead entertains the reader.
- The lead establishes the tone of the story.
- The lead establishes the expertise of the writer.

That's a lot to cram into the top of your stories, but it can be done. How long should a lead be? In general, the lead of a news story is about three paragraphs. The lead of a feature story should be no longer than *about* one tenth of the complete story. If you have a 10-screen (10-page) story, then the lead could be up to about one page long. If you have a five-screen (five-page) story, then the lead could be about one-half page. If the lead is too long, you risk having a reader ask, mentally, "What's this about and why am I reading this?" No matter what type of lead you have, it should come to an obvious conclusion. The more you know about types of leads, the better you will be as a writer, because you will have considerable choices of methods of beginnings.

Many sports writers who cover a game in progress—a university football game, for instance—will write the game as it progresses, on a laptop computer in the press box. When the game is over, they will scroll up through the story and "top" the story, by then adding the lead. The lead will usually come to them as the game progresses and "topping the story" is an easy method of adding the appropriate lead. *In all cases, the story dictates the lead, not vice versa.* There are at least 25 recognizable types of leads appropriate for sports writing. They are discussed in the following sections. When you are comfortable with all 25, don't forget they can be combined. In writing leads, you are limited only by your imagination.

The Anecdotal Lead

An anecdote is a small, presumably true story about someone, showing character, behaviour, or motivation. An anecdote placed "on top of" the complete story helps the reader understand the principal figure in the story. All anecdotes should be meaningful—and should have an ending. Here's a key to writing a story with an anecdote: When you are interviewing, ask Person A: "What is your favourite story?" That favourite story may well be a good anecdote to use to begin a feature. Here Charles W. Hall of *The Washington Post* uses three anecdotes (high school lawsuit, college achievement, and a place on the Silver Bullets) to begin a feature about Julie Croteau, who always wanted to play baseball. (This also has elements of the timeline lead.) This article was run on *The Washington Post* wires in early April 1994. Since the age of 6, when she swung at baseballs perched on a tee, Julie Croteau has been a pioneer, a girl willing and able to play hardball with the boys.

At her Prince William County, Va. high school, she sued for a chance to play on the varsity. As a freshman in college, she became the first woman to play on a men's NCAA baseball squad. And this week, Croteau won a place on the first women's professional baseball team in four decades.

Croteau, who gained national attention when she played at St. Mary's College in Maryland, was named a first baseman with the Colorado Silver Bullets, a touring team that will play against men's minor-league and semi-professional players.

> "I'm just elated," said Croteau, 23, who was one of 24 players chosen out of 1,300 women who tried out nationally. "I think this team will make a big difference for girls who are in the same shoes I grew up in."

Here is a perfect example of how a single anecdote is used to begin a story. Richie Whitt, writing for the Fort Worth Star-Telegram, shows quarterback Steve Beuerlein's personality with a brief glimpse at what he thinks of his championship ring, received when he was a member of the Dallas Cowboys. Beuerlein has since moved on to the Phoenix Cardinals. This article was run on the wires September 19, 1993:

> PHOENIX—In a remote hallway of Steve Beuerlein's new, 4,000-square-foot home is a Super Bowl trophy replica from last year's championship season with the Dallas Cowboys. But the ring and the memories have been locked away.
>
> "I showed the ring to the guys before the season started," Beuerlein said. "Then I put it in a safety deposit box. It's not my style to go flashing it around. Besides, I've got a new life now."

The Cowboys' backup quarterback last year, Beuerlein is the Phoenix Cardinals' handsomely paid saviour. In return for a three-year, $7.5 million contract (the most lucrative in team history) he signed as a free agent April 21, Beuerlein is expected to give a passing game, experienced leadership and a play-off berth to a franchise that is 42-86-1 the past nine seasons. The Cardinals last finished with a winning record in 1984 and last qualified for a non-strike postseason in 1975.

Tim Layden, writing for *Newsday*, uses an anecdote lead about Florida State University football star Charlie Ward's basketball techniques in an article run on the wires December 10, 1993:

> When football season is finished at Florida State, players often congregate in the belly of the Moore Athletic Centre, on the concrete-walled basketball court adjacent to the weight room. They play pickup games, fierce and serious, without form, only with bravado.
>
> "Every man for himself," said defensive back Clifton Abraham. "Bring your best."
>
> In the spring and summer, when his basketball season is finished, after the NCAA Tournament, Charlie Ward joins them. And wouldn't you know it?
>
> "He's out there trying to set people up, use his basketball technique, playing team ball," Abraham said. "Everybody else is just firing it up. Charlie, he's not much for street ball."

Alan Page, once a key player with the Minnesota Vikings, is now a respected jurist in Minnesota. Here Jeremy Schaap uses an anecdotal lead to show Page as a member of the Minnesota Supreme Court. Schaap's article, headlined, "NOW HE TACKLES INJUSTICE," appeared in *Parade magazine*, the Sunday supplement, May 15, 1994.

The article was subtitled " Alan Page, once a mainstay of the Minnesota Vikings' defence, now fights for equality as a state Supreme Court justice."

"Would you please all rise for the honourable justices of the Supreme Court of Minnesota?" says the court clerk. One by one, four women and three men enter Courtroom 300 of the Minnesota Judicial Centre. The junior justice, Alan Page, bespectacled and bow-tied, leads the procession. He is wearing a black robe. He used to wear purple and white—the uniform of the Minnesota Vikings.

When he was elected to a six-year term in November 1992, Page moved from the state attorney general's office to the Minnesota Judicial Centre, only a few miles from where he once anchored the Purple People Eaters, the Vikings' fearsome defensive line of the '70s.

> "I love what I'm doing," says Page, Minnesota's first African-American Supreme Court justice, who looks distinctly judicial with his white beard and dark suit. "What you do on the playing field is great—for a moment—but what one does in a courtroom can have some real meaning, some lasting effect."

The "Big Play" Lead

The home run that won a World Series game; a last-second touchdown that won a major college bowl game; a sprinter who lunged to break the tape and win by a millisecond. They often furnish sports writers ideal leads but the sports writer must watch and recognize the "big play" when it occurs. As a football game, an Olympic event, or a baseball game is in progress, sports writers must make mental notes regarding the lead to the story. A big play lead may present itself; the sports writer needs to recognize it when it takes place. John Ferro of the Gannett News Service uses a key play—a missed field goal—to begin his story of the 1993 Army-Navy game.

Note: In any game story, the names of the teams, where the game was played, and the score should all be somewhere in the top three paragraphs. Other items, such as a key play or the weather, if it was a factor, should also be in the lead.

This article was run early in December 1993.

EAST RUTHERFORD, N.J.: The Navy football team could not have gotten much closer. Just one yard from the goal line, the Midshipmen were achingly close to a come-from-behind victory over Army, the Commander In Chief's trophy and a chance to honour a fallen teammate. But the weightiest of moments fell on the shoulders of a freshman kicker with just two attempts in his career. And so it was that Ryan Bucchianeri's 18-yard field goal try with six seconds remaining sailed wide right and gave Army a 16-14 victory before 67,852 at Giants Stadium Saturday.

The key to a game may not necessarily be a play on the field. Here Leonard Laye, writing for The Charlotte Observer, uses a key halftime event as the lead to a story about a Louisville-University of Minnesota basketball game, from late March 1994:

> SACRAMENTO, Calif.: At half-time, his team trailing Minnesota by a dozen points, Louisville coach Denny Crum zipped into the locker room and headed straight for Clifford Rozier.
>
> "Coach just asked me to do one thing. He begged me to do it," said Rozier, an All-America centre. "He said, 'Son, we can't win if you keep forcing things'."

Rozier got the message, albeit along with some very un-All-America States. And the Cardinals got a 60-55 victory Sunday in Arco Arena, earning a spot in the NCAA Midwest Regional semifinals Thursday in Los Angeles.

The Classified Ad Lead

If you are stuck for a lead and nothing fits—no good quotations, no good descriptions, no question lead is apparent—and nothing works for your lead, turn to the nearest Sunday newspaper. How many categories of classified ads are there?

Dozens? Hundreds? You may be able to use a variation of a classified ad as the lead to a sports article. In the following article, Neil Hohlfeld (1994) of the *Houston Chronicle* uses a help wanted ad to begin a story about baseball managers. (Notice also the interesting simile in his fifth paragraph: "Like building a fire or running a hotel, everyone in America believes he can do a better job managing a baseball team. " That also, it seems to me, is an exceptional lead). Use of a variation of a classified ad for a story lead is limited only by your imagination, but bear in mind, this is a bit of a novelty lead—used once every hundred articles is about the right average. Otherwise, the uniqueness of this lead quickly fades.

Help Wanted

Brilliant tactician, media darling, ticket salesman, matinee idol. Must be able to think on feet 162 times a summer. Knowledge of baseball essential. Communication skills a must.

> Compensation: Low to mid-six figures—but be advised you will earn one-tenth the salary of some of your employees.
>
> —By Neil Hohlfeld *Houston Chronicle*

So, you want to be a baseball manager? It looks easy, right? Make out the lineup card, bunt when you should bunt, pull the pitcher when you should pull the pitcher. Go on the talk shows, sit in first class, drive a big car, and let everyone hail your genius. Explain, then, why every manager—in the language of baseball-ese—is on a day-to-day basis. Why every manager is an interim manager. Why the managerial carousel never stops, but merely slows to toss one victim off and take on another. Just five managers in the 14-team National League have held their jobs longer than 18 months. Since 1984, seven of the 12 NL teams (not counting the two 1993 expansion franchises) have had five or more managers. Chicago and Cincinnati have had seven apiece, an average job life span of less than 1½ years.

Like building a fire or running a hotel, everyone in America believes he can do a better job managing a baseball team than the 27 men who currently hold the coveted major-league jobs.

The Comparison-contrast Lead

Compare two athletes, two coaches with different coaching philosophies, or two teams with different training styles and you pull your reader into your story:

- Which athlete is better?
- Which coach has the better technique?
- Which team should win and why?

Here John Jeansonne of *Newsday* uses this technique lead to compare two ice skating teams in the Lillehammer Olympics: Gordeeva and Grinkov and Mishkutenok and Dmitriev. This article was run on the wires February 15, 1994, during the Lillehammer Olympics.

HAMAR, Norway—Gordeeva and Grinkov were formal, Mishkutenok and Dmitriev industrial. The first couple seemed to be at a royal ball, the second in some Russian factory. Actually, they all were in the middle of the best Olympic pairs figure-skating final anyone could remember.

Gordeeva and Grinkov were precision, taking traditional pairs skating—with him as the quiet straight man and her as the smiling, graceful butterfly—shining it up and putting it on display the way it rarely can be seen. Mishkutenok and Dmitriev were passion, beginning with their costumes already slashed open at the thighs and arms, working as equal partners in an effort of creativity bordering on anger. Mark Woods of the Gannett News Service uses a comparison of Shaquille O'Neal and David Robinson to begin a story about an April 30, 1993 game between the Orlando Magic and the San Antonio Spurs. Note that Woods uses the key word contrasts in the first paragraph. ORLANDO, Fla.: The first meeting of the All-Star centres turned into a study of contrasts. Shaquille O'Neal was youth, relying on muscle and anxious energy. David Robinson was experience, turning to patience and the flick of a sore wrist.

And, at least this time, the flick won. Robinson, still hampered by a sprained thumb on his shooting hand, scored

23 points and grabbed 16 rebounds Sunday to lead the San Antonio Spurs out of a slump and to a 94-90 victory over the Orlando Magic. With my hand the way it was," Robinson said, "I didn't want to try and get it slapped a lot. So I really tried to isolate (O'Neal) on the floor. I think the key was that I made him work." Rich Hoffman, writing for the *Philadelphia Daily News*, compares Duke's Grant Hill and Purdue's Glenn Robinson in the southeast regional NCAA basketball tournament, late in March 1994:

KNOXVILLE, Tenn.: Two dunks. We will begin there. Duke's Grant Hill takes the ball somewhere near Nashville and begins his drive. He leaps; he flies. The poor fellow between him and the basket is Marquette's Jim McIlvaine, all 7-1 of him. Hill ends up dunking the ball, fiercely. McIlvaine ends up in a heap. Hill stands over him, then ends up woofing—at his teammates.

"I was excited," he said. "I just wanted to share the emotion."

Next game in the NCAA Southeast Regional. Purdue's Glenn Robinson is down at the same end of the Arena. His victim is Greg Ostertag, a 7-2 guy from Kansas. Robinson annihilated him. After the dunk, Robinson just stood over the body. He stared Ostertag down, until Ostertag reacted in the perfect way. He shook Robinson's hand. Congratulations. Hill and Robinson. Make that Robinson and Hill. They are the two best players left in this NCAA Tournament. Jalen Rose and Juwan Howard of a Michigan will make a lot of money in the NBA, as will Connecticut's Donyell Marshall. But Robinson is best and Hill is next. After today, only [one] will be left. The life of two University of Michigan basketball players is compared in a story by *Detroit Free Press* writer Greg Stoda. He clearly uses a comparison-contrast lead in his article about Bobby Crawford and Dugan Fife. This article was run in early December 1993.

ANN ARBOR, Mich.: One sat on the bench, and sometimes played. The other sat in the living room, and sometimes dreamed. A year ago, the distances from the bright lights of Michigan basketball were vastly different, but in another way much the same for Bobby Crawford and Dugan Fife.

Life on the fringe.

Fife was then a Michigan freshman. He arrived in Ann Arbor with a reputation as a big scorer after averaging 27.7 points as a senior at Clarkston (Mich.) High, where he threw in a 49-point outing along the way.

And promptly made not a single field goal in his first season as a Wolverine.

> "That was the hardest thing—not shooting," said Fife, who took only nine shots last season. "That was an adjustment."

So Crawford, then a high-scoring senior at Houston Eisenhower who had signed with Michigan, saw little of Fife when he tuned in Michigan games on the family television.

After five games as a freshman this season, Crawford hasn't experienced the scoring frustrations Fife did, but there have been troubling moments.

> "It was tougher than I thought it would be coming in," Crawford said. "An open shot is an open shot, but you have to do so much more to get one."

Alan Truex, sports writer for the Houston Chronicle, clearly uses a comparison lead in a story about Art Howe, fired manager of the Houston Astros and his replacement, Terry Collins. This article was run under a headline "On Top and Nonstop," and subhead "Collins' revved-up style will give Astros a new look" and was published in the *Chronicle* on December 24, 1993. There are obvious contrasts between Terry Collins, the Astros' new manager, and his predecessor, Art Howe.

Howe is tall—6-1. Collins is short—5-8.

Howe is bald. Collins can be hair-raising.

Howe seemed incapable of anger. Even when he stalked an umpire, it seemed he was operating out of a sense of obligation rather than conviction. Howe was stoic, imperturbable, laid-back. Collins is animated, intense, involved. Pausing for an interview after a recent whirlwind day at the Astrodome, Collins said: "I'm not like Art. I have a temper. I won't kick any water coolers, but I might swear on the bench."

The Delayed Climax Lead

Occasionally, a writer may delay the point of a lead; the reader has to read down through the lead to discover the point. Thus the name *delayed climax.* Here Charlie Meyers of *The Denver Post* uses a delayed climax lead for his story of the Italy-Norway cross-country ski race during the Lillehammer Olympics. This was run on the wires February 22, 1994. His key line (the fourth paragraph): "In the Super Bowl of Nordic skiing, Buffalo won."

LILLEHAMMER, Norway: To the shock and chagrin of 105,000 Norwegians, interlopers from Italy stole the grandest cross-country ski prize of these Olympic Games, the men's 4x10-kilometer relay. The Italians did it when their youngest racer outkicked Norway's great champion, Bjorn Dahlie, on the final leg. And they did it by selecting a 43-year-old in his final season to start the race. When Silvio Fauner, a 25-year-old with a modest portfolio, beat Dahlie to the finish line by four-hundredths of a second following a dramatic side-by-side sprint, a roaring throng fell deathly silent as if someone had flipped a switch. In the Super Bowl of Nordic skiing, Buffalo won.

Here is a perfect example of a delayed climax lead. Michael Murphy, writing for the *Houston Chronicle,* profiles a Houston-area pitcher, Ronny Carroll, who had decided to attend Southwest Texas State University in San Marcos. After a key telephone call, he changed his mind and decided to attend Texas Christian University in Fort Worth. This article was published in the *Houston Chronicle* May 11, 1994. The headline is shown under the lead.

Ronny Carroll still smiles when he talks about "the phone call." A senior pitcher for Langham Creek High School, Carroll was home icing his arm last month after a District 20-5A victory over Cy-Fair when the phone rang. Carroll picked up the phone and heard an oddly familiar voice. "Hi, Ronny," the voice started. "This is . . ." Before the caller could finish, Carroll knew. He was talking with Nolan Ryan.

> "I knew right away (who it was)," he said. "I recognized the voice from somewhere. I just said, 'Whoa.' It was wild."
>
> *It would get wilder.*
>
> "I was wondering why he was calling me," Carroll said. "I figured there was no way he was calling to congratulate me on the game I just pitched. Then, he told me about TCU."

Ryan, a restricted-earnings coach at Texas Christian, was calling in an official capacity. He had seen a pitcher he wanted on the Horned Frogs' staff. In other words, he wanted Carroll.

> "I just liked him," Ryan said. "He had good command of his breaking ball, and he throws the ball with good velocity. I think his velocity will improve, too."

Ryan should know. So it was goodbye, Southwest Texas—where Carroll was originally planning to go—and hello, TCU.

> "When Nolan Ryan calls, you go," said Carroll's father, Ronny Sr. "What a huge recruiting tool. He wanted Ronny, so that's where he's going."

It didn't matter one bit that Carroll, who has compiled an 8-3 record with a 0.79 ERA for the Lobos, has only one arm, his left.

The *Houston Chronicle*'s headline for this story was: "What handicap?"

The Descriptive Lead

Descriptions can often mean exceptional leads for sports features. The keys to writing description are:

- If you are writing about a location so well known that readers may have *icons*—mental pictures of it in their minds—like the Kentucky Derby or a typical major university football stadium, go behind the scenes to show the reader some aspect of the location they could not imagine or have not seen on ESPN.
- If you are writing about a remote location, fill in all the details so readers can see that location in their own imagination.
- If you are in a remote location, don't naturally assume your readers know what to look for.
- If you are on location to witness an event, "talk the details" of the scene into a tape recorder. Listening to the tape later will help you reconstruct the picture you need to show in your lead.

In this descriptive lead Sandra Blakeslee shows a remote and captivating location for kayaking—the Sea of Cortés—to begin her article "Kayaking In Splendor for Cardiac Fitness." Her article appeared in *The New York Times Magazine*, April 24, 1994.

Dawn is breaking over the Sea of Cortés. The horizon, an inky blue, is crowned with an iridescent, salmon light that paints the underside of meandering clouds with the rays of a sun that has not yet climbed up to the edge of the earth. In utter stillness, the little sea kayak moves easily out towards the Mercenaries—a jagged outcrop of volcanic and sedimentary spires two miles from the coastline of Baja California Sur in Mexico. Bestrewn with osprey nests, the rocks also shelter flocks of cormorants, blue-footed boobies, peregrine falcons, ravens, hawks and score of pelicans preening before breakfast. Near the kayak, six porpoises leap from the water, their backs glistening in the rising light.

Halfway to the rocks, a pair of fins stick out of the water. Actually, they turn out to be flippers, and they belong to a sea lion, asleep on its back. It seems to be snoring, but opens one eye, sees the kayak and, with a comical, shocked look, dives below.

The "epic game" Lead

How often can you call a game an epic? One game in a season? Perhaps not even one in a season for many college and university football teams. One game in a hundred? One game in a decade? Bob Ryan, writing for *The Boston Globe* called the October 2, 1993 Boston College-Syracuse University football game an epic. Boston College won 33-29 at Syracuse. Notice Ryan calls the game an epic without the use of overblown style. Nothing wrecks a true epic story as quickly as excessive gushing on the part of a sports writer.

SYRACUSE, N.Y.: There are 106 Division I-A teams playing college football, and they are going to play a whole mess o' games this season. Not many will be better than Boston College-Syracuse.

This will be remembered as the Great Carrier Dome Shootout. This is one game which will surely be recalled when the Boston College team members get together in their future reunion guises as insurance agents, high school coaches, Commonwealth of Massachusetts political appointees and perhaps even NFL players. As the years roll by, they're going to be telling taller and taller tales about who did what in the Carrier Dome, making even more of Saturday's epic 33-29 conquest of Syracuse than they were doing in the immediate aftermath of a victory which might very well send them on the way to a highly satisfying season.

Dennis Georgatos, writing for the Associated Press, called the October 2, 1993, California—Oregon game "one of the greatest comebacks in college football history." California came back from a 30-0 deficit to beat Oregon 42-41. His lead read:

BERKELEY, Calif.: California staged one of the greatest comebacks in college football history Saturday.

Dave Barr threw three second-half scoring passes, the last a 26-yarder to Iheanyi Uwaezuoke with 1:17 left as the Golden Bears overcame a 30-0 deficit to beat Oregon 42-41.

> "People were going crazy," Barr said. "I don't know if I'll ever have a feeling like this again. We were down, beaten. We were hurting. We weren't feeling good about ourselves, and we came back. We wouldn't accept no for an answer."
>
> The return from 30 points down to win was second only to two 31-point comebacks, by Maryland in a 42-40 victory over Miami on Nov. 10, 1984, and Ohio State's 41-37 win over Minnesota on Oct. 28, 1989.

It was the biggest comeback ever by Cal, surpassing a 29-28 win against Arizona on Nov. 4, 1989, in which the Bears overcame a 21-0 deficit.

The "False" Lead

Writers don't lie to their readers. But occasionally, an ingenious writer *can leave out* one element of a lead—to suggest a different place, time, idea, or possibility. Here is the title: "I'm not just a jock." It appeared in *The Houston Post* on September 14, 1993. Here is writer Bonnie Gangelhoff's first two paragraphs:

First the pale pink nail polish. Then the gold stud earrings and the monogrammed purse. Is this any way for a football player to dress? Well, you think, some players wear ear studs. Joe Namath used to wear pantyhose under his Jet uniform. Pale pink nail polish? Could be. Monogrammed purse? Errrr, maybe. Here is Gangelhoff's third paragraph: It is if she's a girl. Gangelhoff omitted Erin Shilk's sex momentarily, in an attempt to convince the reader that she was talking about someone else; someone male.

Here are Gangelhoff's next few paragraphs: Meet Erin Shilk, 5-foot-3 and 108 pounds: lover of the Aggies, boys, soccer, country & western music, cooking and chemistry. She's a girl blazing a trail for the '90s.

Two weeks ago, amid a media blitz, Shilk, 15, kicked her way into the history books of the Cypress Falls sophomore football team. The barefoot place-kicker made two extra points and became the only area girl to play high school football. Then, last Thursday, Shilk kicked another two extra points against Sharpstown High School. Her team won, 14-6. Shilk is one of five girls in Texas taking advantage of a University Interscholastic League rule passed last year, which for the first time allows girls to participate in the Sports.

She's grabbed headlines for her football abilities, but happily consented to an interview off the playing field because she wants people to know, "I'm not *just* a jock." This is a variation of the delayed climax lead, discussed earlier. How can the false lead be used? Like Gangelhoff's article, the sex of a subject can be omitted. The writer could omit the age of an athlete, to convince the reader that a golfer, for instance, is a national tournament-calibre player. The actual player could be a teenager (or younger) or the player could be a senior citizen, shooting well under his or her age.

As in the Michael Murphy story about Texas Christian University pitcher Ronny Carroll, the writer can let the reader assume the pitcher has both arms. Murphy tells the reader at the end of the lead that Carroll has only his left arm. The writer could omit the time (date) when the action occurs to convince the reader that the sports event took place years ago, or the writer could omit the time to convince the readers that a decades-old boxing match took place this year, for instance.

The writer could omit the time and details to convince readers that a gladiator was dressing for the Roman arena. In fact, the story could be about a pro football player today (although a football players as gladiators or football as war is something of a cliché).

There is a great deal of current interest in re-enactments of Civil War battles, with 1990s "summer soldiers and sunshine patriots" in blue and grey, to quote Kuklick (1989) "The Crisis Papers" (*Thomas Paine: Political Writings*). Clearly, this is an ideal story assignment for use of a false lead. Should your readers be thinking of the original Battle of Gettysburg, or a re-enactment of that battle? Leave out the date and let them believe, momentarily, that the re-enactment is the original battle.

The "I" Lead

The first-person "I" is the writer talking to the reader. This technique is often used in a personal column, but can be used in a participant article (*This is what I did when I ran the Boston Marathon . . ..*). Here Steve Wilstein of the Associated Press uses the "I" form in a piece about how many players in the 1994 college basketball Final Four Tournament had tattoos. In addition to Corliss Williamson, who is mentioned in the lead, Lee Wilson, Corey Beck, and Darnell Robinson of Arkansas all had tattoos. Marty Clark of Duke and four members of the Purdue women's team had tattoos. This article was run on the wire services on April 4, 1994. CHARLOTTE, N.C.: I'm at the Final Four and I have to get a tattoo. It's the thing to do.

I'm wondering how an ornery Arkansas Razorback, tusks and all, would look side by side with a Duke Blue Devil. Or maybe the Corliss Williamson look: Tasmanian devil near his heart, his initials on the right side of his chest, and his nickname, "Nasty." I asked him why he did it and he said: "It's just one of the wild things you do when you first get into college." Raoul Estlinbaum of *The Houston Post* went fishing for redfish in the Gulf of Mexico near Houston and not only came back with a big one ("maybe 35 pounds") but also an "I" lead for a story, run September 23, 1993, under the headline "With redfish, it's a fight to the end." Estlinbaum omitted the "I" form after the first six paragraphs of the story.

The strike caught me off-guard, almost yanking the rod out of my hand. The line ripped sideways as a big redfish surfaced briefly, then executed a power dive, taking out 30 yards of line. For the next 15 minutes, the bronze brute and I engaged in a game of tug-of-war, a seesaw battle that went back and forth with neither side gaining much ground. Slowly, the battle started to swing my way, but not without considerable effort. Finally, an exhausted red, maybe 35 pounds, came belly up, no longer able to resist. Mike Williams lifted the hardy fish out of the water, removed the hook and revived the weary warrior, sliding it gently back and forth to get water moving through its gills.

"These reds are big-time fighters," Williams said, watching the fish swim away. "Like tarpon, they give it everything they've got." Steve Howland, of *The Houston Post*, uses an appropriate "I" beginning in an article about deer hunting in east Texas. He also uses the "I" form throughout the article. His article was published December 2, 1993, under the headline "Patience pays off big time for hunter." BRUSHY CREEK EXPERIMENTAL FOREST: This place is definitely a successful experiment. I'm sitting here in a ground blind, being eaten alive by a large family of mosquitoes, and not feeling a thing because I'm looking at the biggest deer *I've* ever seen in the flesh.

I haven't been to Champion International's 25,000-acre game and timber reserve since 1988, when *Houston Post* carpentry supervisor and master deer hunter Henry Duran and I made a visit to gather venison for his booth at *The Post's annual Chili Cookoff*. That was my first visit here and I got a nice nine-point, my best buck in seven years of deer hunting, on the first night out. Howland's end paragraph refers to his colleague Henry Duran and Duran's promise that Howland would get his deer.

The ending was:

Henry and I meet up in camp. He has harvested an antler less for the chili pot. He will get the venison from my deer, and I'll settle for the horns and a backstrap or two. Henry casually looks at the deer, congratulates me and sums it all up: "I told you," he says, shaking his finger my way, "I told you he'd be there."

Fred King of *The Houston Post* uses an "I" lead to begin a story about how *not* to begin hunting season. *The Houston Post* ran this article under a headline "Abundance of game makes Hill Country hunt a snap" on November 18, 1993. (*The Hill Country* is a huge swatch of woodlands beginning west of Austin. Fredericksburg and Kerrville, Texas, are in the middle of the Hill Country.) I breathe and exhale, and the crosshairs settle exactly where I want them. Baalowww! . . . Damn! I've drawn blood with my first shot. But the season's not open yet. And it's my blood. I'm at Bayou Rifles checking my zero two days before the whitetail season starts in most of Texas. Since I got a hard case for my rifles, the zero has changed little. However, things happen. In my book, it is unethical to go hunting unless you have checked your zero.

And, this year, for the first time in many years, I'm not using my favourite handload in the 264 Winchester Mag. I just ran out of time to reload and was lucky to find both my license and a box of 140-grain factory ammo in the same place. I'm going with new ammo to a new place, Bill Carter's Apache Springs Ranch at Hunt, in the Hill Country. What was eagerness a moment ago feels like dumbness. The spots on my finger confirm it's my blood, from just above my right eyebrow. Settling in on the bench, wearing the field jacket I'll wear if it's really cold at Carter's, I've held the rifle too loosely and edged too close to the scope.

The Interior Monologue Lead

Try to think about how other people think. It's almost impossible, and there is seldom a perfect method in print to show how people think, brainstorm, and scheme. The novelist James Joyce used interior monologues, or *thought processes*, in his book *Ulysses*. (The voice-over in some films is often the thought processes of the hero, especially a detective tracking a case: *I thought he was a crook because of his shifty eyes*, or words to that effect, so viewers can better follow the film.)

It's possible, however, to sometimes use thoughts of others in articles. You first have to know—by interviewing—what they were thinking, what they were planning, and what they were trying to do. Then you can attempt to get this on the page, usually by fragmented sentences, often set apart typographically with italic type or boldface. In this article by Jim Reeves of the *Fort Worth Star-Telegram*, from March 1994, the thought processes of Jose Canseco are shown in the fourth paragraph, beginning: "The trade to Texas? No big deal. . . ." Later in the article, Reeves quotes Canseco explaining what he was thinking, which is always a good idea to backstop the thought processes. PORT CHARLOTTE, Fla.: The thought came to him in his darkest hours over the last year, when he could see no way to slow the careening, runaway horror that his life had become.

"Suicide."

On the outside, Jose Canseco laughed.

The trade to Texas? No big deal. The divorce? Shrug. Lots of women out there. Blow an elbow trying to pitch? Just another of life's little speed bumps.

On the inside, Canseco twisted and writhed in the stew of his own despair. He seriously considered, on more than one occasion, taking his own life. A future lead could begin something like this: By the year 2010, Japanese teams will have won the Super Bowl three times and be aiming for a fourth win.

That string of consecutive Super Bowl wins was triggered when Jimmy Johnson was fired as coach of the Dallas Cowboys after the 1993-1994 season. The actual chain of events that culminated in the Japanese victories began when Johnson was hired by a group of Japanese officials three years after he left the Cowboys. That management group, headed by officials from *Sony with virtually unlimited financing, allowed the Japanese to buy an available NFL franchise and move it to Tokyo.* And never again would a Super Bowl victory be guaranteed for USA teams. Do you recall a sci-fi film called Rollerball, about futuristic gladiators in massive "pinball" roller-derby events? That film, starring James Caan, was originally a short story in *Esquire* magazine.

The "letter to" Lead

Every newspaper publishes a letters-to-the-editor column or page. Sports writers might occasionally use a "letter to" or "memo to" technique, either as the lead to a feature article or, usually, as a column or opinion piece. Here Mike Cochran, staff writer for the Dallas-Fort Worth bureau of the Associated Press, uses a "letter to" format in an article about the Dallas Cowboys. He uses this technique throughout the article. This was moved on the AP wires January 29, 1994.

Last year, AP correspondent Mike Cochran followed the Dallas Cowboys to Super Bowl XXVII to report on the offbeat activities of the Boys in La La Land. This year, with no sand, sea, surf or starlets in Atlanta, he is sending a letter.— By Mike Cochran, *Associated Press.* DALLAS—Hey, there, Big Guys, how's it going in the land of grits and gravy?

I know you plan to kick some serious Buffalo tail today, but some folks felt a letter from home might be in order. Frankly, we're a bit worried about Super Bowl XXVIII. A rematch with the Bills doesn't exactly light a roaring fire. And after La La Land, and that Southern California sun, it's gotta be tough. No stars and starlets. No Sunset Strips and

Beverly Hills. No beaches and bikinis. No sushi and champagne. Mark Purdy, of the *San Jose Mercury News*, writes a letter to Joe Montana, late of the San Francisco 49ers, traded to the Kansas City Chiefs. This article, under the headline "Dear Joe: Steve gives thumb up to Week 1" was run in the *Houston Chronicle* on September 7, 1993 with the subhead "Commentary." The entire article, some 29 paragraphs long, was written as a letter. Purdy signed the letter: "Yours truly, The scarlet Heroes of Yore."

PITTSBURGH—Dear Joe: Howdy. It's us. Your old pals, the San Francisco 49ers. Hey, congratulations on the victory. We had a great opener, too. Wish you could've been here. It was a swell weekend for us, except for Ricky Watters' interesting career decision to become a pro wrestling promoter and provoke the entire Steelers roster into a Three Rivers death match. Anyway, since you weren't able to see the game—which we the Niners won, of course—let us give you a summation in the form of a riddle.

Question: How many Pittsburgh Steelers does it take to screw in a light bulb?

Answer: Only one. But if you are linebacker Kevin Greene and no light bulbs are handy, you try and screw Steve Young into the ground instead.

The "list" Head

We use the term *menu* daily regarding computers and computer usage; sports writers may also use a menu or "list of ingredients"—usually highlighted with black bullets, asterisks, or boxes. Highlighting this list material on the page helps readers comprehend it visually. Here John Hillyer of the San Francisco Examiner uses such a list to highlight the competition between the Golden State Warriors and the Portland Trail Blazers. (This is also an example of a comparison-contrast lead). This article was moved on the wires March 8, 1994.

SEATTLE: The Warriors meet the Trail Blazers again Thursday night in Oakland. After Monday night's precedent-setting 137-108 loss in Portland, what might the world expect in the rematch? "We got 'em right where we want 'em," Don Nelson said. Golden State's coach must be counting on the Blazers showing up overconfident. After what happened Monday, it would be a remarkable example of mental discipline if they didn't.

Just count the new season highs—or lows, depending on your perspective—to emerge Monday night:

- Biggest margin of defeat by the Warriors.
- Biggest margin of victory by the Blazers.
- Most points allowed by the Warriors.
- Most points scored by the Blazers.
- Most first-quarter points (38) scored by the Blazers, and a tie for the most allowed by the Warriors.
- Most fourth-quarter points (44) scored by the Blazers.
- Most baskets (59) made by the Blazers.
- Most baskets allowed by the Warriors.
- Most assists (38) by the Blazers, and a tie for the most allowed by the Warriors.

The Literary Reference Lead

One of the never-to-be-violated commandments of sports writing should be: Never use a cliché. It is, however, occasionally clever to turn a phrase sideways or upside down and come up with a fresh lead to captivate your readers. Here Mike Conklin of the *Chicago Tribune* recasts the old phrase "No greater love . . ." for a clever lead, run February 15, 1994. GJOVIC, Norway—Greater love hath no U.S. hockey player than to donate two front teeth to the Olympic cause. In the case of left winger Craig Johnson, the gap he displayed after getting introduced to the stick of a Slovakian player late in Tuesday's 3-3 tie meant everyone in the U.S. contingent could keep smiling. But, as you might suspect, it wasn't pretty.

This was the second tie in as many games for the Americans, who must finish no worse than fourth in its six-nation pool to advance to the quarterfinals. The United States is deadlocked with Slovakia, which tied Sweden in their opener, in the third spot with three games remaining. It is also possible to use song lyrics, lines of a poem, or a quotation from a novel or play, either in the lead or above the byline. The more sophisticated the quotation, the more sophisticated your lead.

On December 26, 1993, the *Houston Chronicle* used the first page of the Sports 2 section (p. B19), their section of sports features, and ran a banner headline: "HELLO, GOODBYE." It was in 1¼-inch high type, blue with black shadows. On the right was a major story about the year in Sports, nationally. In the middle of the page was a six-column-wide colour photo of Michael Jordan during his last press conference. Down the left-side column was a highlight story of key sports events of 1993 in Houston. Jayne Custred wrote the national wrap-up story and because sports and country music are king in Texas, she began with a Garth Brooks lyric, for her story, subheaded:

Dance Ends Far Too Soon for Big Stars

And I'm glad I didn't know
The way it all would end
The way it all would go
Our lives are better left to chance
We could have missed the pain
But we'd of had to miss the dance.

—Garth Brooks, By Jayne Custred, *Houston Chronicle*

Davey Allison danced through life, living it to the fullest, embracing its wonders along with its dangers. Heather Farr never missed a beat, never lost a step despite her battle with cancer. And Reggie Lewis was dancing at the end, doing what he loved best despite the risks. The music stopped for many in 1993, long before the dance was supposed to end.

Yet the melodies of their lives remain with us, reminding us that tragedy comes to everyone, whether superstar, hero or idol. It was an amazing year in sports. The Chicago Bulls captured a third straight NBA title—then saw their hopes for a fourth virtually disappear when megastar Michael Jordan shockingly retired; the USA hung on to the coveted Ryder Cup trophy; Joe Carter ripped a dramatic homer that handed the Blue Jays a second straight World Series; and Don Shula broke George Halas' NFL record for career wins.

But the triumphs and victories were so overshadowed by the tragedies and the losses that 1993 will best be remembered as the year of goodbyes. Neil Best of *Newsday* uses a Thoreau quotation to begin an article about runner Keith Brantly who found the heart of Africa in, as Best writes, "of all places, Concord, Mass." Best's article ran in November 1993.

"The mass of men lead lives of quiet desperation."

— Henry David Thoreau By Neil Best *Newsday*

NEW YORK: Not Keith Brandy. He rejected the notion American men can't win the New York City Marathon anymore and boldly struck out in search of the figurative heart of Africa, home to many of the world's best long-distance runners. He's found it in, of all places, Concord, Mass., site of an early battle in the Revolutionary War and hometown of Henry David Thoreau—about as American a place as you'll find. Brantly, a 31-year-old Floridian, spent most of August there. He trained with elite Kenyan athletes, living their Spartan lifestyle, sleeping in a dorm at Concord Academy (where Thoreau studied in the late 1820s) and running the perimeter of Thoreau's beloved Walden Pond. It was an anthropological adventure in his own land. "You can't be successful unless you emulate success," Brandy said of his decision to accept an invitation to join the Kenyans.

Shannon Tompkins, outdoors writer for the *Houston Chronicle*, uses an old song lyric from the Lovin' Spoonful to begin a nice piece about the simple magic of fishin'. This article, under the headline "Childhood bass-fishing memories live," appeared in the *Chronicle* on August 1, 1993.

"Do you believe in magic? . . . It'll free your soul."
—The Lovin' Spoonful, circa 1967

Magic is everywhere when you're a kid.

Whitey Ford and Mickey Mantle were magic. So was a grove of trees where the shadows and bushes became Yankee soldiers that you vanquished with a saber made of cane. Every day was a new adventure and no seam separated the physical from the metaphysical. But then you grow up, read *Ball Four*, see the unspeakable horrors of war, learn other brutal truths of life . . . and the magic evaporates. Childhood's magic becomes like a cup of coffee left out too long, eventually, all you're left with is the ugly crust of what once was something enjoyable. If you're lucky, a few faint embers of that early magic hide somewhere deep in the synapses, waiting for just the right breeze to fan them back to life.

It wasn't much of a breeze—more a breath of humid fog than wind—but it was enough. Standing on the banks of a little lake an hour before sunrise a week ago, that feeling of magic surged out of the past. It was the magic of a topwater plug and summer bass. In this lead, Neal Farmer, sports writer for the Houston Chronicle, uses a quotation from Tennyson to begin an article about Rice University's long losing streak in football against the University of Texas. (This lead also contains elements of a timeline lead.) This lead, in a story headlined "Rice looking to snap skid against Texas," was run in the *Chronicle* on September 28, 1993 (PS: Rice lost again to Texas, 55-38).

"Forward the Light Brigade! Charge for the guns," he said: Into the valley of Death Rode the 600.

—from Alfred Lord Tennyson "The Charge of the Light Brigade"—By Neal Farmer *Houston Chronicle*

Twenty-seven times the Rice Owls have ridden into battle against the University of Texas, and 27 times they have lost.

Twenty-two starters over 27 years means 594 Rice starters—nearly 600—have lost to the Longhorns.

It is the second-longest such current streak in NCAA football, behind only the 29 consecutive decisions Notre Dame has over Navy. Fifth-year Rice coach Fred Goldsmith said his troops have not lost 27 games, just four since he has been here. And the burden is not as big as one might think. Larry Dierker, TV-radio analyst for the Houston Astros, uses a quotation from Jim Bouton above paragraph one to begin an article about Black National League President Len Coleman. Dierker's article appeared in the *Houston Chronicle* on March 21, 1994. "You spend a good piece of life gripping a baseball, and in the end it turns out that it was the other way around all the time." — *Jim Bouton*

KISSIMMEE, Fla.: Last week, when Len Coleman addressed the media at Osceola Stadium, it became evident that you do not have to actually play in the major leagues to feel the grip of the game. Coleman grew up in New York. His mother, who taught him about baseball, was a Dodgers fan. His father liked the Giants. And directly upstairs lived a beighbour who rooted for the Yankees all the way. That was how it started for the new president of the National League. "I was a Dodgers fan like my mother," Coleman said. "But as you can imagine, things got pretty lively around the house when the topic turned to baseball." Like his predecessor, Bill White, Coleman is a black man who grew up in the era of Jackie Robinson. Now as an adult, he looks back on the game of his youth and sees something uniquely American. And as he embarks on his own baseball odyssey, Coleman knows he is treading on hallowed ground. *Houston Chronicle* writer and columnist Ed Fowler used a quotation from Shakespeare above the first paragraph to begin a story about the 1993 Ryder Cup matches. This piece appeared in the *Houston Chronicle* on September 24, 1993.

> Young Cassius has a lean and hungry look. He thinks too much. Such men are dangerous. —*Julius* Caesar, from William Shakespeare's Julius Caesar

SUTTON COLDFIELD, England: Tom Watson, freckled-faced and gap-toothed, has been compared to his fellow Middle American Tom Sawyer often enough, but never to a scheming Roman. Perhaps he has been transformed here in Warwickshire, which as the road signs remind us is "Shakespeare's country." This weekend it's the land of high tea and sniper fire as that serialized international incident known as the Ryder Cup returns to the Belfry. We recently have seen that there is room enough on this mortal coil for Israelis and Palestinians, but can it accommodate American and British golf pros?

At a black-tie dinner Wednesday night, Watson, the U.S. captain, instructed his players not to sign autographs and himself twice refused to sign for Sam Torrance, a member of the European team. Man the ramparts, boys. The battle is joined. A quotation from Pat Riley's book was used above the lead paragraph to begin an article about the Knicks and the Bulls. This article, by Rich Hofmann of the *Philadelphia Daily News*, was run in May 1994.

Knicks overcome loss of Harper to take control

"In every contest, there comes a moment that defines winning from losing. The true warrior understands and seizes that moment by giving an effort so intense and so intuitive that it could only be called one from the heart."—from Pat Riley's *The Winner Within* By Rich Hofmann, *Philadelphia Daily News*

NEW YORK: Gifts from the sky. Free throws from the heart. The Knicks have survived a Game 5 against the Chicago Bulls. And there is a pattern developing here.

They came from behind early. They came from behind late. Three times out of four in this series, they have won the end game when the end game was in doubt-including Wednesday night at Madison Square Garden 87-86. The Knicks have seized the moment, as Riley wrote. But this night, they seized it after it was dropped into their laps.

Terry Blount of the *Houston Chronicle* uses a memorable Dickens line to begin a story about Jerry Glanville's tenure as head coach of the Houston Oilers. This article was run in December 1993 when Glanville was fired as head coach of the Atlanta Falcons. The headline was "Oilers recall Glanville era with mixed emotions." To hear the Oilers players describe the Jerry Glanville era, it sounds like the start of a Charles Dickens novel: *It was the best of times. It was the worst of times.*

"Jerry is a complex individual," quarterback Cody Carlson said. "I think down deep, he's a good man. But I could see what was coming here. It was a circus and we should have put a tent around the facility. "A lot of people had gotten tired of him because they really didn't understand him. And I don't know that he wants to be understood." Glanville was the head coach for four full seasons in Houston (1986-89) and led the team to the playoffs in his last three years. The players who were here at the time have mixed feelings about his tenure, which sometimes seemed like a roller-coaster ride in the dark.

Shannon Tompkins uses another literary reference, to the novel *The River Why?*, to begin an article about duck hunting. His article, headlined "Of dawn, ducks and memories," was published in the *Houston Chronicle* on November 25, 1993. In his transcendental novel, *The River Why?*, author David James Duncan lead character is a young adult man consumed by fishing and trying to come to grips with it. The character, Gus, comes to understand that some people don't share his commitment, but can live happy lives nonetheless. But Gus also understands that *his* life is and almost certainly always will be defined by fishing, both in the physical and metaphysical sense. That epiphany hits him when he realizes he can remember every one of the hundreds of fishing experiences he's had. And that, he sees, is not so much a sign of his cognitive ability as it is a manifestation of fishing's hold on his soul.

"It's not an ability to remember," Gus says to himself. "It's an inability to forget." A couple of hours before dawn Saturday morning, with the stars of Orion the Hunter hanging in the cold sky overhead, I stood in the coastal marsh I've hunted for almost 25 years and felt a lot like Gus. Kevin Kernan, writing for the *Copley News Service*, uses a reference to Norman Rockwell's nostalgic paintings to begin an article about Lenny Dykstra. This article was run the first week in October 1993. Kernan uses an apt reference, but with any such dated references the question should be asked: Because many baseball fans are, say, under 25, how many of them will know who Norman Rockwell was? PHILADELPHIA: Picture a Norman Rockwell painting of a baseball player surrounded by young fans. Phils centre fielder Lenny Dykstra wouldn't be the ballplayer, he'd be the dirty-faced kid trying to sneak onto the field.

If there's one player who epitomizes the hard-nosed style of the Phillies, it is Dykstra. While the Braves may be America's Team, the Phils are painted as America's Bad Boys. As reliever Mitch Williams said of the National League Championship Series battle that begins tonight at Veterans Stadium, "(The Braves) were expected to win. We were expected to be in prison." Kevin Blackistone, writer for *The Dallas Morning News*, refers to the Addams Family (and Clyde the Glide and Earl the Pearl and Magic Johnson) in the lead of his article about Arkansas basketball player Dwight Stewart. This article was run late in March 1994. DALLAS: Dwight Stewart stands 6-8. He weighs at least 260 pounds. Much of his bulk looks to be in his shoulders, which are hunched and rounded like Morticia and Gomez's butler.

But Stewart is no Lurch. He's Nimble B. Quick on, of all places, the basketball court. In the second half of an NCAA Tournament game last weekend against Georgetown, Stewart dribbled into the paint like Clyde the Glide, made an Earl the Pearl twirl and passed with Magic precision to a cutter on the baseline for a slam.

And Stewart's real speciality is 3-point shooting. On the tip of his toes he stroked four against the Hoyas without a miss.

> "He . . . can pat it. He can dance with it," Stewart's coach, Nolan Richardson, said of him. "I'm not going to take the gift the good Lord gave to him. I told him in practice one day. 'Hey, Big Dog, you're a guard, son. Go on and shoot your shot.'

The NCAA Tournament is supposed to be a fair contest. But with guys like Stewart, it isn't. Mike Lopresti, of the Gannett News Service uses a variation of an Elizabeth Barrett Browning poem: "How do I love thee? Let me count the ways. . . ." in an article lead about the Nebraska Cornhuskers. His article was run on the wires Christmas, 1993, prior to the Orange Bowl.

LINCOLN, Neb.: How does the nation disrespect Nebraska? Let us count the ways:

- Ranked No. 1 in the CNN/USA Today poll, Nebraska nevertheless is a 17-point underdog against Florida State in the Orange Bowl, an unprecedented position for a top-ranked team.
- When the Cornhuskers left the field in Lawrence, Kan., having slipped by the Jayhawks 21-20, the Kansas crowd stood and shouted at them, "Overrated! Overrated! Overrated!"
- Nebraska hasn't been out of the *Associated Press* rankings any week in 12 years, and hasn't had fewer than nine victories in a season in a quarter century. The *AP* media poll ranks the Cornhuskers No. 2 behind Florida State. All that, and if Notre Dame hadn't lost to Boston College, the Cornhuskers may never have even had a chance to play for the national championship with an 11-0 record.
- One oddsmaker in Las Vegas said there were 10 teams in the country better than the Cornhuskers.

"We can't please anybody, it seems like," linebacker Mike Anderson said.

Here Mike Kern of the Philadelphia Daily News uses a turn of phrase on the old sports quote "Win one for the Gipper." This article appeared in the Anchorage Daily News on December 31, 1993, under the headline "Bowden's had it with poll racket."

MIAMI—Win one for the quipper.

That's what some coaches, most notably West Virginia's Don Nehlen, have said the media are trying to do.

It's become a political thing, they contend. Bobby Bowden is a decent guy, always there with a catchy quote, win or lose, and the writers who vote in the *Associated Press* poll want to see him rewarded with his first national championship. Or so the theory goes. Here Steve Aschburner of the *Minneapolis-St. Paul Star Tribune* uses a variation of the "inmates running the asylum" cliché to profile the San Antonio Spurs. His article was published the first week of March 1994. When inmates start running the asylum—and the asylum starts running better than it did before—people take notice.

No NBA team has been hotter over the past six weeks than the San Antonio Spurs. Since a 108-98 loss to the Timberwolves at Target Centre on Jan. 11, the Spurs are 14-2 and have wiped out the Rockets' seemingly insurmountable lead in the Midwest Division. Spurs centre David Robinson has emerged as a leading candidate for the league's MVP award, rainbow-haired Dennis Rodman brought a pot o' rebounds with him from Detroit, and John Lucas could wind up as coach of the year. One key to San Antonio's success, most of its players agree, is Lucas' willingness to let them take a significant role in running the team. His "board of directors"—made up of Robinson, Terry Cummings, Willie Anderson and Dale Ellis—is consulted on many decisions. From what plays to call during a timeout to the team's practice schedule to trade proposals and disciplinary action, the Spurs have a say.

A News Lead

Some sports articles are simply news articles. Here Linda Leavell of the *Associated Press* writes a news article, with a summary news lead, about a fire in Texas Stadium on Wednesday, October 13, 1993. IRVING: A three-alarm fire that raged Wednesday evening at Texas Stadium severely damaged a dozen luxury suites and set about 10 rows of general admission seats ablaze. No one was injured.

Irving Fire Battalion Chief Jimmy Sims said the fire damaged seven suites on the lower level and five on the upper level. Three more received extensive water damage. The boxes' contents, including television sets, furniture, mini-bars and other amenities, also were destroyed, he said. No events were taking place Wednesday, a Dallas Cowboys' spokesman said. *Associated Press* writer Nasha Starevic covered the trial of German Guenter Parche, who stabbed Monica Seles while she was on the tennis court in April 1993. This article ran on the *AP* wires on October 13, 1993. Starevic's lead was:

HAMBURG, Germany: A tennis fan who stabbed Monica Seles out of an obsessive love for her rival, Steffi Graf, walked away free Wednesday when the court that convicted him gave him a suspended two-year sentence. Guenter Parche, 39, an unemployed East German lathe operator who had been detained since the April 30 attack at a Hamburg tournament, could have received a three-year, nine-month jail term. But Hamburg District Judge Elke Bosse said she took into account a psychiatrist's testimony that Parche had a "highly abnormal personality" that could have diminished his ability to reason.

NEWS REFERENCE LEAD

In early November 1993, Cleveland Browns coach Bill Belichick cut quarterback Bernie Kosar, who was the most beloved athlete in Cleveland in many, many years. Belichick thus became the most hated man in Cleveland. The Browns went nowhere the rest of the season, and Kosar went to Dallas, where he played backup to Troy Aikman and earned himself a Super Bowl ring.

Terry Blount of the *Houston Chronicle* referred to a cut of an entirely different kind in the lead of an article headlined: "Angry fans cutting Belichik no slack." The *Chronicle* ran this article on November 22, 1993.

CLEVELAND: The most painful banner of all was unfurled with a few seconds left in the game:

"Hey Bill: Lorena Bobbitt wants to make your next cut."

Browns coach Bill Belichick continues to be the most hated man in northeast Ohio after Sunday's 27-20 loss to the Oilers. Never has so much animosity been directed at anyone involved in the Browns organization, although team owner Art Modell is running a close second. Most of the 71,668 fans at Cleveland Stadium weren't about to let Belichick and Modell off the hook for their decision two weeks ago to waive beloved quarterback Bernie Kosar. Sunday was the team's first home game since the decision was made.

THE PROMINENT NAME LEAD

The use of a key name is often a valid method to begin a story—as the name prompts reader recognition—whether the name is a local, regional, or nationally known figure. In Texas, Troy Aikman, quarterback of the Dallas Cowboys, would qualify as a "name" player. Denne Freeman of the *Associated Press Dallas* bureau uses Aikman's name to begin a story about a then-upcoming Cowboys—49ers game. This story was run on the *AP* wires on October 16, 1993. IRVING—Troy Aikman puts Sunday's showdown with the San Francisco 49ers in this perspective: "It's as important as an NFL game can get in October."

The Dallas Cowboys want to know how far they've progressed since a stumbling 0-2 start, and they figure the 49ers will let them know in the Texas Stadium rematch of NFC title opponents. The Cowboys are 6½-point favorites. The Super Bowl champion Cowboys and the 49ers, who lost 30-20 in the NFC championship game at Candlestick Park, have had their problems as they've each posted 3-2 records. The Cowboys have bounced back since Emmitt Smith ended his holdout to defeat Phoenix, Green Bay and Indianapolis after losses to Washington and Buffalo. The 49ers, one of the NFL's best road teams in recent year, have lost at Cleveland and New Orleans. Here Indiana's Bobby Knight is used as the key name in the lead of a story by an unnamed *Associated Press* writer. This event took place in December 1993.

BLOOMINGTON, Ind.: Bob Knight swung his foot. Whether his son was the intended victim or just happened to be in the way, the reaction from Indiana fans was enough to send the General into another tirade. It's nothing new, of course. Just the first time this season. But considering the No. 12-ranked Hoosiers' campaign is only three games old, their coach already appears in midseason form. His outburst in Tuesday night's 101-82 victory over Notre Dame was triggered by some sloppy play in the closing minutes by the Hoosiers' mop-up crew, which included his son Pat, a 6-foot-6 junior.

Indiana was up by 28 points when the younger Knight made a bad pass that Notre Dame's Ryan Hoover intercepted and took in for a fast-break layup. That was too much for the old man, who already was in a bad mood after scolding some fans for displaying a sarcastic sign directed at the Irish. During a time out, Knight went face-to-face with his son, screaming at him as the players went to the bench and sat down. Knight apparently kicked at something, and some fans thought it was his son's leg and started booing. That's when Knight turned from his seat and glared at the anonymous offenders behind him, his face as red as his trademark sweater.

You didn't need to be a lip-reader to make out his four-letter response. The crowd of players surrounding the bench prevented most people from seeing the apparent assault. Knight refused to speak to the news media after the game and did not return a phone call to his office on Wednesday. Athletes with unusual names or nicknames can also offer sports writers interesting ways to begin articles. One of the most interesting U.S. athletes to emerge from the Lillehammer Winter Olympics was women's skiing champion Picabo Street. This *Associated Press* article, sent on the wires the third week in February 1994, during the Olympics, stressed the pronunciation of her unique name:

RINGEBU, Norway: Pronounce it Peek-a-boo, then keep an eye on her. "Watch for her tomorrow and the rest of the season, and next year, and in four more years," said Picabo Street's mother, Dee. Street won a silver medal in the women's downhill at the Olympics on Saturday. And America now has four Alpine skiing medals—one shy of its all-time best in 1984, courtesy of this 22-year-old daughter of former flower children Dee and Stubby Street of Sun Valley, Idaho. "There's a little tiger in me that comes out of the middle of nowhere that I really don't have control of sometimes," Street said. "I'm just glad I didn't freak out."

Robes Patton of the *Fort Lauderdale Sun-Sentinel* uses a litany of names to begin an article about the big, *big* men in basketball. This article was run in October 1993. LAKE WORTH, Fla.: Even in a league brimming with tall men, there remain some who stand above the rest. Manute Bol, Mark Eaton, Chuck Nevitt, Shawn Bradley, Gheorghe Muresan.

At 7-4 and up, they are the tallest of the tall.

As such, they occupy a rarefied niche reserved for those who lack the package of skills required of others. When the Miami Heat signed Bol on Tuesday, it landed one of those rare players whose mere presence makes others—even near 7-footers such as Rony Seikaly and John Salley—appear small.

THE QUESTION LEAD

Can you begin a story with a question?

I just did.

Features can begin with questions because they involve the reader in the story, but they should be clear, understandable, and answerable. Give the reader an answer

No other game provides its fans with such an intimate view of its competitors' raw emotions. The fan can almost reach out and touch the NBA's heroes and villains. Here Dale Robertson, sports writer and columnist for the Houston Chronicle, uses a key quotation from a previous Michael Jordan interview in *Playboy* to begin a story about Jordan's retirement. This article was run under the headline "He's Michael to the bitter end" and appeared in the *Chronicle* on October 7, 1993.

> "People say they wish they were Michael Jordan. OK, do it for a year. Do it for five years. On one road trip, we got into Denver at 3 in the morning and there were people sitting around the hotel lobby. I was tired. I said, 'I'm sorry, please. I'm tired.' Then I heard, 'I guess that's the Jordan rules.'
>
> "I just kept on walking. One of these days I'm going to say, 'Go screw yourself.' Maybe when I'm walking out of the league." — Michael Jordan in *Playboy*

Michael Jeffrey Jordan walked out of the NBA on Wednesday morning, and if you listened to his farewell news conference—Jordan is so big, the networks carried it live—you would have heard him say essentially that. Not in so many words, of course, but the greatest basketball player who ever drew a breath is leaving the game he loves—a game he practically reinvented and one that made him unfathomably wealthy—a bitter man. The painted-on smile, the upbeat rhetoric and the happy prospects of spending quality time with his family couldn't hide this.

It came through loud and clear.

Jim Litke of the Associated Press uses a quotation by Mickey Lolich to begin an article about pitcher Dave Stewart. Litke's article ran on the AP wires on October 23, 1993. "I have a name now. They'll be looking for new heroes next season. But I will be remembered by someone some day."—Detroit's Mickey Lolich, after beating Bob Gibson and the St. Louis Cardinals in Game 7 of the 1968 World Series.

—By Jim Litke, *Associated Press*

TORONTO: The World Series is like a beacon. By October, the light diffused over an entire season has tapered to become a single beam. It lengthens the shadows behind a very select few hitters and pitchers. It exposes the weaknesses of most of the rest. "You get nervous when you don't really want to be in a situation," Dave Stewart said before taking the ball to the mound for the Toronto Blue Jays in Game 6 on Saturday night. "But I'm really looking forward to this." Those were brave words, but perhaps only Stewart really knew how much he risked this particular night. Already acknowledged as one of the greatest playoff performers ever—he is 8-0 in league championship play, an even more incredible 4-0 in pennant-clinching games—Stewart had yet to be similarly recognized in the best-of-seven sets that followed. And that task never seemed more daunting Saturday night.

Bob Kravitz of the *Rocky Mountain News* uses two quotations above the first paragraph of an article about Denver Nuggets" player Mark Macon. This article was published in November 1993. "He's the next Oscar Robertson." — Dick Vitale on Mark Macon

"He'll be much better as a pro. He has some very good point guard skills. He has skills people don't even know about." — NBA scout Marty Blake

DENVER: It is the strangest thing. How did Mark Macon become such a certifiable bust? How did it all go so wrong, so haywire that in only the third year of his career the Denver Nuggets had to admit his selection as the eighth pick in the draft was a mistake? The real story of Friday's deal to Detroit is not Denver's acquisition of Alvin Robertson but the unfortunate demise of Mark Macon, a young man his former coach at Temple University, John Chaney, calls "one of the most extraordinary human beings I've ever known." Steve Wulf, staff writer for Sports Illustrated, uses a quotation from the late Branch Rickey to begin an article about the new alignments in baseball. His article appeared under the headline "Scouting Reports" in SI on April 4, 1994. Baseball people—and that includes myself—are slow to change and accept new ideas. I remember that it took years to persuade them to put numbers on uniforms. —Branch Rickey, 1954

Forty years after the Mahatma said that, baseball people are again wringing their hands over a fundamental change in the game. For the first time the World Series can conceivably be won by a team that finishes . . . painful as it is to write it . . . second. Yes, there are now three divisions (East, Central, West) in each league and a new best-of-five round in postseason play. In that new format, the division winner with the best record meets the second-place finisher with the best record while the other two division winners play one another, with the victors moving on to the time-honored best-of-seven league championship series, which determines who's in the best-of-seven World Series, which could possibly produce—if delayed by weather a day or two-baseball's first Mr. November.

Can you use a single word as a quotation lead?

Yes.

Here Christopher Clarey of *The New York Times* uses such a one-word quotation in a story about the 1993 Ryder Cup golf matches in England. This article was run in *The New*

York Times on September 24, 1993, under the headline "When Continents Collide, In New Blazers and All." SUTTON COLDFIELD, England: "Apprehensive" was the word Tom Watson chose to describe his mood just before lunch. He would feel considerably better as he headed off to dinner.

Trailing by three points after losing three of four Ryde. Cup matches in the morning, Watson's United States team roared back Saturday afternoon. With two notable exceptions, the U.S. team lived up to its considerable potential, winning three matches to narrow the European edge to 8½-7½. The biennial match-play event between American and European teams concludes today with 12 individual matches that will start with two former Masters champions, Ian Woosnam and Fred Couples, teeing off first, and end with sizzling Nick Faldo playing Paul Azinger.

THE SIMILE (OR METAPHOR) LEAD

A simile compares Item A to Item B. Strictly speaking, the usage is *A is like B*. The more unusual the match, the more interesting the simile. Ken Rodriquez of *The Miami Herald* uses a simile lead in his story about the January 1994 Fiesta Bowl game in Tempe, where Arizona beat Miami 29-0. TEMPE, Ariz.: Under a shadow of mountains, cactus and blood-red Arizona fans chanting, "U of A! U of A!," the University of Miami went down like a wounded gunslinger Saturday, ambushed in the desert. A dynasty lay sprawled. A rising challenger stood tall, strutting into the sunset after a shocking Fiesta Bowl massacre: Arizona 29, Miami 0.

"They just kicked the living heck out of us," said Miami coach Dennis Erickson, whose No. 10 Hurricanes (9-3) completed their worst season since an 8-5 record under Jimmy Johnson in 1984. "We never could get anything going." Mike Lopresti of the Gannett News Service uses a nice simile ("College basketball looks like . . .") to begin an analysis piece about college basketball. This was run in January 1994.

Here at the season's halfway post, college basketball looks like a messy closet, where No. 1 is a revolving door and the biggest story has been a walkout that didn't happen, but still might. There is no place to turn for neatness. Parity is cluttering up the college game. Not to mention energizing it. We could start by talking about the top-ranked team, but that's assuming there is one, which may be stretching things. Four teams have been there—Kansas, North Carolina, Duke and Arkansas—and four teams have lost, two of them at home. Larry Dierker, TV-radio analyst for the Houston Astros, uses a simile lead in an analysis article about the Phillies. His article appeared in the *Houston Chronicle* on August 23, 1993 under the headline "Primordial Phils reflect Fregosi."

In this age of artificial intelligence, the Phillies are like cavemen. They're way behind the times. The Phillies don't have a nutritionist on staff. "Our nutrition is a hot dog and a beer," says manager Jim Fregosi, sitting with his legs crossed in the visitors' dugout at the Astrodome, grinning as he watches his warrior clan stretch lazily on the turf. The Phillies don't employ a psychologist, either. They like to hang around in the training room after the hunt, in an area where outsiders are forbidden. It's a let-your-hair-down, let-your-feelings-out sort of place. It's an ice house, an infirmary. A healing place. A cave. You can also use a metaphor instead of a simile. The simile is A is like B; the metaphor is A is B. In the cases of the similes shown here, the metaphor versions would be:

- The University of Miami was a wounded gunslinger Saturday. . .
- College basketball is a messy closet. . . .
- The Phillies are cavemen. . . .

When should you use a simile and when should you use a metaphor? There is no rule; the choice simply depends on how you want the sentence to sound.

THE STATISTICS LEAD

Occasionally, a sports writer can use statistics to show winners and losers. After all, many sports fans are numbers junkies. Statistics must be clean and clear; you don't want to sink a good story in an unfathomable sea of numbers. Controversies about Black student athletes and Black coaches erupted in 1994. Liz Clarke of the *Knight-Ridder Tribune News* service uses statistics in the lead of an article about this issue. This article was run on the *Knight-Ridder Tribune News* wires in January 1994.

Behind the war of words that nearly triggered a college basketball boycott earlier this month is an issue larger than scholarships: It's the lack of black voices in debates that produce NCAA rules—such as the one limiting men's basketball to 13 scholarships per team. Blacks account for just 3.2 percent of 312 key NCAA delegates—composed of college presidents, athletic directors, top women's administrators and faculty members—from schools in the nation's eight biggest athletic conferences. In the nine-member Atlantic Coast Conference, none of 36 campus delegates to the NCAA is black. It's the same in the 12-member Southeastern Conference, where none of 48 campus NCAA delegates is black. It's that lack of representation—mirrored to a less dramatic but consistent extent throughout the NCAA—that spurred the Black Coaches Association to call for a basketball boycott on Jan. 15, the Rev. Martin Luther King Jr.'s birthday. The boycott has been postponed while the Congressional Black Caucus and the Justice Department mediate the dispute.

THE STATEMENT LEAD

Simplicity is often best. Short declarative sentences have impact. You have just read two, short, single-sentence paragraphs. The statement lead is not as elegant as some other types of leads, but is workable in many cases. Here

Bill Knight of the *Seattle Post-Intelligencer* uses this type of lead in a story about the NBA. This article was written in January 1994. Success breeds hostility. At least that's the way it seems in the combative relationship of professional basketball fans with rival players and referees.

Fans who follow winners take the outcome of every game more seriously and are more abusive in the stands, according to an informal survey of NBA teams. "Fans seem to get a lot more hostile when it's a big game that means something," said Dale Ratermann of the Indiana Pacers. "One or two plays can incite a crowd in a hurry. When all games mean something it does make a difference in how people behave." Elizabeth Leland of *The Charlotte Observer* uses a simple statement of fact to begin an article about the death of Michael Jordan's father. This article was published in August 1993. CHARLOTTE, N.C.: There's a lot of James Jordan in his superstar son. Father passed on his looks to Michael Jordan—broad nose, prominent cheekbones, a smile that curves at the corners into dimples—his high spirits and sense of mischief.

And now, after James Jordan's slaying, a world of Michael Jordan worshipers struggles to understand why anyone would kill the hero's father. Bill Sullivan of the *Houston Chronicle* uses a simple statement lead to begin an article about Jimmy Johnson and Cowboy "problem players." The article was run under the headline "Cowboys try Roper experiment" in the *Chronicle* on August 20, 1993.

AUSTIN—JIMMY Johnson has been down this road. Tony Casillas, you might recall, came to the Cowboys from Atlanta with the reputation of being a bad actor. Charles Haley, whose behaviour in San Francisco could be considered "colourful" only on the best of days, was a virtual giveaway when the 49ers decided enough was enough. But in Dallas, each found a place in Jimmy's Home for Wayward Boys. Each contributed greatly to a Super Bowl win. Each, by the way, is still around. Small wonder, then, that Johnson is willing to roll the dice again. " John Roper won't make or break our football team," the Cowboys' coach said after picking up the former Yates and Texas A&M star in Tuesday's trade with the Bears. "But if he fits in, and the chemistry is right, then we've got a bonus because he's a talented player."

On the other hand. . . . Malcolm Moran used a simple statement of fact to begin an article about former University of Washington Husky head coach Don James. This article appeared in *The New York Times* on September 3, 1993, under the title " Don James Finds That Roses Outnumber The Thorns." SEATTLE—The former coach will arrive by yacht. As the players, coaches and fans at the University of Washington continue to cope with emotions usually reserved for a death in the family, Don James will begin his season outside football the way he has always wanted—relaxing on Lake Washington as he approaches Husky Stadium Saturday. Less than two weeks after his sudden, emotionally charged resignation, touched off by a two-year bowl ban imposed on Washington by the Pacific-10 Conference, James has begun to grow apart from the programme he led for 18 seasons.

Cynthia Thomas of the *Houston Chronicle* uses a statement lead to begin an article about Karen Voight, workout expert. This article, published on September 9, 1993 was run under a headline "Woman of Steel," with an accompanying colour picture of Voight in front of a workout class. The woman with "the perfect body" leads a boring life. Glamour magazine dubbed her "the Empress of Abs." *The London tabloid Today* called hers "the $3 million body." She's one of the most sought-after instructors in the fitness industry, commanding five-digit fees to teach at conferences. Still, given the hours she and husband Henry Siegel put into their business, her lifestyle can sound more akin to that of a worker in a family-run grocery than a fitness guru flitting from the aerobics studio to the television studio. (Granted, the grocer doesn't get to tutor Tina Turner on her "abs").

When the couple opened their studio in Los Angeles in 1981 they did everything themselves. She taught. He ran the business. Between classes they cleaned the mirrors and swept the floors. They started early in the morning and worked into the night seven days a week. Now the Voight Fitness and Dance Centre teaches 3,500 students a week in classes such as Step 'N' Pump; Bodysculpt; and Abs, Thighs and Buns. Voight's six videos are well-reviewed and have sold hundreds of thousands of copies. Robes Patton of the *Fort Lauderdale Sun-Sentinel* uses a statement lead in an article about the 1993 Sugar Bowl, in which Florida beat West Virginia, 41-7. This game was played New Year's Day, 1994.

NEW ORLEANS: This is why they play the games. After a month of whining and bemoaning a perceived lack of respect and poll unfairness, West Virginia was muzzled by Florida 41-7 Saturday night in the Sugar Bowl. It was a Florida performance that was dazzling in its completeness. "Overall, I think this is one of our best games of the season," said Florida senior running back Errict Rhett. "I wanted to go out just like this right here. It'll be the game I'll always remember as a Gator, so it felt really good." A simple statement can often be used effectively to underplay a dramatic event. Mike Monroe of *The Denver Post* uses such a lead in a copyrighted story (often stated incorrectly as a "copyright story" in the press) announcing the retirement of Michael Jordan.

> This article was moved on the wires late on October 5, 1993 in advance of Jordan's announcement, and was run in the October 6, 1993 *Houston Post* under the headline "Jordan to announce basketball retirement today". —By Mike Monroe, *The Denver Post*, 1993,

The Denver Post Corp. The Michael Jordan era in professional basketball has ended.

Jordan, the Chicago Bulls superstar who is one of the most popular personalities in the world, today will announce his retirement from the game after nine amazing seasons that brought him three Most Valuable Player awards, seven NBA scoring titles and the highest career scoring average (32.3) points in NBA history. A source close to Jordan told *The Denver Post* of Jordan's plan to announce the end of his career, and Bulls coach Phil Jackson confirmed it Tuesday night.

THE SUMMARY LEAD

Who played, where and when, the score, and a key play or key statistics: These are the key elements of a summary lead. Here is a perfect example, in an article about a Bulls-Knicks game in December 1993. CHICAGO—B.J.: Armstrong scored 20 points, 11 in the final 6:06 Friday night, boosting the Chicago Bulls to a 98-86 victory over New York that snapped the Knicks' five-game winning streak. Charles Oakley's 18-foot jumper from the corner with 8:16 left gave the Knicks their first lead of the game at 76-75. After an exchange of baskets, the Bulls scored the next eight points, four by Armstrong, for an 85-78 advantage with 5:39 left.

John Starks, who had 19 points, responded with a 3-pointer at 5:13 and another basket at 4:14, closing the Knicks to 85-83. But Chicago coasted to its eighth victory in nine games after Scottie Pippen, who had 18 points, scored on a layup with 1:54 left and Armstrong hit a 3-pointer 25 seconds later for a 90-83 lead. In some cases, the most natural lead for a sports story is the summary lead, in which the writer summarizes or capsulizes the achievements of a player, team, or coach. *Associated Press* writer Dave Carpenter used a summary lead to begin an article about the triumph of U.S. speed skater Dan Jansen. This article was run on the *AP* wires on February 18, 1994 after Jansen's dramatic victory in the Lillehammer Olympics:

LILLEHAMMER, Norway: Skating for redemption and a gold medal, Dan Jansen got both emphatically Friday with a world record in his final Olympic race after seven failures over a decade of heartbreak. "I guess good guys do win," said Jansen's coach, Peter Mueller. The world's fastest skater thrust his arms up triumphantly after crossing the finish line in the 1,000-meter race and put his hands to his head, no doubt as much in relief as in ecstasy. The crowd erupted as the record time flashed on the Viking Ship Hall scoreboard: 1 minute, 12.43 seconds, .11 faster than Canadian Kevin Scott's 2-month-old world record. After 10 years of agony, Jansenstill had to wait for another 1 1/2 hours before his long-awaited gold was made official, with three dozen competitors skating behind him.

THE "THEME" LEAD

Writers can sometimes use a continuing *lyric* or theme line to emphasize a lead throughout a story. In this story, Claudia Feldman of the *Houston Chronicle* uses "Pow!" to show how golfer Teri Lee not only swings her golf clubs, but also how she visualizes conquering cancer cells. This article, under the headline "Hard Hitter" and the subhead "Cancer scare teaches CPA to fight, relax," was published in the *Chronicle* on October 4, 1993. A lyric word or theme line should be short or concise to emphasize the writer's point.

Teri Lee was practicing her golf swing in preparation for today's First Annual CAnCare of Houston Golf Classic.

Pow!

She had a radical mastectomy in the spring, three years ago.

Pow!

She's a CPA. It was tax season. She still got her work done.

Pow!

It was her right breast, and she's right-handed. Her teacher said it might help her swing.

Pow!

She didn't play much golf before her surgery. She didn't have time. But if she learned anything during her cancer scare, it was to slow down, spend more time with her family and enjoy herself.

Pow! Whoa! Ouch! She almost brained a man crouched 10 yards away who was trying to take her picture.

Pow!

Every time she swings that club, she sees herself pulverizing cancer cells.

Pow! She's a hard hitter. She has golf gloves, golf clubs, golf shoes and a golf bag with her name inscribed on it. But no, she doesn't take her golf score that seriously. Life's too short.

Houston Chronicle columnist Fran Blinebury uses the same technique in an article headlined "Cowboys smart but get wiser". This article ran in the *Houston Chronicle* on November 22, 1993.

ATLANTA: It was the game when the silver and blue became black and blue. An afternoon when the sides of their helmets weren't the only place they saw stars.

The Cowboys expected a nice day at the beach and wound up washed away by a tidal wave. They probably thought the worst thing that could happen was a little fender bender on the road back to the Super Bowl and nearly found themselves smack in the middle of the Hindenburg disaster.

Boom!

Kenneth Gant had to leave the game with a dislocated left shoulder.

Boom!

Nate Newton hobbled out with a bruised right knee.

Boom!

Kevin Gogan limps off with a twisted left knee.

Boom!

Bernie Kosar stayed on the field, but had visions of Quasimodo running around inside his skull after having his bell rung in a big way by the Falcons' Jessie Tuggle.

Boom!

Emmitt Smith had to be taken to the locker room on a cart after going down to the artificial turf in a heap late in the second quarter. The next explosion you heard figured to be the Cowboys' dynasty collapsing upon itself like one of those old buildings that has been rigged with so many sticks of dynamite.

THE TIMELINE LEAD

Sports writers can use a chronology to show the progress of an athlete, a team, or a Sports. This can be used with the earlier date first, or today's date, then a flashback to previous months, years or conditions. Here Christine Brennan of *The Washington Post* used such a lead to show how long the British team of Jayne Torvill and Christopher Dean have been champions of the Sports of ice dancing. This article was published in February 1994, during the Winter Olympics in Lillehammer, Norway. HAMAR, Norway: Ten years later, the perfect 6.0s still popped onto the scoreboard and the Union Jacks still waved in the stands.

Torvill and Dean are back, and they are precisely where they are expected to be, leading the ice dancing competition at the Winter Olympics. With tonight's free dance portion remaining, Jayne Torvill and Christopher Dean hold a slight edge over two Russian dance pairs after 50 percent of the competition. The 1984 Olympic gold medalists took the lead with an elegant original dance Sunday night at the Olympic Amphitheatre after falling behind two nights ago in the compulsory dance. Here is another version of the timeline lead. Dave Goldberg, writer for the *Associated Press*, uses it well in a 1993 article about Miami Dolphins coach Don Shula.

MIAMI: Oct. 5, 1963. Don Shula is standing on the sidelines at Wrigley Field in Chicago, watching George Halas coach the Bears to a 10-3 victory over his Baltimore Colts. "I was just in awe of him," Shula says. "Here I was this 33-

year-old rookie and I was standing there trying to coach against this legend." Oct. 30, 1993. Scott Mitchell, who the next day will quarterback the Miami Dolphins to the win that ties Shula with Halas for the most ever by an NFL coach, is recalling when he first met Shula in 1990. "I was standing there when he came up to me, stuck out his hand and said 'I'm coach Shula,'" Mitchell recalls. "Of course I knew him. I'd seen him a million times on television. I was born in 1968 and he was already a legend by then."

Cathy Harasta uses a timeline lead in a story about UCLA-Houston basketball, 1968 style and the same teams, playing each other in 1993 for the first time since that 1968 game. Her article appeared in *The Dallas Morning News* on December 20, 1993, under the headline "Hayes played large role in biggest game." Abdul-Jabbar still was Alcindor. The Astrodome still was an anomaly. At the time, Elvin Hayes wondered if anyone would be there for the Jan. 20, 1968, UCLA-Houston game. "Anyone" was a relative term, because some fans certainly would show for a No. 1 versus No. 2 matchup of undefeated teams. But this game was an unusual test, not just of the Cougars, then 16-0 and ranked second, and the top-ranked Bruins (13-0). This game would chart the future of the Sports. It would become a touchstone for basketball, for Hayes, for sports television, for arena management and for millions of fans.

Hayes and his Houston teammates were to be part of a new-fangled notion. Basketball never had been played in a domed stadium. Regular-season college basketball had yet to enjoy national television exposure. Nobody knew the sport's potential, what it could be worth, or if anybody cared. The game, in a novel building in a football state, would be known as The Game of the Century. But nobody knew it, going in. Hayes did not feel like a frontiersman. "The players were conscious of a building of that size and magnitude," said Hayes, whose No. 44 will be retired during a ceremony at halftime of UCLA's game at Houston Monday night. "We wondered if there would be any people in the stands. Was anybody going to come?"

What came out of that game was a national awareness of college basketball and its potential. The game drew 52,693—a record paid crowd for basketball at the time. Hayes, a 6-9 senior, led the Cougars to a 71-69 victory. Fouled with 28 seconds left, he made the decisive free throws against the Lew Alcindor-led Bruins. Hayes played all 40 minutes, scored 39 points and had 15 rebounds. On Monday night, UCLA will play the Cougars in Houston for the first time since that 1968 landmark game. This time, the Bruins will meet UH in Hofheinz Pavilion. Many of Hayes' teammates plan to be there. Here, sports writer Melanie Hauser of The Houston Post uses a timeline lead to show how long Billie Jean King has been a tennis star. Hauser's article appeared under the headline: "King part of gala to combat AIDS". The article appeared in *The Houston Post* on February 15, 1994. Twenty-five years ago, a visit to Houston changed Billie Jean King's life and the face of women's tennis. Still another King visit here in 1973 helped change the perception towards females and female athletes.

Two decades later, King is out in front once again, this time teaming some legendary Virginia Slims players with headline entertainers Liza Minnelli and Angela Lansbury for a nostalgic weekend benefiting the American Foundation for AIDS Research. As a lead-in to this year's Virginia Slims of Houston, the 50-year-old King has helped put together Virginia Slims Legends weekend—a two-day affair March 19-20 that includes a pro-am, a concert by Minnelli and a round-robin exhibition featuring King, Martina Navratilova, Virginia Wade and Tracy Austin.Here Owen Davis, writer for the *Detroit Free Press*, uses a timeline lead to show the progress of a U.S. luge sledder, run on the wire services February 18, 1994.

LILLEHAMMER, Norway: Mark Grimmette grew up sledding down hills in Muskegon, Mich., in the wintertime. "One day I heard some noise on my favourite sledding hill," Grimmette said Friday. "All these bulldozers were carving out a luge track. I helped them." An Olympian was born. Ten years later, Grimmette and Jonathan Edwards finished fourth in Olympic luge doubles, the best performance ever by American lugers—singles or doubles. Chris Thorpe of Marquette, Mich., and Gordon Sheer were fifth. Alan Solomon, writing for the *Chicago Tribune*, uses a timeline lead to show how much difference a year makes. This article, about Michael Jordan, was run on the wires March 21, 1994.

SARASOTA, Fla.: A year ago, Michael Jordan was a member of the NBA champion Chicago Bulls, cheered by thousands. Monday, he was a member of the Prince William Cannons, cheered by 32. As the national anthem was being sung by a sellout crowd in full throat at Ed Smith Stadium, a few hundred feet away the greatest basketball player who ever played the game trotted out to right field on a place with a decidedly unmagical name: Field 4. He is a minor-leaguer now. He will play, for the next week or so, on whatever White Sox farm team has room. "Today, it's (Class A) Prince William," said general manager Ron Schueler. "Wednesday, it might be (Class AAA) Nashville. It's where we can get him in games or where we can get him the most at-bats."

Writer Joe Gergen of *Newsday* uses a timeline lead to begin a story about Louisville basketball coach Denny Crum's induction into the Basketball Hall of Fame, late in March 1994. With the lengthy association of Crum and John Wooden of UCLA, such a timeline lead is a natural. LOS ANGELES: Denny Crum doesn't get nostalgic about buildings. He didn't shed a tear when he walked inside the Sports Arena on Wednesday although it might have been appropriate.

It was here in 1968 that he sat on the UCLA bench alongside John Wooden as a celebrated centre named Lew Alcindor led the Bruins to a second consecutive NCAA championship. It was here, four years later, that he first opposed the man he still calls Coach (with a capital C) in the semifinals of another Final Four. The centre on that UCLA team was Bill Walton so don't bother asking if he won. Still, it was a great moment for Crum in his first season as head coach of the Louisville Cardinals.

"That was a long time ago," Crum said. Were you alive when Franklin Roosevelt was president? Ken Grissom, Outdoors Editor of *The Houston Post*, uses a timeline lead to begin a story about a gulf fishing tournament, held annually in Port Aransas, Texas. His article was published on March 20, 1994. (My pocket calculator tells me that the tournament began in 1935. If you use numbers, dates, and years in a story—make sure they add up correctly. Grissom's numbers did add up: Roosevelt's first term began in 1933.) Franklin Delano Roosevelt was in his first term when the first Deep Sea Roundup was held in Port Aransas. They're doing it again—the 59th annual—July 1-3 with separate competitions in the Offshore, Bay & Surf, Junior and Piggy Perch divisions.

More than 500 anglers are expected in Texas' premier saltwater tournament. If one of them happens to break the present state record for kingfish, 711/5 pounds, the prize is $50,000. For winning catches in the regular categories, trophies, plaques and other prizes will be awarded. Entry is $60 per angler before June 15, $70 afterward. Categories are: Offshore—Amberjack, barracuda, bonito, ling, ... If you ask "whatever happened to . . .?" you may be able to develop a fascinating sports story of an individual, a team, or an era. Curt Brown, of the Minneapolis-St. Paul *Star Tribune*, uses a timeline lead to write about the NFL "Class of '83." His article was published in November 1993. Most classes hold their 10-year reunions at some posh hotel, toasting plastic champagne glasses while comparing hair lost and weight gained. The NFL's rookie class of '83 was never like most classes, though.

> "We were a class of our own, the cream of the crop, we were amazing," said Vikings running back Roger Craig, one of five members from the Class of '83 who played in Sunday's Vikings-Broncos game. "Our class made a serious, serious impact. I mean, man, we kind of made the league at the time by giving fans a whole new corps of guys."

The bulbs behind the marquee names of Terry Bradshaw, Bob Griese, Mean Joe Greene, O.J. Simpson, Roger Staubach, Frank Tarkenton, Alan Page and Franco Harris had burned out by the early 1980s, leaving the NFL in a black hole. When the '83 draft rolled around, the stars were instantly realigned with the likes of John Elway, Jim Kelly, Dan Marino, Eric Dickerson, Curt Warner, Richard Dent, Joey Browner, Darrell Green, Karl Mecklenburg and Charles Mann.

THE "YOU" LEAD

Every article "talks" to the reader. Style is a matter of how your material "sounds" to your reader's inner ear. The use of the second-person "you" lead speaks directly to your readers. This technique makes it seem as if you are speaking to a good friend, telling them exactly what will happen to them if. . . . Here Ken Grissom of *The Houston Post* tells you what will happen to you when you first take a snorkeling trip to the Florida Keys. Notice the use of the key word *you*. The complete article is published so you (there's that word again) can count the *you*'s if you like. This article was published under the headline "Snorkeling off the Keys opens eyes to new world" and was published March 27, 1994.

LOOE KEY, Fla.: You won't know the half of it until you step off the *Emerald See* into the invisible water over this fabulous, accessible coral reef. As you swing around and make your approach from the south, the world is a slightly rumpled sheet of azure Atlantic, with the Lower Keys just a smudge on the horizon. In the immediate foreground is an orderly line of boats, some passengercarrying 40-foot catamarans like the *See* and some smaller private craft. What makes the anchorage so orderly is the line of anchor buoys you're required to use to avoid dragging your hook over the precious creation below. Capt. Alex Creedon has gotten you here. Now divemaster Margi Austin takes over, showing you how to apply anti-fog lotion to your diving mask, outfitting you with a flotation vest should you get tired of kicking. Maybe you don't need such attention, but some of those on the half-day tour have yet to clamp their teeth on a snorkel. It doesn't matter. You can float on the surface right by the boat and see a big barracuda lazing 20 feet below. The coral bank becomes shallower, more profuse, vastly more colourful as you swim southward towards its crest within a foot or so of the surface. By comparison, the world above the surface is monochromatic, blue on blue.

The sea life is abundant, too. One of the youngsters in your group babbles excitedly through his snorkel at the sight of a dazzling parrotfish. The fish is used to human sightseers and allows the boy to follow it on its rounds of the reef. All of this comes without having to hold your breath. If you do want to swim beneath the surface, there are sand-bottom channels through the reef which give the snorkeler a taste of what scuba divers call "wall diving." Snorkeling is something that can be done by people with a wide variety of skill levels and physical conditions, from relaxing on the surface with your personal window on the underwater world to the very taxing "free-diving" done by those who spearfish without the aid of scuba in the same spirit that some deer hunters like to use archery equipment or muzzleloaders.

Equipment is fairly inexpensive, too. Of course, dive boats like the *Emerald See* have all the equipment available.

The *See* is operated by Strike Zone Charters out of a marina on Big Pine Key (mile 29 1/2). Cary Estes (1993) writing for the *Birmingham Post-Herald*, talks to the reader most dramatically in this article about Alabama's George Wilkerson. Note the nice touch after the lead: "He is 'The Club' in human form". BIRMINGHAM, Ala.: He is in your face. Right there. A living shadow, relentlessly following your every step. You move right, he stays with you. You juke left. No good. He sticks to you like gum on a shoe. You cannot simply shake him off.

His breath hits your face. His taunts pierce your ears. You feel his sweat. He senses your fear. He is in constant motion, even while standing still. His hands flicker. His eyes dart. He is tightly coiled and ready to strike. Finally, out of frustration, you shoot the ball. You know you are off balance and too far from the basket. You know he will extend his arms and make you put too much arc on the ball. Still, you have to do something. So you shoot. Clang. And so ends the first possession. In less than a minute, you have to do it all over again. This is the nightmare faced every game by the player who is guarded by Alabama Birmingham's George Wilkerson. Wilkerson's statistics seldom make much of an impression. He is averaging five points and four rebounds per game. He will make a few steals, dish out a couple of assists. Nothing special overall.

But Wilkerson's contribution to the Blazers goes far beyond mere stats. He is "The Club" in human form. He clamps down on the opposing team's top perimeter scorer and never lets go. Gannett writer and columnist Mike Lopresti uses a "you" lead on the new NFL rule that will allow a 2-point conversion. This column was moved by Gannett late in March 1994. (This lead is especially appealing for all the fans of the NFL who believe—Monday morning—that they could do better than that sorry fellow who was coaching their team Sunday afternoon.).

Imagine you're an NFL coach (headphones are optional). Your team has just scored a touchdown late in the fourth quarter to go ahead by seven points, and now you walk the sideline and face the PAT dilemma. You can take the easy kick for one. Go by the book. But your heart is whispering something else into your ear. The wind is against you. Your defence is hurt and tired. Go for two. Get a nine-point lead, put this game away, slip a shiv into the back of that team across the way. The fans will cheer your bold move. The players soon will be pouring Gatorade upon your head. Or. You'll blow the game. You'll fail on the two-point PAT and the other team will come back to win, and the fans will be dialing up radio talk shows to call you names, you dummy. You pace, you wonder. What would Lombardi have done? Or Noll? What would Don Shula be deciding right now? Well, that's the point. Or, to be more precise, the two points. Lombardi and Noll and Shula and the rest never have had to ask themselves that question. Not on the pro level, anyway. The PAT was a pat hand. You scored a touchdown, you sent out the kicker. One point was the only item on the menu.

COMBINATION LEADS

Previously we have cited several leads that are a combination of techniques. Lead techniques can often be combined for a solid article beginning. Here Brian Ettkin of the Scripps-Howard News Service uses a statement and then a comparison of Kevin Johnson of the Phoenix Suns and Mark Price of the Cleveland Cavaliers in an article about the sports marketing attractions of various players. This article was run on the Scripps-Howard wires in March 1994. Combinations of various types of leads are limited only by your imagination, and your knowledge and use of various leads.

There's such a fine line in sports between marketable and dull. Phoenix all-star point guard Kevin Johnson is flashy, exciting and plays for the Western Conference champion

Suns. Advertisers find him marketable. Cleveland all-star point guard Mark Price is plain, equally talented and plays for the Cavaliers. He is dull—advertisers often lose his phone number. As the market for athletes who endorse everything from shoes to frozen pizzas has become saturated, companies aren't shelling out their money as freely.

Here's an unusual combination lead and story. Ken Grissom of *The Houston Post* begins with a "you" lead, that leads to a "test" style. He had four questions in the article. One is reprinted here. This article, under a headline "Patience key in trophy hunting," ran in *The Houston Post* on December 9, 1993. Take this quick test: You are on a big South Texas ranch, sitting in a tripod stand on a narrow sendero, hunting for a big deer known to be in the area. The buck—and it *is* a monster, heavy and wide with 10 points—suddenly appears in the sendero about 250 yards away. It turns and weaves down the edge of the sendero, coming towards you—now in the open, now in the brush. Continually moving.

What do you do?

(1) Shoot.
(2) Don't shoot.

The correct answer is don't shoot. Why risk a moving shot at 200-plus yards when the animal is still coming towards you? Using the "you" of the reader and the "I" of the writer *can* be done. Here Vin T. Sparano of the Gannett News Service uses both in an article about hunting and fishing trips. This was run early in December 1993. Sportsmen can spend months, even years, planning that great hunting or fishing trip, but everything still can go wrong and destroy a journey. Unless you are an experienced traveler, you may not be aware of the problems that can ruin your trip. If you're a hunter or fisherman, there are some precautions to consider.

Several years ago, I decided that I would no longer travel with sporting arms. It was just too much trouble at most airports. I would carefully pack my shotgun or rifle and tape all hinges and latches of the case with duct tape to protect them from the usual battering inflicted by baggage handlers.

To repeat, combinations of lead types are limited solely by the writer's imagination:

- A *quotation* from an athlete, player or coach might be followed by a *description* of that person.
- An *anecdote* about a person might be followed by a *rhetorical question* at the end of the lead: "Do you think he did the right thing in that circumstance?"
- A *statement.*"It was the highest scoring football game ever played (in the state of . . .)" might easily be followed by *contrasting quotations* from, or *contrasting anecdotes* about, the winning and losing coaches.
- A *false lead* (perhaps about a Civil War battle re-enactment) might be followed by a *quotation* from a participant in that battle re-enactment.

A Reminder: All leads must come to an obvious conclusion, before the writer (and eventually the reader) begins the body of the article. In *Modern Sportswriting* (1969), Louis I. Gelfand and Harry E. Heath Jr. wrote:

> Regardless of the type of story being written, however, the sportswriter should examine his notes carefully, select his lead elements, and make a mental outline of the story before proceeding. The beginner will find it helpful to number the facts in his notes in the order of their importance. *The veteran automatically turns over lead possibilities in his mind as the game is played. In many cases he has mentally concocted a half-dozen leads before the contest has ended. This procedure is second nature with him; indeed, he may be entirely unaware of it. The beginner will develop it only through practice.*

SPORTS LEADS

On occasion, even the best writer "runs dry" at the beginning of a story. The writer has no lead; no beginning. The blinking cursor just seems to say: "No lead. . . . No lead. . . . No lead. . . . No lead. . . ." There is nothing like that cold, empty feeling when there is no lead in sight for a story that has to be written—especially if the writer is on deadline and can hear the ticking clock as the deadline grows nearer. Fortunately, there are some keys to help the writer find that ideal lead for the story in progress. Answering these questions may help the writer find the best type of lead for the article in progress.

- What is the best anecdote I have in my notes?
- What is the best quotation?
- What is the best description?
- What did I see when I was covering the story?
- Was there anything important behind the scenes?
- What would the reader expect to know?

It may help the writer discover the right lead by considering the category of the story. In the following, a list of leads is offered after each type of story. These are leads that, in general, may be the most appropriate for these types of articles. Although this is not a completely fail-safe method, these charts may help the writer select the lead based on the type of article in progress. (You can consider this a rudimentary computer-check programme in type form).

Are you writing about yourself as observer or participant in a sports event? Consider:

- A first-person lead
- The anecdotal lead
- A big play lead
- A descriptive lead
- An interior monologue lead
- Combinations of two or more of these types
- Other type of lead or leads

Are you writing a profile or biographical article about an active or retired player or someone else in sports? Consider:

- An anecdotal lead
- A descriptive lead
- A quotation lead
- A timeline lead
- Combinations of two or more of these leads
- Other types of leads

Are you writing about any active sports event (baseball game, football game, tennis match, etc.)? Consider:

- A summary lead
- A prominent name lead
- A big play lead
- A descriptive lead
- A quotation lead
- A comparison-contrast lead
- Combinations of two or more of these types of leads
- Other types of leads

Are you writing about a trend in sports or a problem in sports and society? Consider:

- A question lead
- A summary lead
- A statement lead
- A timeline lead
- Combinations of two or more of these lead types
- Another type of lead, or leads

Are you writing an *essay, editorial, or personal philosophy?* Consider:

- A first-person "I" lead
- A statement lead
- A question lead
- An anecdotal lead
- A summary lead
- Combinations of two of these leads
- Other type of lead or leads

Are you writing about *a specific scene or location?* Consider:

- A descriptive lead
- A second-person "you" lead

- A summary lead
- Combinations of two or more of these leads
- Other types of leads

Are you writing about *an accident or other incident that includes a fatality, injury, or property damage (or potential for such)?* Consider:

- A summary lead
- Prominent name lead
- A descriptive lead
- A statement lead
- A quotation lead
- Combinations of these types of leads
- Other types of leads

Are you writing *how-to-do-it material*? Consider:

- A descriptive lead
- A statement lead
- A second-person "you" lead
- A summary lead
- Combinations of two or more of these types of leads
- Another type of lead or leads

Are you writing *inspirational or motivational material?* Consider:

- A first-person "I" lead
- A second-person "you" lead
- An anecdotal lead
- A question lead
- A statement lead
- Combinations of these types of leads
- Other types of leads

Are you writing *publicity material, press releases, or formal documents?* Consider:

- A prominent name lead
- A summary lead
- A statement lead
- Combinations of these types of leads
- Other types of leads

Are you writing about sports and government, sports in the courts, sports and the law, or sports and politics? Consider:

- A summary lead
- A prominent name lead
- A statement lead
- A timeline lead
- A quotation lead
- A question lead
- Combinations of these types of leads
- Other types of leads

Are you writing about sports and medicine or sports *and science?* Consider:

- A descriptive lead
- A summary lead
- A question lead
- A statement lead
- An anecdotal lead
- A quotation lead
- Combinations of these types of leads
- Other leads

Are you writing for *radio or TV?* Consider:

- A comparison-contrast lead
- A summary lead
- A prominent name lead
- A descriptive lead
- A big play lead
- An anecdotal lead
- A quotation lead
- A first-person "I" lead
- A second-person "you" lead
- A statement lead
- Combinations of these types of leads
- Other types of leads

Are you writing an *advance* story? Consider:

- A comparison-contrast lead
- A summary lead
- A statement lead
- A prominent name lead
- A quotation lead
- Combinations of two or more of these types of leads
- Other types of leads

Are you writing a *follow-up* story? Consider:

- A summary lead
- An anecdote lead
- A big play lead
- A comparison-contrast lead
- A quotation lead
- A prominent name lead
- A statement lead
- Combinations of these types of leads
- Other types of leads

LEADS CHARTED BY GENERAL DEGREE OF DIFFICULTY OF USE

The following list indicates how hard these types of leads are, or how often they can be seen in general sports usage. Although this is *not* a fail-safe guarantee either, the numbers indicate the degree of simplicity or complexity of use for the writer.

1-3 indicates generally easy to use and often seen;

4-7 moderately harder to use, takes more planning or is more complex;

8-10 difficult to use in most situations.

An asterisk after the number indicates that this type of lead is seldom seen in most sports articles.

- The anecdotal lead: 2-3
- The big play lead: 3-5
- The classified ad lead: 4-6

- The comparison-contrast lead: 4-6
- The delayed climax lead: 4-6
- The descriptive lead: 3-5
- The epic game lead: 3-5
- The false lead: 8-10
- The future lead: 7-9
- The "I" lead: 1-3
- The interior monologue lead: 9-10
- The "letter to" lead: 2-3
- The list lead: 2-4
- The literary reference lead: 6-9
- The news lead: 1-3
- The news reference lead: 2-5
- The prominent name lead: 2-3
- The question lead: 2-4
- The quotation lead: 2-4
- The simile (or metaphor) lead: 8-9
- The statement lead: 1-3
- The statistics lead: 3-5
- The summary lead: 1-3
- The "theme" lead: 3-5
- The timeline lead: 4-5
- The "you" lead: 2-4
- Combination leads?

Guide to Game Stories

In general, the complete game story, no matter what Sports, should contain these elements or items:

- The final score, usually in the top three paragraphs, often in the first paragraph
- Names of the teams
- When the game took place and where (the where is often in the dateline)
- Key players or outstanding plays or both
- Coaching strategies
- Crowd

- Quotations from players or coaches
- Injuries
- Records set during the game
- Effect of game on league standings
- Any oddities, length of game, number of penalties, etc.
- Weather—if a factor in outcome.

OUTLINING AND TRANSITIONS

How important is the outline? Extremely important. In *Modern Feature Writing* (1949), DeWitt Reddick offered five rules why outlining the article is important:

1. ***A Good Outline Insures Logical Development of Thought:*** The outline permits the writer to view the structure of the whole before he begins writing. By looking at this skeleton he can make sure that each major idea has a proper relationship to the central theme.
2. ***A Good Outline Helps to Secure Unity:*** For every article the writer should gather more information than he uses. It is important that he see clearly what to leave out as well as what to include. The outline aids in proper selection of material.
3. ***A Good Outline Aids in Securing Proper Emphasis on the Various Elements:*** After the author has selected his material, he still faces the task of deciding the emphasis to be placed on each of the items or groups of facts. An outline clarifies the main points to be introduced as topic sentences and indicates the material to be subordinated.
4. ***Careful Preparation of an Outline Permits the Writer to Consider in Advance the Style to be Used in Developing Each Important Section:*** One idea in the article, perhaps, can be presented most clearly by a narrative incident; another is complex and needs clarification by means of a hypothetical situation; a

direct quotation from an authority will give greatest force to another important thought. As he prepares his outline, the writer can decide upon the literary devices for the effective presentation of each idea.

5. ***An Outline Aids Spontaneity in Writing:*** The preparation of an outline exercises the mind of the writer, steeps it in the material, and creates the mood of the article. Thus, when he begins to write, he will have less trouble overcoming initial inertia and will be able to move along more swiftly because he knows in advance how he will approach each section.

SIX NO-FAIL TRANSITIONS INSIDE AN ARTICLE

In long, complicated articles, such as those written in the diamond structure, the writer may encounter three or four or as many as nine or ten subsections. Certainly, in the diamond format, there will be at least three separate sections: the lead, the body of the story, and the end; or four: the lead, the theme segment, the body, and the end. Many articles will have subtopics or subsections inside the body of the story, anecdotes from various personalities, short profiles inside the article, summary material, and other necessary material.

Trying to tie all these subsections together involves the use of transitional devices. Most writers don't have trouble with transitions *inside* the subsection that may be one or two or three pages (screens) long: The problem lies in bridging the gap between one major section and another. Following are seven types of transitions that the writer may use to bridge this gap. (They appear in order from the easiest to use to the most complex.).

1. ***The Concluding Statement:*** In a personality section of an article, in which the writer is profiling subject "X", the writer may effectively draw the section to a close

by using a quotation from "X" that is very clearly a definitive statement by the speaker: For example: "He squinted into the sun and shuffled his feet in the dust. 'I've had a good life. I wouldn't have changed it for anything. Not for anything at all'." This type of concluding statement is often followed by three ellipsis points (. . .).

2. *The Spacebreak:* This is a physical separation of text on the page (or on the screen, when you are using a word processor). If you are typing double-spaced copy, when you need a spacebreak transition, jump six lines. The "air" or white on the page will indicate to the reader that a different topic is upcoming. Many writers use one or more *bullets*—large, heavy dots (or the asterisk key on the keyboard)—in the middle of the spacebreak to indicate to editors and readers that this jump is deliberate. (On a word processor, a jump of a few lines is very easy to do accidentally).

   The English call this *line white* because it is literally a line of white space on the copy. It is also literally a line of white added by word processors.

   The spacebreak should not be overused. In a 10-page article, for instance, the spacebreak should only be used perhaps three times; otherwise the writer has copy that reads "too choppy," as if the reader is watching a freight train moving across a highway intersection. The white between the article sections is like the space between individual freight cars. If the writer uses too many spacebreaks, the article may read like many brief freight cars, passing the reader.

On the page, the spacebreak looks like this:

"XXXXXXXXXXXX. XXXXXXXXXX.
XXXXXXXXXXXXXX."

"XXXXXXXXXXXX. XXXXXXXXXXXXXXXXX.
XXXXXXXXXXXXXXXXXXX."

3. *The Spacebreak-With-Filler Material:* This is the spacebreak on the page, with additional material inserted, such as a headline or subhead, song lyrics, poetry selections, an excerpt from a short story, or perhaps a quotation picked up from later in the article. Use this material with discretion. If you are citing the work of a poet or writer, or lyricist, be sure to get formal permission to quote material that may be copyrighted. Use small amounts of filler so as not to confuse or sidetrack the reader. The filler material should read like a headline, for it is exactly that, a subhead inside the article.
4. *The Dateline or Diary Transition:* This is a simple time technique: "By late 1992, Joe Smith had gone to Canada and had become involved in. . . ."
   This offers a quick and clean transition into an anecdote or other subtopic within your article. It may be used with a spacebreak or without.
5. *The Argumentative:* Let one personality (A) in your article make a statement: Let another personality (B) answer pro or con as a way to transition into a subtopic about (B). For example:
   "I think such-and-such is true," "A" said finally, resting his arms on the table and looking out the window. "I've always believed that."
   "I just don't believe in such-and-such at all," "B" said later. "That's never been true as far as I am concerned."
   "B"'s life, from the early 1940s, indicates that . . . .
6. *The Metaphor Transition:* Here the writer uses a fanciful style to move smoothly from one subtopic to another. The metaphor is a connection between two items—a sports writer can use it to transition from one of the items to another, like this:
   'Joe Jock paused during a practice climb up western Massachusetts's Mount Greylock. He carefully re-

coiled his climbing rope and slowly re-tied his bootlaces.'

"The thing about climbing, he said, gazing at the top of Greylock, shrouded in haze, "is, the closer you are to the top, the faster you think you can get there."

In fact, during the last six years of his career, the closer he got to the top, the faster he got there. When he isn't climbing, his career as a sports equipment developer and innovator has moved him from rock bottom to the pinnacle of success faster than he or anyone else could have guessed. His business, ...

Here, of course, the comparison is mountain climbing to career ladder. The metaphor transition is a very difficult one to use because it is rare that such a combination of literal and figurative combinations would occur (or probably occur to the writer to use). Other transitions are much easier to use.

TWO TYPES OF ARTICLE STRUCTURES: THE INVERTED PYRAMID AND THE DIAMOND STRUCTURE

When newspaper or magazine readers read sports articles, they are seldom concerned—or perhaps never notice—the structure of an article: the *internal order* or organization of that article. There is, in fact, no reason for a reader to be concerned about structure. Readers read articles for entertainment, information, education, and amusement.

But there is every reason for writers to be concerned about how they structure articles. There are two key structures writers need to be familiar with. The *inverted pyramid* is an old, old structure that can be seen in every newspaper in the United States every day. The diamond structure is a more complex form, originally a magazine-oriented form. Writers can usually write inverted pyramid articles by instinct after some practice, whereas the diamond form is more complicated and usually requires an outline (and often requires more time to complete). To use a simile, the inverted pyramid is like a plain pine box: You can carry things in it (in this case articles—information) but the box is not elegant. The diamond structure is like a toolbox lined with velvet. One is plain, the other is fancier, but both boxes could carry the same tools. Both the inverted pyramid and the diamond structure carry information to the reader, but you can fit a lot of different tools inside the diamond format—and carry them better (and even impress the reader more). Sports writers should know when each is appropriate to use and particularly why it is appropriate in some cases and inappropriate in other cases.

THE INVERTED PYRAMID

This is an article structure that has existed since about the Civil War. With the advent of the telegraph as a means of distributing news stories (the "wire story"), wire editors looked for a story structure that would be universally acceptable to editors of different newspapers with differing news styles and differing design and editing formulas. They looked for a story structure that editors would need and readers would accept. The inverted pyramid met everyone's expectations. The inverted pyramid style is a news article or sports article that is written like an upside down triangle, with the base at the top and the point at the bottom. The top contains (usually) a summary lead, with the key elements of *who, what, where* and *when* in the top three paragraphs or so. Other elements, *why* and *how*, may be left until later in the story. This summary form using *who, what, where,* and *when* is universally appropriate for news articles, at the national, regional, and local level.

For example, a hypothetical news story might begin like this:

> WASHINGTON: PresidentClinton announced a "complete package" of reform measures for the National Park System Wednesday.

The package, labelled "Parks for the Next Century," will cost $250 billion and will involve upgrades for user services in Yellowstone, Yosemite, and many of the other major parks in the National Park system. The $250 billion package will be paid for in a special proposal which will be presented to Congress soon. It is expected that user fees for all national parks will increase, although administration officials did not estimate the increase for individual park users. Here is the *who* (President Clinton); the *what* (announced the National Park package); the *where* (the Washington dateline) and the *when* (Wednesday).

On national wire stories, the *where* is usually a dateline before the first sentence and then *when* (Wednesday) often "fits best" at the end of a sentence or paragraph. Generally, a summary of the most important key facts, financial costs, key facts, key details, and key quotations are used in the top three paragraphs. If the news article in the inverted pyramid form is nine paragraphs long, a general rule would be this: The first one to three paragraphs would be a summary lead of the key elements of the story. The middle three paragraphs would be major facts, major details, and major quotations in the order of importance, most important at the top, least important details towards the bottom. The bottom of the article, written in this inverted pyramid, should contain the least important material in the story. The inverted pyramid should be written in such a manner that if the article was 9 inches in column form, and there was only 7 inches of space for the article, the last 2 inches of copy could literally be cut off the story *without crippling* the meaning of the story.

The inverted pyramid is "top heavy" with *key facts,* details and quotations. This type of article structure is perfect for international, national, regional, and local news and is mandatory for front-page articles that involve fatalities, whether they are airplane crashes, automobile crashes, shootings, accidents, or weather stories, such as hurricanes and other storms. In general, everything in an inverted pyramid story is immediate. In the newspaper business, yesterday's news is on today's front page. In the Clinton parks story, earlier, the Wednesday announcement of the parks package would (presumably) be on the front page of Thursday newspapers.

In general, *everything* in the inverted pyramid story is "yesterday": yesterday's announcement by the president, yesterday's air crash, yesterday's areawide tornado, or yesterday's local town elections, but the day is used to avoid confusion. The focus of the inverted pyramid is *immediate news*. Details, facts, and information become less important as the writer works through the middle of the story. Minor details are used towards and at the bottom of the article. This becomes an instinctive form for daily newspaper news writers. It is just as appropriate in sports writing, especially for sports news articles. The sports writer often answers who's involved, what's happening, where, and when at the top of the article, then works through the key facets or key topics of the story, to the minor details at the bottom.

Here is a similar example of an inverted pyramid sports story. This article, by Gary Long of *The Miami Herald*, was published in the *Houston Chronicle* on February 12, 1994 under a four-column headline and subhead:

> "Bonnett dies pursuing his dream, Driver suffers fatal head injuries as car crashes in Daytona 500 practice" —By Gary Long Miami Herald

The lead of this article runs four paragraphs, down through the paragraph about the time of his death.

DAYTONA BEACH, Fla.: Neil Bonnett, a popular stock car driver who had raced only twice since an April 1990 crash that caused severe head injuries and temporary amnesia, died Friday afternoon trying to keep alive a high-risk career that he wouldn't give up.

Bonnett, 47, from Bessemer, Ala., suffered massive head injuries when his Chevrolet slammed the fourth-turn wall nose-first. He was practicing for the 36th annual Day-tona 500 a week from Sunday. Bonnett would have tried to qualify for his 16th Daytona 500 this afternoon. Instead, he became the 25th fatality in all forms of racing at Daytona International Speedway since its 1959 opening. He was pronounced dead at nearby Halifax Medical Centre at 1:17 p.m., less than an hour after the accident. How the accident happened is described here, towards the middle of the article. Bonnett, who ran fifth in his first Daytona 500 in 1976, lost control of his Chevrolet as he exited the 31-degree banking in Turn 4. The car skidded down on the flat apron and then veered straight back into the outside wall brutally hard.

Bonnett had to be cut from the wreckage, and NASCAR officials promptly ordered that a tarp be placed over the Chevrolet, a grim signal. Initially, there were rumours that he might have hit an oil slick. Briefly into the practice, a red flag had been waved so that oil-dry powder could be spread between Turns 1 and 2. But NASCAR official Chip Williams said there was no sign of oil in the fourth turn and that other drivers reported no problems there. Williams said indications were that Bonnett lost control. Bonnett's car hit just a few feet from where ARCA rookie Andy Farr knocked a hole into the concrete in a crash in practice Thursday. Track officials worked overnight replacing a section of the wall and catch fencing that had been torn out.

Farr remained hospitalized in good condition Friday. Summary of his career begins here. Bonnett, survived by wife, Susan, and two children, interspersed 18 victories through a successful NASCAR Winston Cup career that appeared at an end after a serious accident in the 1990 TranSouth 500 at Darlington, S.C. had been most visible since as a television analyst for CBS, WTBS and The Nashville Network on race telecasts. But he began subbing for close friend Dale Earnhardt during off-season testing before the 1993 Winston Cup campaign. Then, at the invitation of Earnhardt's car owner Richard Childress, Bonnett qualified an Earnhardt backup car for the midsummer DieHard 500 at Talladega, Ala. He was running in midpack in his first race in more than three years when he got caught up in a multicar tangle in which his car became airborne and ripped apart fencing that kept it from sailing into packed grandstands. Not only did Bonnett escape injury, but his appetite was whetted.

Minor details, quotations, and facts are used towards the end of the article. "You can't walk away from the Sports you've spent your entire life around," he said after signing a limited six-race 1994 contract to drive the Country Time Chevrolet for James Finch of Panama City, Fla. "Television was a good avenue for me to get involved in racing again," he said. "It opened the door for me to come back and be around all of my friends. But it also stirred up that interest to get back inside of a race car." A year ago, Bonnett worked in the CBS booth with Ken Squier and two-time NASCAR champion Ned Jarrett as Jarrett's son Dale raced past Earnhardt on the final lap to win the Daytona 500. "I'm sure a lot of people wonder why Neil Bonnett ever got back into a race car again after what he had gone through in 1990 and then the things he had seen happen to his very close friends, the Allison family," Jarrett said Friday afternoon. A protege of Bobby Allison, Bonnett provided support through Allison's recovery from near-fatal injuries in a June 1988 crash and also after the deaths of Allison's racing sons Davey and Clifford 11 months apart.

"But having been a former racer myself," Jarrett said, "I can understand. Neil wanted to drive a race car. That's what he wanted. "He knew the risks that could be involved, but he was willing to accept those risks." There is one obvious problem with the inverted pyramid form. As Brooks,

Kennedy, Moen, and Ranly wrote in *News* Reporting and Writing (1985), "For all its strengths, the inverted pyramid has a telling weakness. It cannot maintain, let alone build, reader interest as the story progresses. After the first three paragraphs, it's not going to get any better". The diamond structure, or the newsmagazine diamond described in the following section solves that problem—the diamond format article becomes richer, more detailed, and more interesting paragraph by paragraph as the article continues. That's why the diamond structure form is preferred for sports features, profiles, trend articles, and all types of sports articles other than the "game" or "score" article.

THE DIAMOND STRUCTURE

Although few textbooks identify this form, it is an obvious structure for many general articles and many sports articles. It differs from the inverted pyramid, but is just as easy to learn. The key difference between the inverted pyramid and the diamond structure is this: *The diamond allows room for historical perspective in the article.* Everything in the inverted pyramid is the immediate past. Saturday's football games are in Sunday's newspapers; Sunday's games are in Monday's newspapers. A summary of the growth of baseball, ever since Abner Doubleday "invented" the game, however, would likely be written in the diamond structure, allowing the writer room in the article for the early days of the game.

A profile of any athlete would likely be written in the diamond format, which allows the writer space in the article for the player's youth, education, and early playing days—in short, a biography of the player. The inverted pyramid article is usually one "block" of material. The diamond article consists of at least three separate elements: the lead, the body of the story, which begins with "the historical past," and the end segment. Unlike the inverted pyramid article, which can be cut from the end towards the middle of the article, the diamond article *cannot* be cut from the end. The diamond format article has a specific and important end segment. If the diamond article must be cut anywhere, it must be cut carefully somewhere in the middle. Long profile articles and trend articles and articles that have a rich historical middle may have three or four or as many as eight or nine subtopics in the middle of the article. Writers using the diamond format should make it a practice to outline their articles as carefully and as completely as possible to make sure they have included all key facts, anecdotes, and quotations.

Although many sports feature writers know that the diamond format involves at least three divisions of the article—lead-body-end—freelancer William B. Hartley believes that article writers should consider four elements in the article. In "Building the Magazine Article" (The Writer, March 1972), he suggested: "In general . . . the usual magazine article has four basic sections. Generalizations are notably dangerous, but I would suggest that most successful articles are built with a *lead, a statement of theme or intent*, the *body* of the article which supports and advances the theme, and a *conclusion*."

Hartley suggested that "an old nursery rhyme provides a simple illustration of four-element construction":

Jack and Jill went up the hill
(*Anecdote lead*)
To fetch a pail of water:
(*Statement of theme*)
Jack fell down and broke his crown
(*Body: the story itself*)
And Jill came tumbling after.

The theme section need only be a concise paragraph that summarizes the article. It certainly need not be a major section. It acts simply as a reminder to the reader of what the article is about. Additionally, if the article begins with a person "A," then it ends with "A": if the article begins in the present, it should end in the present; if it begins with a description of scene "X," it should end with "X" again.

Returning to the same individual, theme, time, or location gives the reader an instinctive sense that the article has come full circle and the writer has completed the story. In some cases, the end segment will offer the reader a *glimpse of the future* or an educated guess of the future.

Here is an example of a diamond structure article. This profile, of Kansas Cityarea student athlete Lisa Davies, was published in *The Kansas City Star* on May 15, 1994, under a two-column headline and subhead:

(15 varsity letters, but she still ranks No. 2 in her class Top girl scholar-athlete has been chosen All-Metro five times, in four sports).

—By Terrance Harris Staff Writer

The *Kansas City Star*reporter uses an anecdote lead—how hard she studies for an upcoming exam. Her eyelids grew heavier and the temptation to allow them to simply shut grew stronger as night turned into Wednesday morning for Lisa Davies.

"I just have to do well on this psychology test," she repeated, often in concert with yawns. Davies was forced to study past midnight after a whirlwind Tuesday, which began with morning classes in Oak Grove, continued in Boonville at 1:30 for the Missouri River Valley Conference track and field championships and finished at Adair Park in Independence for an early evening game in the Greater Kansas City Softball Tournament. We're talking mileage. In the process, Davies gathered conference titles in the triple jump, high jump and long jump in helping the Panthers bring back the league championship with three points to spare. She later blasted a bases-empty homer in the bottom of the seventh inning, but it didn't prevent a 5-2 loss to Truman.

"It was definitely a very stressful day," she said. "I didn't feel right leaving the track team because I could have possibly given them more points had I run the 400. But I also would not have felt right not showing up for the softball game because I have a commitment to them.

> "I've always been taught that you honor a commitment no matter the personal sacrifice."

This paragraph and the next summarize the theme of this article. That strong sense of dedication and devotion has propelled Davies to the highest levels in all her endeavors at Oak Grove, whether in the classroom, on the basketball court, in front of a volleyball net, on a softball diamond or floating through the air in track and field competition. Davies' selfless commitment and never-tiring work ethic have not gone unnoticed. She was selected The Kansas City Star's top girl scholar-athlete for 1994. Statistics help prove how exceptional she is. In addition to winning 15 varsity letters in four sports since her freshman year, Davies holds three academic letters for her 3.95 grade-point average on a 4-point scale. She will graduate this year as salutatorian in her class of 109.

Davies also serves as the National Honor Society president and vice president of Interact Club, and she is a member of student council. Quotations from others begin to appear in the article. "Lisa is just very self-disciplined, goal-oriented and motivated," said Leland Loux, Davies' counselor. "To be able to juggle as many things as she does also says a lot about Lisa's organizational skills. She budgets her time and uses it wisely. Lisa doesn't waste time."

> "She realizes that she has so much time for academics, athletics and extracurricular activities. And she balances it out real well. Better than most."

Through this all, Davies manages to be a popular person outside of sports. The consensus at Oak Grove is that Davies is as caring and genuine away from sports as she is fierce and competitive as an athlete.

> "Lisa has always been a person I could come and talk about anything and no matter what is going on in her life, she will make you feel that your problem or situation is the only one that matters," said Sarah Munson, a close friend since fifth grade. "And one

of the things I've always really enjoyed about Lisa is that she is really modest about her accomplishments in sports and in academics. She's never been like 'Hey, look what I did.'

"You often have to drag things out of her. Lisa doesn't ever make other people feel less than her. Come to think of it, she's actually quite humble about all of her accomplishments."

Jim Borland, her math teacher and a longtime friend of the Davies family, said: "Lisa doesn't flaunt anything, which is another one of her many admirable traits. She's just like everyone."

Strong Background: The historical background part of the article begins at this subhead. To know Ron Davies and Beverly Davies and their backgrounds leaves little to wonder about the foundation of their youngest of four children. Both Ron and Beverly competed in athletics in college, and both are now educators. Beverly played basketball for Kansas during 1964-68 and now is a teacher in Blue Springs. Ron played football and baseball for Central Missouri State during the 1960s and now is superintendent of East Lynne School, kindergarten-eighth grade, near Harrisonville.

"If young people get anything from their parents, I'm sure Lisa gets a lot from them," Borland said. "I guess you could say she's a chip off the old blocks."

But Davies and her parents, who are divorced, said Lisa carved her way independent of their influence. "My parents didn't really value one thing over the other," Davies said. "Their outlook was 'As long as you work hard and try your hardest, then we'll be happy with whatever you do.' They made it clear right from the beginning that if I didn't want to play any sports, then great, or if I got all C's, then great also.

"Their only concern was that I worked my hardest." Beverly confirms her daughter's appraisal, but she added that Lisa displayed an uncommon inner drive at an early age that made it easier to let her daughter define her own level of achievement.

> "Lisa is a very self-motivated person who has never needed to be pushed at all," Beverly said. "We never had to push her to study or participate in athletics. Her selfmotivation has always pushed her to go above what's required, which is why she has achieved so highly in so many different areas."

Beverly, however, also a recalls a brief period in her daughter's life when achievement did not come easily. She was placed in a low reading group during first grade in Colorado and second grade in Alabama. Beverly Davies attributes it to the family moving around, but by the time she was in the fifth grade and had returned to Oak Grove, Lisa had climbed to the top of her class.

> "She just kept gaining momentum by the time she reached fourth and fifth grade, and we just kept being surprised at how well she did," Beverly said. "Watching her grow up and develop into the person she is today has been a lot of fun and enjoyable. Lisa just never ceases to amaze us with the things she can do."

Oak Grove basketball coach Brad Gaines recalls a tall and scrawny seventh-grader who used to come around during his varsity practices, shooting at one of the vacant baskets. Shot after shot, seldom making as much as a peep. "When she'd come over we never really said much to each other," Gaines said. "I'd just give her a ball and let her shoot. I'd be on one end of the court doing my thing, and she'd be at the other end just shooting.

> "You could tell back then, and even in elementary school, that she was going to be a gifted athlete someday." "I remember one day Dr. Roger Nelson (Oak Grove principal) and I were watching her shoot from upstairs, and I told him then that he was looking at the next Oak Grove stud. This is Lisa Davies."

Call Gaines a prophet or a vulture, but Davies roared onto the high school set as a freshman starter in varsity volleyball, basketball and track. She added softball to her list as a sophomore. But her basketball draws the most attention, and it is basketball that will pay for her education beginning next fall at Southwest Missouri State in Springfield. She passed on offers from Notre Dame, Alabama, Louisiana State, Northwestern, Illinois and Colorado. Additional details prove what an exceptional athlete she is. During her four years of basketball at Oak Grove the Panthers were 105-15 overall and 32-0 in the MRVC, including an undefeated Missouri 3A state championship season in 1992. Davies averaged 21.1 points and 11 rebounds, receiving All-Metro and all-state honours last season.

Davies, who is 5 feet 11, leaves Oak Grove No. 2 on the school's career rebounding (979) and steals (462) lists. And her 1,657 career points rank third. The volleyball team also went undefeated in the conference since 1990, and it won district titles in 1991 and 1993. For her efforts, Davies received All-Metro accolades as a junior and senior. Finally, in her three-year dual spring seasons, Davies has contributed equally in softball and track. Last season she was All-Metro in softball after hitting .413 with 15 RBIs, 16 stolen bases and three home runs. All-Metro teams have not been selected this spring, but she is batting .508, with 27 RBIs and 12 stolen bases. A box with a feature story helps the reader quickly understand her achievements. Gerri Hirshey article, "Arc of a Diver," a profile of diver Greg Louganis, is also a classic example of how the diamond structure should be used. This article appeared in the September 22, 1988 issue of *Rolling Stone* magazine.

"Arc of a Diver" To stay at the top of his Sports for ten years, Greg Louganis has had to face down a lot of fears. The article begins with a spectator's view of high diving. "SHEL, IT'S FOUR FLIGHTS UP, WILL YOU *LOOK*, SHEL?"

Shel, a straw-hatted retiree, squints into the Florida sun, up to the ten-meter diving platform at the Mission Bay Aquatic Training Centre. "Like jumping off a brownstone, huh? *Meshugah*. Nuts," Shel says, shaking his head. "But beeyootiful, I gotta say." Shel and his wife, retirement-condo shoppers, have wandered out to the pool grandstand from the real-estate office also located in the Mission Bay centre. In matching shorts sets, with floor plans in hand, they stand watching some of the nation's best divers arc and plunge. It was the condo developer's idea to put an Olympic-quality diving and swimming facility in his Boca Raton Utopia, hire one of the best diving coaches in America and make a Family Attraction that would elevate his tracts of stucco duplexes above the others gouged into the sandy scrubland north of Miami.

He's planted young gods amid the pensioners, and it's working. Mission Bay hosts worldclass diving and swimming meets, collects fat media fees for photographing and videotaping and runs clinics and camps that draw hopefuls from all over the United States and Canada. This is the business end of Olympic dreams, with a sweet real-estate tie-in. And bunking in the heart of it, in a rent-free model unit, is the most beeyootiful dreamer of all. The two paragraphs beginning "high up" are summary paragraphs proving his international expertise.

High up on the tower, preparing to jump from brown stone height, is Greg Louganis, who swept the platform and springboard gold meals in the '84 Olympics and hopes to repeat in Seoul. He has been called the best ever; he's the only man in history to earn over 700 points in a single Olympic diving event, the only human—ever—to score seven perfect 10s for one dive in national and world competition. He is the gold standard for the Sports. Single-handedly, Greg Louganis raised the degree of difficulty in world competition. The diving competition was not diluted by the Eastern-bloc boycott in '84; this year, as it was then, the chief rivalry will be between the Americans and the Chinese. Most of his competitors, but especially the Eastern-bloc teams, are known to study tapes of Greg Louganis, who has dominated the Sports for the last ten years. He was just sixteen when he won a silver medal in Montreal in 1976 and became the One to Watch. Since then, he has been the One to Beat, and to that end, they fret over the tapes, freeze-frame his dives and analyze the parts. But they cannot come up with the impossible sums that judges award Greg Louganis.

"The Soviets and the Chinese seem to have developed programmes that teach Louganis techniques to every one of their divers," says Louganis's coach, Ron O'Brien. "[The communist countries] have developed an acrobatic, a mechanical copy of Greg. They haven't been successful at teaching a rhythmic, dancelike quality." They've called him a Nureyev, a Baryshnikov. No one is better at aquatic, serial, kamikaze ballet. He walks like a dancer, back straight, shoulders square and high, legs turned out slightly. Louganis has been pacing along the platform, unrolling a chamois that he squeaks over a diver's hard torso and a dancer's outsize thighs. He has been dancing since he was eighteen months old, diving since he was eight, and the resulting sculpture draws stares even while he's performing this high-rise toilette. Poolside, and in the grandstand, they gawk as water sluices down a pair of Rodin-quality calves. In sacks of letters, in poetics and porn, men and women inflict their reactions, say they cannot help themselves, he is so . . . so . . . beeyootiful.

Even Shel, who doesn't know an inverted triple from a club sandwich, is spellbound as Louganis readies himself for liftoff. One, two, three. He always eyes the water, then, counts it down in his head. Arms out, head straight, Louganis pushes off the concrete, rises straight up, high, higher, with a vertical leap that has been measured at thirty-three inches, blocking the noon-day sun in a gleaming brown flash. Now he is tucked, spinning, falling at 40 mph, counting the revolutions, looking for his spots, the visual reference points essential to spinning ballet divas. And trapeze artists. And fancy divers.

Top of platform, *kick.*

Bottom of platform, *kick.*

Bottom, water, open and *stretch.*

The astonishing silhouette is torn from the blue sky, slipped beneath the water with a mere surface dimple and a sound they call the rip.

Good feature articles should offer the reader material they cannot get from television.

There should be a "gee whiz—I didn't know that" quality to good nonfiction. In this case, the explanation of "the rip." It sounds like taut silk tearing. Blazered, stat-fed guys like Jim McKay wax lyrical about the rip on TV, but you cannot hear it on any network satellite feed. The rip is the diver's sonic boom, the aquatic Mach III. It's the screech of water molecules giving it up to a force greater than their pissant specific gravity. Louganis's rip is followed by an instant of reverent silence and a cacophony of claps, whistles and the crack of wet chamois slapped against the concrete deck.

"Way to rip it, Lugo!" "Nine point five," rasps O'Brien, who is scoring practice dives over the poolside P.A. "Real soft, Grego." In a hard, competitive Sports, a soft entry is highly prized. Despite the intricate acrobatics of the three-second performance, the entry, or bottom, is the last thing the judges see. And if Louganis has any chronic weakness, it is the bottom of his dives. He says he wishes he could rip consistently, like the Chinese; he wishes he could concentrate on the end better. "The problem I have," Louganis says, "is getting in the water." The problem he *had*, says O'Brien, was getting out of himself. Ask O'Brien about the greatest reward of coaching the world's best for over a decade, and there is no talk about pikes, triples and perfect scores.

"To see him grow as a person," O'Brien replies. "He used to be very introverted. He was in a lot of turmoil. I've seen him grow to being a very relaxed, confident, comfortable person who can deal with media, speak in front of crowds and just be happy. When I first started coaching him, he wasn't a real happy kid." He was always a brave, strong diver, O'Brien says. "But he was a scared kid. Scared of so darn many things."

LOUGANIS IS SMALLER AT EYE LEVEL, JUST FIVE FEET NINE, a god turned garbage man. He has put himself on trash detail, his tough feet scudding on the griddle-hot concrete, picking up empty Gatorade cups discarded during the last session of Mission Bay's summer diving camp. In a second, the children are on him, shy but insistent, a knot of brown, peely-nosed kids in wet Speedos and BODY AND SEOUL T-shirts. Some just stare; some are nudged by parents aiming Canon Sure Shots. Louganis poses with tiny springboard fliers, signs T-shirts. The bolder ones ask the questions he hears over and over: "What if you get scared?" "What if you wipe out?" "What if you get all the way up there and you *just can't do it?"*

Here is the underlying theme of the article: overcoming fears. Notice the author's nice phrase "Louganis thinks there are more kinds of fear than Baskin-Robbins flavours." He talks to them gently, patiently, about fear. Sometimes Greg Louganis thinks there are more kinds of fear than Baskin-Robbins flavours. He's tasted quite a few, has rolled them around in his mouth, taken their measure, given them their quarter of respect. He admits he's been scared of a lot of things. Dangerous dives. New dives.People. Failure. Success. "And snakes," he is saying as he stuffs towels and a wet Speedo into his battered Gap tote bag. "I really had a thing about snakes as a kid. But the thing about fear is that sooner or later you have to face it down or you'll be, like, nuts." So he faced down some snakes?

"I saved up and bought one," he says. "A boa constrictor. Not too big. But a *serious* snake." He made himself feed it live mice and sacks of squirming worms, and he came to see it as a thing of beauty and strength. "It was kind of gross at first," he says. But he got past it. "The other thing about fear?" he says, posing his own question. "Is that there's always another one to take its place. It doesn't have to be a bad thing if you *deal* with it." Eat the boa before it eats you? "Nah," he says. "Just remember to buy the mice." The author uses the spacebreak technique to separate sections of the article.

HERE'S THE BIG BOA NOW: LETTING ONE OBSESSION GO AND committing to another. He wants very much to act; he has studied the craft for nine years, since he majored in drama at college. He signed with William Morris right after the '84 Olympics, has kept studying, auditioning, chatting up casting directors. He is looking forward to what he calls an emotional rather than a physical obsession, but he wants to go out of diving just right. Can he rip it, leave the Sports with a clean, golden finish? And when should he leave it? In October? Or in '92? Divers are said to peak in their mid-twenties, and he is twenty-eight.

> "I am totally consumed by the limitations of age," he says. "The young kids on the team say, 'Show us how to do it, Grandpa.' I keep reminding myself that Dr.Sammy Lee was thirty-two when he won his last Olympic gold medal. And I'll be thirty-two at the '92 Olympics."

Once before, after the '84 games, he announced his retirement, then ignored it. Leaving is scary in itself. It means the end of an obsession that's fueled half his life. Diving cleaves the years, neatly, into a progression he can understand. "I went through so many stages," he says, and proceeds to tick them off:

> Grammar school through junior high: "When I first started out, this [diving] was the one area of success.

So it was almost like my survival."

High school and college: "It became something I was good at but I wasn't really enjoying. And then it was something that I wanted to do well at."

From eight to twenty-four, he lived his life hungry, troubled, pressured by great expectations and deferred payoffs. Like so many American athletes, he endured an eight-year wait for his gold because of the '80 U.S. boycott of the Moscow games, and it nearly unnerved him. Before '84, says Ron O'Brien, "he was not a happycamper." And then, after the Los Angeles Olympics?

"I was doing it because I enjoyed it," says the camper, happy as a clam. "I was having fun, so really, these last four years have been for the enjoyment." He stops and smiles, then he shakes his head. "I never thought I could get to this point."

He has described the common pathology of obsession. It was keenest when he was hungry. But he has been losing some over the last year, which is to say placing fourth or fifth in Olympic tuneup meets that he used to win by 50 or 100 points. Right now he has to control his appetite for other things—quit reading the scripts, auditioning, forget about the appearances and endorsements. Since December 1st, he has been training hard at Mission Bay, two work outs a day, six days a week. Right now he has to summon up the hunger that used to come unbidden.

"I AM AFRAID OF GETTING FAT. SOMETHING HAPPENED TO my metabolism when I hit twenty-five."

Louganis is fretting over the menu at a Boca fern bar, which is pushing pastas, pizzas and other enticing carbs. He does not wish to go an ounce over his 160 pounds, and he normally lunches on liquids—soup and water—and a salad of some sort. He endures two workouts a day, more exercises, weight workouts, a nibble of chicken for dinner, more vegetables. Milk. Sleep. Do it again. Louganis orders up some Spartan gazpachoand green salad but cannot resist a small side order of fried calamari. He is an enthusiastic foodie, conversant with Korean bar-becue, Szechwan lobster, Greek *dolmades*, but he fears his fat-burning capacities are sliding towards the levels of the silver-haired seniors tearing into early-bird specials at surrounding tables.

> "Stop me," he says. "Don't let me eat that garlic bread. I mean, when the time comes, feel free to say, 'Meal's over, Greg.''

HE'S ALWAYS HAD TROUBLE WITH ENDINGS, BE IT A SINGLE dive, a diving career, a lite lunch. The first time Greg Louganis had trouble finishing his act was in his first dance recital, in El Cajon, Southern California. He'd been at it since eighteen months, when he begged to join his older sister's class. At three and a half, he was good enough to have a solo song-and-dance number in tiny top hat and tux.

Owing to the lights, he couldn't see to find his exit. So he sat down on the edge of the stage, where he could watch the show and see his mom in the audience. Frantically, the teacher waved him off, but he sat there grinning. "I was having a great time," he says. Twenty-one years later, when the stage was global, he stood on the ten-meter platform at the Los Angels Olympics—at the very end of his performance; perhaps, he thought then, the end of his Olympic career—and it was no fun, no way. His mom was there, along with 13,497 people holding their collective breath at the USC pool and about 35 million people nationwide on TV. You couldn't have staged a better, a more dramatic Olympic Moment.

It was down to one dive. Oh, he had won before he was finished; the nearest competitor was over fifteen points away; even if he missed the dive entirely, the gold was his. The only competition was with himself. Louganis's score stood within reach of the 700 mark, which no man or woman had ever achieved. He stood above the silent crowd and prepared for the last dive on his list, number 307C, a reverse three-and-a-half somersault. Degree of difficulty, then the highest that had been done. A year earlier, in another meet, Louganis had beenabout to climb the platform when 307C fatally injured Soviet diver Sergei Shilbashvili. And as the ambulance bore him away, Louganis' performed 307C flawlessly. He was not afraid of the dive; his trajectory is always too high and far and fast to send his skull crashing into the platform like the doomed Russian. Nonetheless, as he prepared to do 307C at the end of his programme in the '84 Olympics, he says, "I *was* scared. The fear was a number of things. The fear was a fear of failure. Coming so close and not achieving that [breaking 700], especially at the Olympic games. Another fear was fear of success. If I achieved breaking 700, then *what else can I do?* So it was fear—of many different fears that were just kind of hitting me."

He knew they were there, but he would not let them in: "I just didn't *acknowledge* it." Louganis stood on the edge of the platformand said this to himself. "No matter what happens, my mother still loves me." His early history appears well into the middle of the article, well after the lead. ALWAYS, THROUGH SOME VERY BAD TIMES, FRANCES LOU-ganis has loved her adopted son. His birth parentswere both fifteen when he was born: his father wanted to raise him as a brother but was persuaded to give him up. Peter Louganis, a hard-drinking tuna fisherman, brought the nine-month-old boy home to his tall, fair Texan wife and vowed to raise him strong and strict. No nonsense, no coddling. He would study and work on the tough docks near San Diego and obey, and if it was a matter of honor, he would fight. He would be a man—in the old way.

There were plenty of chances to get in a fight, but the boy never did. Instead, he got beat up, day after day. He would fib about the bruises and fret about the reason.

"Nigger!" they called him at school. His birth father was Samoan, and as a child, Gregory Efthimios Louganis turned very, very brown in the California sun.

"Stupid!" they taunted before dyslexia was a commonly diagnosed reading problem. He inverted sentences, flip flopped letters. Mistakenly, teachers had him tested for mental impairment. "Reeeetard!" He was too shy to answer back, too scared. And he stuttered—badly enough to require speech therapy. When he sought haven from it all, it was in Frances Louganis's kitchen. "My mother is Scotch-Irish, and my father is Greek, so my mother had to learn how to cook Greek," he says. "We learned—I always helped my mom in the kitchen, because this is where I felt most comfortable."

It was a safe place for a dark-skinned, stammering, dyslexic loner. They made spinach-filled *spanikopita*. He drizzled honey over the transparent pastry dough for world-beating *baklava*. "To me, it's relaxing," says Lou- ganis. "I had companionship, you know, from my mother. It gave me a good sense of self-esteem." He hated when his father dragged him to a club for boys and made him wrestle, loathed the combative contact. But he loved to dance. "Sissy! they called him then, and that bothered him more than the other stuff, but not enough to make him stop. No one understood him better than his dance partner, Eleanor Smith. They were a team from age threeto twelve. Almost every day, they went to the dance studio; when one changed teachers, the other followed. They moved alike, thought alike, were best of friends. Eventually, Eleanor headed off towards gymnastics, and Greg followed, but there was no men's gymnastics team in SanDiego. Knee injuries were aggravated by gymnastics and dance. "So," he says, "I learned to dive."

Early on, he was exceptional. Ron O'Brienhas watched thousands of grade-school hopefuls with Olympic dreams and chlorine-pink eyes. But he can still remember his first look at Greg Louganis at a Florida meet: "I saw him when he was ten and I was coach at Ohio StateUniversity. He had a different quality to his diving than I had seen with anyone else. He was stronger. His body lines were sharper. For a ten-year-old, he was extremely strong. And he had a presence about him." On the springboard, still his strongest event, there was no hesitancy. No fear. "As long as I had water under me," Louganis says, "I wasn't afraid."

When he calls diving his "survival" during that early period, he means that it raised him above other, darker things—the torments of school and the increasing difficulties at home. Peter Louganis proved a hardman who could not understand his more vulnerable son: the sweet, strong boy could not bear the drinking, the yelling, the strain on his mother. Once, when he was thirteen, they came to blows, and Greg was hauled to juvenile hall. Despite the turmoil, his diving got stronger, and as it did, each year took him farther outside of El Cajon.

> "I went to Europe when I was thirteenfor a world competition," he says. "When I was fourteen, I lived in Arizona for the summer with a diving family so Icould get coaching. When I was fifteen, I spent the summer in Decatur, Alabama, in RonO'Brien's camp."

He also worked. Diving, coaching and travel was expensive. Peter Louganis helped his son getcoaching, and he also made sure Greg had work at the tuna dock in which Peter owned an interest. Greg started at fifteen, mending the heavy tuna nets, putting his well-developed shoulders to the work of cutting the nets away from the buoys and loading the gunlike needle with the marinegrade twine that repaired the nets. Later, in high school and college, he worked three part-time jobs at once, in two clothing stores and a recreation centre. He paid his expenses, and he put some money away. Since he was fifteen, he's had a special savings account.

> "For a house," he says. "I always wanted a house. It was like something that was out there that I was never going to get."

Other fifteen-year-olds were saving for surfboards and Pink Floyd tapes. But a house?

"See, I needed a place to go. I wanted out of the house, but I needed a sense of security, a sense of roots. I think that's what I was most obsessed with. It is something that's mine . . . my roots."

But there were more immediate goals. In January of '76 when he was sixteen and about to begin training for that year's Olympics, he left home entirely and moved in with the family of his coach, Dr. SammyLee, himself a 1948 and 1952 gold medalist. A busy ear, ose and throat specialist, Lee took as much time off as he could to coach the boy he felt could be the very best diver in history. Once again, Louganis felt himself adopted andfound himself headed for the warmest room in the house. "Dr.Lee is Korean; Mrs. Lee is Chinese," Louganis says. "I always helped her out in the kitchen, too, so I learned how to cook Chinese and Korean stuff." His new high school was more of a culture shock. "I went from an upper-middle class high school to a school that was seventy to eighty percent Chicano. They had seven security guards. The week before I got there, one of the security guards was put in the hospital by some students. So I was a little nervous. But I kind of fit in because I was dark haired and dark complected." He says he kept his mouth shut and focused on diving. When he came home from Montreal with a silver medal in springboard and some headlines, he went back home to El Cajon and Valhalla High, which, despite its name, was not necessarily a hall of hero worship.

The nigger-dummy-sissy was a hero, but a lonely one—even though more people said hello in the halls. He kept saving for his house, training, going on college-recruiting trips. He chose the University of Miami, largely because "it was far away" from California. He says he really "grew up" in south Florida, majoring in theatre and hanging with drama students who knew virtually nothing about his diving. He stayed there from 1978 to 1980, when he transferred to the University of California at Irvine. By then he was swimming under Ron O'Brien at the MissionViejo Club, a worldclass tank near San Diego. And he was not a happy camper. He was withdrawn, uncommunicative. He began a quiet assault on the body and the image that had so far ensured his survival. Aware that it could have gotten him booted from the team, he smoked. A lot. "My smoking was out of rebellion," he says. "Ididn't want to fit the mold of this 'goody-goody-two-shoes jock." So he swaggered around with the burning cylinders hanging off his lip. He thought they said, "I'm bad."

He drank, too, mostly beer and fruity swill wine. And he worried, convinced that owing to his home environment, he was destined for alcoholism. He says he was desperately unhappy, he was spinning. He was in danger of losing the water—the thing a diver fears most of all. Like "the rip," the author explains an insider's knowledge of diving—the fear of "losing the water." LOSING THE WATER—GETTING DISORIENTED AND LANDING badly—happens to everyone at least once, even the best. But fear of it can cripple a diver's nerve the way a bad entry can bend his body. Ron O'Brien can only recall one time whenhis student seized up with serious angst on the platform, when he was trying to teach him the inward three-and-a-half tuck. It involves three and a half tight, dizzying revolutions in the direction of the platform, and when O'Briencame at Louganis with it, the dive had just been entered into the official book. It was so new, so difficult that no one else was doing it.

They worked on it in stages, and Louganis had done it on dry land, in a spotting belt. Finally, says O'Brien, "it was time for him to do the dive. He went up to do it, and he wouldn't go. He'd stand on the end of the platform and stand

and stand and step back." They got to the end of the practice, and he still hadn't done it. He was trying to sneak off when O'Brien caught him. "I told him he just had to learn that dive. That if he wanted to bring his lunch and dinner the next day, to do so, because he was going to stay up there till he did do it. Do it or else." Ask Louganis about it, and he grins. "Yeah, that was probably the most difficult dive I had to learn. Because I spin pretty fast. And I was afraid that I wasn't going to know where I was in the air." It is easy to lose the water in a tight spin, and there is nothing worse, tumbling upside down, falling at 40 mph. It's a thirty-three-foot drop to the surface, another seven-teen feet to the pool bottom. Hit on your side, and you can puncture an eardrum; land on your back, and you can do worse.

The day after he had balked on the inward triple, Louganis thought about losing the water, and he thought about losing his nerve and his place on the team, and he climbed up to the platform and nailed the dive on the first try. Good anecdotes help the reader understand the subject. That was in 1982. He was diving well then. But on dry land, he still didn't know where he was at. He was sneaking the smokes, chugging beers he had no taste for. He thought about cleaning up, but he had no motivation until one day, at a meet, he ran into a subteen diver, a kid puffing absurdly at a cigarette.

"Why are you doing that?" Louganis asked him. "I want to be just like Greg Louganis."

Stupid, too stupid. He decided to cut the crap. He cut it all out in '83, the year before the Olympics. He did it himself, no counseling, but with the help of friends. "I don't think anybody can do it all by themselves," he says. "I had a support group . . . Ron O'Brien and his wife, Mary Kay. And Jim [Babbitt, a UC-Irvine friend who is now his manager]. And Megan Neyer, another diver.

"I found I even had to stay away from my dad," he says. He realized this one evening when Peter

> Louganis took him out to dinner. "Every time he'd order a drink for himself, he'd order one for me. By the end of the meal, I had five untouched beers lined up in front of me, and I said, 'Dad, I won't be coming around for a while."

He says that people have told him that he overreacted, that he probably wasn't a real alcoholic, and he says yes, maybe it wasn't so bad, but he wasn't going to keep drinking and find out for sure. Besides, the worst part was why he did it.

> "I was scared," he says. "And I guess I wasn't real happy with who I am."

He was just twenty-three, a year from the Big Test in Los Angeles, but he felt he was being tested all the time, especially the day he Lost the Water for real. Earlier the author explained the idea of "losing the water." Here is what it means when that really happens to a diver.

LOUGANIS HAS HAD INJURIES, A DISLOCATED SHOULDER, chronic wrist problems aggravated by a ganglion cyst, one horrible crackup where he knocked the base of his skull on the platform and was unconscious for fifteen minutes. But he says the worst was a wipeout at a meet in New Zealand in early '84, because it bruised him body and soul. He can remember it all too well:

> He is standing on the platform during practice, looking down at this strange pool with stripes across the walls and ceiling, long narrow stripes that ripple if you look at them too long. He is preparing himself for an inward three and a half. He counts, springs up, out, spinning, seeing the stripes fly by, and then he loses the water. Is it up, down, where? No time to decide. He sees the windows at the far end, stretches for them and lands, hard, flat on his back with a sickening slap.

Around the pool, there was silence. "Because everybody on the team was just like 'Oh my God, Greg Louganis just *wiped out*." He's not sure how, but he got out of the water laughing. The next day, he couldn't get out of bed. "I just ached so much, I felt like I had the flu," he says. "I had trouble walking, because I had hit my calves on impact, too. I broke a lot of blood vessels in my back and the back of my legs. It had welted up." He was in serious pain for four days and decided not to compete in the meet. He didn't want to screw himself up in a lousy striped tank of water.

> "I was afraid," he says. "I was afraid if I had wiped out again, then I would have to go back to easier dives. I didn't feel that I could afford to do that during the Olympic year."

His coach agreed, but, Louganis says, "I got a lot of flak from other divers. Had it been anybody else, they probably would have been consoling, saying, 'It's okay.' But I caught so much flak." "Chicken!" they were calling him behind his back. The flap was such that a team meeting was called, and while he was still sore and welted from losing the water, Greg Louganis finally stood up for himself. He talked back. He did it in front of a group of people. And it felt okay. Now Louganis talks to many groups: organizations for the dyslexic, youth clubs, drug- and alcohol-rehab places, diving clinics. He talks easily, about what it was like to be dyslexic, dependent on alcohol, and dozens, scores of times he has had to reassure young divers about chickening out or losing the water. He's comfortable with people who admit to their fears. He thinks he helps a little.

There are a lot of stories about healing and forgiveness in Louganis's narrative. His parents divorced four years ago, "and they're dating again," he says with a smile and a shake of his head. On his left hand, he wears a diamond ring that once belonged to his grandfather Louganis and was given to him by his father. "He was supposed to leave it to me. But he said that he wanted to see me enjoy it." His parents come to see him compete; recently, he sent his mother and an aunt to Europe on his frequent-flier miles. He often has his parents to a barbecue at his home in Malibu—the one he finally got to buy, the only thing he owns. It has a panoramic view of the Pacific from a bluff above the beach, a redwood deck, a custom-built swimming pool with a one-meter platform. He looked for the right house for two years, searched from Santa Barbara to San Diego, and he works hard at appearances and endorsements to make the mortgage. When he is home, he spends a lot of time in the kitchen. For Christmas, for Thanksgiving, friends, neighbours and relatives come to him, and he loves feeding them.

"At times, you know, I feel guilty," he says of his home, "because it's nicer than anything I grew up in." Like "the rip" and "losing the water," the idea of the social acceptance of perfection is an interesting concept to show readers. There Are Certain Ineffable, Yet In-Your-Face Qualities that elevate an American Olympian to seven-figure, network, cereal-box, Battle of the Endorsement Stars status; there is Pluck 'n Perk, as in a Dorothy Hamill or Mary Lou Retton; there is the outright Yankee Yahoo factor of Bruce "Tropicana Pure Premium" Jenner, the man single-hand-edly responsible for the insertion of "Go for it" into sitcoms, stump speeches and bumper stickers. But there is no direct commercial tie-in for Perfection itself; especially in what remains a relatively esoteric Sports. Diving is not a widely appreciated art form. And at bottom, Americans don't quite know what to do with undiluted male grace.

There is a man trying to help them figure it out. His name is Jim Babbitt, Louganis's friend since their days at UC-Irvine, a rower, psychology major and, since 1985, Louganis's manager. Working out of Louganis's Malibu home, which they share, Babbitt negotiates poster deals, interviews, personal appearance contracts with car dealerships. Despite the beauty, talent and affability of his client, the deal roster is split between name brands and also-rans: American Express and Banana Boat skin-care products. TV is the same: *Hollywood Squares and Double Dare.* Via William Morris, scripts arrive to be read, with some queries from casting directors. Feeling that his client needed a sample of his acting abilities on film, Babbitt urged him to take a bit part in a movie, *Dirty Laundry,* which proved so execrable it went straight to video rental, without theatrical release in the U.S.

It is difficult to assess the dramatic future of Greg Louganis from his appearance as beach bum Larry, a happenin' dude wearing surf baggies and a bimbo on each arm. Larry's few lines could torpedo Olivier: "Hey, Corinne really digs your sound system. I think she wants to check out your tweeters." "I felt good about it," Louganis says of his performance. Asked about the movie, he laughs. "I heard it's terrible." He got the part when a casting director saw him in an L.A. workshop. Unlike Bruce "Can't Stop the Music" Jenner, Louganis has taken years of classes, has gone to cattle calls, readings. He says he's come close—he read for the spacey Prince Valium in Mel Brooks's *Spaceballs,* for the part of a cadet in the miniseries *Dress Gray. Dirty Laundry* may not be much, he says, but he came by it honestly.

> "I got the part based on the showcase," he says. "A lot of people think that the reason I got the part is because they used Carl Lewis and myself—two Olympians—in the same film. They kind of figured I didn't have to audition."

Carl Lewis is a beautiful, talented athlete who won virtually no endorsements, owing to what has been termed an "attitude problem"—and unsubstantiated rumours of homosexuality that created an adversarial relationship with the press. Since sports establishments—organizational and media-are notoriously homophobic, the Wheaties box was more than a world record long jump away. Lewis is talking now, about the bitterness, the pain, the sportswriters in his face bawling, "Are you on drugs?" "Are you homosexual?" It has taken him four years to be able to speak about the whispering campaigns. Greg Louganis has heard all kinds of sighs and whispers, but he is facing them with good humour and no fear. He says he is comfortable with who he is, at peace, even enjoying himself. His sexual preference is nobody's business; his business arrangements are just fine, thank you, despite a recent article that hung Jim Babbitt out to dry.

Louganis "says he is comfortable with who he is, at peace, even enjoying himself". That was when writer Gerri Hershey interviewed him for this 1988 article. But during the last week of February 1995, Louganis admitted publicly that he has AIDS. He also admitted that he knew he had AIDS before the 1998 Olympic Games in Seoul, Korea. It was during the preliminaries of the springboard events in Seoul that Louganis cracked his head on a reverse dive and became "paralyzed with fear" when he started bleeding in the pool. He did not tell the doctor who stitched the wound that he had AIDS. The doctor stitched it without gloves or other precautions. Louganis was taking the AIDS drug AZT around the clock during the Seoul Olympics. He said he was encouraged by his coach and a few others not to indicate he had AIDS. In 1989, Olympic officials set strict guidelines regarding prevention of contact with athletes' blood. Reports indicated that because the pool was chlorinated, there was an almost zero chance that other athletes could have gotten AIDS from his blood in the pool. The theme of conquering fears continues throughout the article.

> "I usually don't read any of my press," he says. And while Babbitt was upset with the portrayal of him as a grasping *arriviste,* his client just giggled when a fellow diver read the article out loud. "It was just so funny," says Louganis. "And it was totally off base."

What the writer didn't seem to understand, he says, is that the "demons he lives with"—the fears, the past hurts—have largely been banished, and he's not about to let others take their place. Louganis is not afraid of Hollywood, not of studio neurotics and agency piranhas, not even of Rumour. He treats it just the way he did the swarm of fears on the Olympic platform four years ago. He just doesn't acknowledge it.

> "I'm oblivious," he says. He listens, and usually he laughs. He's heard that he's been seen chasing women in bars—teammates no less. "I've heard I'm having an affair with [diver] Tracy Scoggin. And then every four years I am having an affair with Megan Neyer."

Beautiful men must suffer this, and more. He says he's also heard a popular rumour that he has been living with a powerful, older Hollywood studio head. He laughs. "Yeah. Right. I'm *sure*." And Greg Louganis wants you to know this, all you enquiring minds. If it's true, if he's being grandly kept by this mogul, *how come he has to run around pumping hands for car dealerships?* What's he doing *living in a free development condo,* driving a sober little compact *on loan from a car-rental company?*

> "I mean," he says. "I'd be living much more comfortably than I am."

While rumour places him in Tinsel Town love nests, he says he is really in Dr. Sammy Lee's back yard, playing Pictionary and wolfing down Korean barbecue with the Lee family, Aunt Mary, her son Herb. He's cleaning dishes and playing Trivial Pursuit. And so, to most of the rumours, he and Babbitt laugh and say yeah, right, they're sure. The author wraps up the idea of conquering fears in this effective concluding section. WHAT IT COMES DOWN TO IS THIS: YOU HAVE TO PICK YOUR fights with fear. You have to know which ones matter and which ones aren't worth the energy. Some fear is good and honest and can teach you buckets, and some of it is flat evil. Louganis has watched a special friend fight that kind of fear for five years now. He explains:

> "I was following this story about Ryan White—he's the boy who contracted AIDS through the clotting agent. And he was going through the court system to fight his way back into school."
>
> And he was going through the court system to fight his way back into school."
>
> It was a real spook show, the six-o'clock news awash with screeching adult fear masks, hate masks. The Whites lived in Kokomo, Indiana, which is close to Indianapolis, where the national diving championships were being held.
>
> Louganis called Ryan White and invited him to the pool. "In a way, I was hoping that if some people saw that I don't have anything to fear, and if I can be accepting..."

Here was a kid in the fatal embrace of the biggest, fiercest boa, facing death and going further still—to Congress, to TV stations and to school-board meetings—a frail kid letting a tidal wave of dread and prejudice break over him. Ryan and his family came to the meet, and since then, he and Louganis have become friends, with frequent phone chats and visits to Mission Bay and to Louganis's home, in California. Ryan is doing well, Louganis says, just got his driver's license and has friends now that the family left the hate in Kokomo for Cicero, Illinois, and a more accepting environment.

> "What's sad about the situation is that Jeanne, his mother, she's probably going to have to let the banks foreclose on her house in Kokomo, because nobody will buy the AIDS house;" Louganis says. "I mean, the Realtors want Jeanne to get some sort of written

statement that nobody can get AIDS from a house.

It is pathetic. It is sick."

For the first time, there is an edge to Louganis's soft voice. "A lot of the fear is out of ignorance," he says.

Stupid people, calling a young boy names. So Ryan is going around talking to anyone who will listen, trying to hold the fears up to the light, and when it comes to valour and insight and calm, Greg Louganis thinks this boy is a perfect master. No matter what happens, Ryan White will rip it in the end. Notice what a nice twist this ending has, compared to the "high dive" lead. "Fear makes a big splash, you know, in the headlines and all," says Louganis. But when everything settles, "it's just a little puddle."

Choosing a Structure

When to use the inverted pyramid structure:

- If the writer is working for a daily newspaper.
- If the article is about a game played in the previous 24 hours.
- If space is short and the writer must be concise.
- If there is no historical nature to the article.
- If it is a news-oriented article.

When to use the diamond structure:

- If the writer is working for a magazine.
- If the article is not specifically a "score" or "game" story.
- If it is a profile story or a trend story or "think" article.
- If the article contains a specific historical section or segment.
- If space is not a significant factor and the writer can "write long."
- If it is clearly a feature article.

OTHER STRUCTURES

There may be cases in which the writer needs to write a story chronologically or nearly chronologically. The inverted pyramid would not be appropriate and the diamond format not necessary. The chronological structure is perfect for showing a trend in sports or for clearly showing the progress of a personality in the sports world. David Ramsey, staff reporter for the *Syracuse Herald American* has used the chronological structure well. He shows the public fall and the unpublicized aftermath of Cleveland State University basketball coach Kevin Mackey. Notice how this article is structured differently from the *Kansas City Star* article about athlete Lisa Davies.

The article was run in the "Herald American" on January 10, 1993 under the title and subtitle: Mackey reaches again for basketball's glory In CBA, former Cleveland State coach tries to escape past. ALBANY—Even on the best night of his basketball life, a night he should have rejoiced, Kevin Mackey couldn't shake his fury. He tried to bask in his triumph. Everyone wanted to be near him, to drink Miller Lites with him in his room at Syracuse's downtown Holiday Inn. He and his no-name Cleveland State Vikings had just defeated Bobby Knight's Indiana Hoosiers in the 1986 NCAA sub-regional. From his room, Mackey seethed as he watched cars whiz by on Interstate. He saw the Carrier Dome, site of his triumph. Boosters and university officials slapped him on the back. Unbelievable upset, they kept saying. Mackey didn't see it that way.

Couldn't they see the endless hours of labour he had put into this team? Couldn't they see his team's 28-3 record, see his team's ruthless hunger for victory? Couldn't they see? Mackey eventually was left alone with his rage. He reached for another beer. And another. And another. He pushed himself and his players with an endless fire, but the acclaim never seemed enough. Always, he sought more. Mostly, he sought more beer. Mackey says now he was an alcoholic, had been since he was 16. A couple of years after his triumph in Syracuse, he was offered cocaine. He said yes. Alcohol, he says, had ceased to entice him. He soon found he couldn't say no. For Mackey, the toast of Cleveland, cocaine was easy to find. "I really didn't have to spend much money," he says. "It was given to me. All kinds of people wanted to give me cocaine." He believed he could master cocaine. He believed he could continue to win games. He believed he could hide his addiction the same way he had hidden his voracious thirst for alcohol.

On July 13, 1990—Friday the 13th—someone called Cleveland police. Mackey's long time of hiding was about to end. Mackey, the caller said, could be found in a crack house on Edmonton Avenue. The same tip was made to Cleveland's Channel 8. Mackey had made a dangerous choice of destinations. He had much to lose by being there. He had signed a $175,000-per-season contract with Cleveland State two days earlier. In seven seasons he had compiled a 144-67 record. He took his 1986 team to the NCAA's Sweet 16 and came within a last-second shot by David Robinson of carrying the Vikes past Navy and into the final eight.

He owned a 13-room home in Shaker Heights, a swank Cleveland suburb. He had a wife, his college sweetheart, and three children. He did commercials for McDonald's. It was perfect; Mackey talking up the Big Mac. "I was the king," Mackey says, closing his eyes as he gazed back at the old days. "The King of Cleveland, that's what they called me." Mackey is now the coach of the Capital Region Pontiacs, a Continental Basketball Association team based in Albany. Nobody calls him the king. He talks, with the thick New England accent of his native Somerville, Mass., as he eats a salsa-smothered burrito in an Albany restaurant. He wears blue coaching sweats and a CBS-Sports hat. He is 46 years old with a deeply lined face. He winces as he thinks back to the crack house on Edmonton. Mackey stumbled out of the crack house, accompanied by Alma Massey, his mistress of several years. He climbed into his Lincoln Town Car. With the police and a television camera crew following, he drove a couple of blocks. The police pulled him over. Out of the car stepped a rich college coach high on crack. With TV cameras rolling, he was frisked, arrested, charged with drunk driving and, later, drug abuse. He was tossed in jail.

"I had no idea," says Shawn Hood, who played for Cleveland State's 1986 team and worked as Mackey's assistant coach when the arrest was made. "The only thing I was aware of was that he was a great coach. He had two lives, basically. He was very intelligent with his madness." Cleveland State fired him six days later. His wife kicked him out of the house in Shaker Heights. McDonald's no longer wanted to pay him to talk up their Big Macs. After being sentenced to 90 days treatment in lieu of conviction, Mackey underwent drug rehabilitation in Cleveland and Houston, where he attended the John Lucas clinic. Lucas was the first pick in the 1976 NBA draft, a brilliant point guard with an appetite for cocaine. He now coaches the San Antonio Spurs.

Mackey says he has, with the aid of Lucas, shackled his thirst for alcohol and his itch for cocaine. He has not, he says, taken a drink or a hit since his Friday the 13th visit to Edmonton Avenue. He is randomly tested, as are all CBA players and coaches, for drug use. He is beginning what he hopes is his climb back. The Pontiacs are 10-11, but on a tear. Mackey acquired Chuck Nevitt, a 7-foot-5 centre and NBA journeyman, to anchor the middle of his defence. The big man's arrival started a five-game winning streak. Mackey has long envisioned a giant on his team. While at Cleveland State, he recklessly pursued a 7-foot-7 African named Manute Bol, a pursuit that left the Vikings with two years of NCAA sanctions.

Now, Mackey watches Nevitt during practices at Albany's Knickerbocker Arena. He strolls the sidelines yelling, "Repetition is the mother of learning." He tells players he is offering defensive techniques "no other coach" is teaching. His players seem to be listening.

> "I don't care a thing about his past," says Pontiacs' starting point guard Sean Gay, who has read and heard all about Mackey's tumble in Cleveland. "Everyone, you know, has a past they would like to forget. He's a good person now. That's what I care about."

The Capital Region CBA team has been a step to the NBA in the past. Phil Jackson, coach of the World Champion Chicago Bulls, once directed the team. So did George Karl, coach of the Seattle Sonics. Mackey wants to follow that legacy. He lives in a small apartment in Troy. He earns $40,000 a season. He coaches in front of only a few hundred fans on most nights. He wants more. He wants what he had in Cleveland—the big house, the big crowds, the big money. That might not be easy. The lurid facts of the past, Mackey says, are still fresh in the minds of many basketball fans. Mackey often hears the volume go down when he enters a room. Those who know the Kevin Mackey Story, those who know about the booze and the coke and the mistress, begin to whisper. They whisper and they stare.

> "I see those people," Mackey says. "I see those people looking at me everywhere I go. I figure they're wondering if I have a crack pipe in my back pocket or a bottle of Jack Daniel's in my gym bag. I wonder that."

He is driven by those doubters, though he admits a continued vulnerability to alcohol and cocaine. He is quick to affirm cocaine's lure, its power. He had been a heavy drinker for years, he says, and always managed to prosper. Drinking didn't stop him from winning four state titles in his nine seasons as a high school coach. When he was an assistant coach at Boston College from 1977-82, he cruised the interstates of the East Coast with a cooler full of Miller Lite in the passenger's seat. He cranked the radio up loud, drank his beers and drove, always, in the inside lane as he searched from town to town for recruits. He found players who helped BC win Big East titles in 1981 and 1983, a feat the school hasn't managed since Mackey's departure. He found John Bagley, a fat kid from Bridgeport now in his 11th NBA season. He found Michael Adams, a short kid from Hartford now playing for the Washington Bullets. He found the players others missed. Somehow, the highway patrol missed him.

"Hey, the troopers don't stop you in the inside lane," he says of those hazy rides. "It's a fact of life, you know." His driving luck ran out on Friday the 13th. Talking about cocaine with Mackey is a vivid experience. His eyes get this dreamy look. His voice grows soft. The tone is wistful as if he is recalling an intense but failed romance. "Cocaine—it takes you to another world," he says. "Cocaine, you get that hit and, ah"—he's smiling now, looking out the window—"you know, it's 'Beam me up, Scottie.' The thing for me, I didn't like it. I, oh, I loved it." Some days, he says, he still misses it. Last spring Mackey coached the Fayetteville (N.C.) Flyers to the best record (41-23) in the Global Basketball Association, another minor-league. After the season ended, he felt a degree of vindication. He also felt the old hunger for acclaim, and he wanted—desperately wanted—to drink and snort.

> "I told myself, 'You done a good job. You deserve something,'" Mackey remembers. "I thought about going off by myself and, you know, rewarding myself. I thought about checking into a hotel."

His word choice in the next sentence is chilling. "I wanted to lay in some alcohol and cocaine." He picked out the hotel. He pictured the entire scenario. He was all ready to jump off the sobriety wagon. But he didn't "lay" in alcohol and cocaine.

> "I'm not sure why," he says. "I don't know if it was because of good reasons. I don't really think so. But I didn't go to the hotel."

He won that day, but not every past scar has been mended. Mackey shakes his finger when asked about his family. He will not say a word about his wife, his children or about Alma Massey. "Nothing about that," he says. Kathleen Mackey, Kevin's wife of 27 years, works as a nursing supervisor at the Cuyahoga County Jail in Cleveland. She answers the phone minutes after returning from her lunch break.

"It was a great, great thing," she says, her voice bright as she remembers the victory night in Syracuse. "It was a natural high, so to speak."

The voice continues to hop as she talks about the fast-talking Irish man she met at St. Anselm's College. She is still married to Mackey. "Kevin, he was a lot of fun," she says. "He was very good-looking. He played ball. We had a very nice relationship. You know, I've known him more than half my life. I met him when I was 19." Her tone changes as the subject moves closer to the present. She says she had no idea her husband had a serious drinking problem, no idea he abused cocaine, no idea he had a mistress. No idea. "The whole thing was quite a shock," she says. "The depth and the breadth of it was quite a shock. I knew maybe he was drinking a little bit too much, but I wasn't looking for anything like what happened. It was shattering." Kathleen still waits for her husband to say he's sorry. He never apologized, she says.

She waits for him to say anything. She hasn't spoken to him in months. He knows the number, she says, but he chooses not to call. "Silence," she says, "is not always golden." Mackey is quiet after declining to talk about Kathleen and his children. He gazes out the window. The sun's rays bathe his face. The former King of Cleveland, today an unknown at a restaurant in Albany, smiles. "I don't feel guilty," he says. "I take full responsibility for what happened, but I don't feel guilty. I've put the guilt down.

"Yesterday is a canceled check." He has so much to do, so far to climb. "I'm not satisfied," he says. "I want it back." His wife is confident he will succeed—on the basketball court. "He really is an excellent coach," she says, her voice cracking at the Cuyahoga County Jail. The writer could even highlight the straight-line time chronology by using a diary format, by beginning key sections or paragraphs with a time. The use of a diary or time format article would be particularly appropriate in an article such as "24 Hours Behind the Scenes at the Indianapolis 500" or other similar articles.

Staff writers and editors for *The Wall Street Journal* have devised their own structure, which bears examination. In *News Reporting and* Writing (1985), the Missouri Group, Brooks, Kennedy, Moen, and Ranly, wrote:

For centuries, writers have used the literary device of telling a story through the eyes of one person or by examining part of the whole. The device makes large institutions, complex issues and seven-digit numbers meaningful. Few of us can comprehend the size of the U.S. budget, but we can understand the numbers on our own paycheck. Not many of us can explain the marketing system for wheat, but we could if we followed a bushel of wheat from the time it was planted until a consumer picked up a loaf of bread in the supermarket. Even though Joseph Stalin was hardly talking about literary approaches, he summed the impact of focusing on a part of the whole when he said, "Ten million deaths are a statistic; one death is a tragedy." Individual newspaper journalists have used the technique often, but no newspaper has seized upon it like *The Wall Street Journal*. In its daily one-column feature examining national and international issues, *The Journal* routinely and expertly puts a literary magnifying glass on the individual involved in an issue or institution.

The Wall Street Journal article has four distinct parts:

1. The lead begins with *a focus on an individual* and his or her problems or concerns about an industry or a work environment.
2. There is a *transition* to a larger level—the same issue across an industry or at the national level.
3. There is a *lengthy report* on the larger scope—the issue at the industry or national level.
4. There is a return to *end the article with the focus again at the local level*—the article usually ends with an anecdote or quotation from the same person cited in the lead, or with a similar person.

The key to *The Wall Street Journal* structure is:

Individual '! Industry '! Individual

Another way of viewing this structure or method would be:

Simple '! Complex '! Simple

The first four paragraphs of a typical *Wall Street Journal* article begin with the individual, then there is a subhead. The subhead acts as the transition to the body of the article, which examines the problem across an industry. At the end of the article body, there is another subhead, which again acts as a transition, and the end of the article is the last four paragraphs, to exactly match the lead. A typical article in this format for *The Wall Street Journal* would be how one auto worker, Joe, has been replaced on a Ford assembly line by a robot welding arm. Then the body of the article is devoted to how many workers throughout the auto industry are being replaced by robot welders and how the human workers are being retrained for other jobs. The end of the article might be a look at how auto worker Joe was successfully retrained for another position at Ford.

This is a variation of the diamond format. Sports writers might use this technique to show how one pro football player's career was ended by a crippling injury, then show

how all injured football players are rehabilitated, then return to show how the single player successfully overcame his injuries. The article may not need to use exactly four paragraphs in the lead, then the body, and then exactly four paragraphs at the end of the article, as *The Wall Street Journal does*.

Choosing a Structure

Use the chronology structure if the writer is writing a trend or profile story, or if there is no real historical nature to the story. Use the diary structure if the writer is covering an event like the Indianapolis 500 or the Kentucky Derby, or if the writer is planning a first-person article about "How I Went Over Niagara Falls in a Barrel" or something similar.

Use *The Wall Street Journal* structure if the writer needs to clarify a problem in terms of one person or one small unit, such as a family. It is also useful when there are clearly smaller and larger components to the story or when the writer would normally use the diamond structure.

CHAPTER

6

How to Write Effective News Endings

Most writers labour over their beginnings, because the beginning—the lead—must be perfect to lure the reader into the story. The same writers, however, are often far less careful with their endings. But the endings shouldn't be just a relief ("Thank goodness that's over!") for the writer or the reader. Rather, the ending should fit the story as well as the beginning. Most articles should have effective, emphatic, obvious endings. Most articles (and *all* feature articles) shouldn't just trail down the last column of the last page and fall off the bottom of the page.

It should be of little surprise to know that techniques for effective beginnings can be used for effective endings. There are, however, not quite as many techniques for effective endings as there are techniques for effective beginnings. Some techniques for effective beginnings simply don't work as endings. The anthology The Best American Sports Writing, 1993 (Deford, 1994) comprises 25 articles that are, indeed, the best writing about Sports in America in 1993. How do the writers represented in this collection use effective endings? Let's see. There are several key techniques for effective endings.

THE ANECDOTAL ENDING

An anecdote can be a short but significant story about an individual that shows that person's character. The anecdote can also show the character of a team or institution. One of the exceptional articles in The Best American Sports Writing, 1993 was a Sports Illustrated article by Rick Reilly about athletic abuses (including severe hazing), human rights abuses, and racism at the Citadel. Reilly's piece, "What Is the Citadel?" appeared in Sports Illustrated on September 14, 1992. Reilly ended his article with a quotation ending, but then, as the article went to press, added a one-paragraph anecdote, as a postscript:

"I can tell you one thing," said the wrestler, Reaves. "I'm going to be hell when I'm a sophomore. I took a lot of crap. I've gotta get *somebody* back." Here's hoping they beat Wofford.

Postscript: Just before this story went to print, a black Citadel freshman told authorities he woke up on August 20 to find a string noose hanging from the bunk above him. Some say the noose was there because the freshman refused an upperclassman's demand that he sing *Dixie* in the barracks shower. The Citadel says it has completed its investigation and has asked the South Carolina Law Enforcement Division to take over (Reilly, 994,p.350).

THE EDITORIAL ENDING

If you write about two boxers, two football coaches, two runners, or two teams, you could begin the article with a comparison of the two. You can end the article with an editorial (or judgment) ending.

Humour columnist and author Dave Barry travelled from Miami (when Floridians were anticipating the first season of the Florida Marlins) to Erie, Pennsylvania, the home of the Erie Sailors, a Marlins farm team. He found the Sailors' stadium quaint, the operation a nickel-and-dime affair, and the players more human and certainly more approachable than in the big leagues.

Barry's article, "The Old Ball Game," appeared in *Tropic* magazine and also in *The Best* American Sports *Stories, 1993*. His ending:

The 1992 Sailors season ended September 1. As I write this, the Marlins haven't decided whether to remain affiliated with the Sailors for the 1993 season. And if Erie doesn't solve its stadium problem by 1994, the Sailors won't be affiliated with any big-league team. Of course, by next year, South Florida won't care about Erie: the Marlins will be playing here. We'll have a big-league team to follow, with big-league stars making big-league money, playing in a big-league stadium in front of big-league crowds. Everything will be bigger. Although not necessarily better. (Barry, 1994,p. 321)

THE "I" ENDING

If you are writing a first-person article, "There I Was, Running the Boston Marathon," and if you begin with the "I" of the author as participant, then the "I" of the author is certainly appropriate at the end of the article. If the "I" of the author does not appear anywhere else in the article, it is usually inappropriate—and jarring to the reader—for the "I" viewpoint of the author to appear *for the first time* at the end of the article. Ray Blount Jr.'s article, "Blunder Road," from *Men's Journal*, is in the tradition of George Plimpton's inept-amateur-as-athlete books. In "Blunder Road," Blount attends the Skip Barber Racing School to learn to drive a formula race car. Of course he does everything wrong, including never learning quite well enough how to anticipate a high-speed turn.

His end:

> But I want them to know this: The next time I drove my Jetta on the highway, I found that if I concentrated I could look further up the road than usual and plot my course smoothly through a series of turns. Well, two turns. A turn and a half. At one point, as I swung all the way to the far edge of the right lane and unwound smoothly back to the far edge of the left, I felt something. A fleeting connection with some Platonic vector matrix stretching from Detroit to heaven. I like to think it was my apex.
> (Blount, 1994, p.30)

THE QUESTION ENDING

Can you end an article with a question? Certainly, but you must give the reader enough evidence—pro or con, yes or no—in the article for the reader to be able to answer the question. Asking a question at the end of a feature requires that the reader *continue to consider* the article.

In his article "A Tragedy Too Easy to Ignore," *Detroit Free Press* writer Mitch Albom chronicled the Damon Bailes story. Bailes, a Detroit native, was shot in the back of the head during a pick-up basketball game, apparently because an opposing player thought Bailes wanted his red basketball shorts.

The bullet, Albom wrote:

> Had hit the lobe that controls vision and left Bailes with only partial sight, paralyzed on the right side. In the months that followed, he would regain a slurred speech, partial vision and some feeling in his otherwise dead right leg and arm. The vision bothered him most. He would cry for hours over his near-blindness. (Albom, 1994, p. 412)

Albom's end:

> What are we supposed to do? The future of our city is being taken down, gangland style, one ambulance

> after another. We have to do something. Tonight is Christmas Eve, they are talking flurries, and that should make our suburbs pretty and white. But try to remember, while you open your presents, that somewhere, not far away, Damon Bailes is struggling to see the drawings on the wall, the ones teaching him how to walk again. For what, you keep asking yourself? For what? For what? For what? For nothing. And the snow falls. (Albom, 1994, p. 415)

If you ask a rhetorical question, as Albom does, the ending also carries an implication of the editorial ending. *Car and Driver* tested the new Dodge Neon and reported the test in the April 1994 issue, in an article under a headline and subhead:

> Dodge Neon :A little car with a big motor and a big grin

Writer Patrick Bedard's ending was:

> Can we live with an $11,552 Neon? Yes, very well, thank you. The lesson of the Neon is that common sense makes a real nifty car. Which is bad news for Saturn and other small cars that have relied on low prices. They simply can't measure up for roominess and performance. Would we prefer a plusher version? Well, yes, and we'll have a test of such a Neon within a few months.

THE QUOTATION ENDING

This is an almost no-fail ending, especially for personality portraits. A quotation from the principal subject of a profile leaves the "voice" of the personality in the reader's inner ear and should, additionally, reinforce the character of the speaker that has been established throughout the article. Writer Pat Jordan (1994) profiled baseball manager Whitey Herzog for the *Los Angeles Times Magazine*, in an article titled "The Wit and Wisdom of the White Rat" (Herzog's nickname).

Jordan's last three paragraphs were:

Herzog today seems less passionate about the game he loves, though still intellectually involved. He seems more determined to enjoy his life outside of baseball, too. So he accepted a no-lose situation. The Angels can only get better, not worse, and the credit will go to Herzog. So what if he was overruled about Joyner and Abbott, if he must listen to Jackie Autry say she had no money to throw around, and to Richard Brown warn that all Herzog's suggestions must be filtered through a committee.

A younger Herzog might have raged, or even quit, over such things, insisting on the last word. The loss of such power doesn't seem to bother him now, because the game has changed and so has his place in it. The power has shifted to the players, and that rankles him.

Suddenly he lurches forward, his elbows planted on the table. "You know what I don't understand," he says. "One year I made six thousand dollars as a player and I had to buy my own tickets to the game for my family. Today, you got players making two million a year and they want five hundred free tickets." He shakes his head in despair. "I just don't understand it," he says. "I never saw so many unhappy millionaires in my life". (Jordan, 1994, p. 266)

THE SUMMARY ENDING

Using this technique, the writer completes the article by summarizing the story. Charles P. Pierce uses such an ending in a profile about Shaquille O'Neal. Pierce article, "The Next Superstar," appeared in *The New York Times Magazine*. His last two paragraphs were:

O'Neal plays with consummate ease and confidence. He blocks shots by catching them. He whips down the lane for a dunk off an inbounds play, and he winks at Leonard Armato's four-year-old son while he does it. He tosses the veteran Pistons centre Olden Polynice this way and that, once bouncing the ball off the backboard, retrieving it with a lightning first step, and then slamming it through as the women from En Vogue rock and Arsenio grabs his head. He ends up with 36 points and 19 rebounds. "Shaquille, the best part about him is that he's mean," Magic Johnson says later. "He's going to be one of those guys that, after you play him, you sleep real good. He's gonna put guys to sleep." He does not look mean. He does not look like a product here. He looks like a twenty-year-old discovering himself all over again. There is a purity that extends from north Orlando to this gathering of gaudy dilettantes. He will be comfortable in both places. He will be a kid and a corporation. He will be for sale and he will be free. He will be a Goliath for everyone to love.(Pierce, 1994, p. 335)

THE "YOU" ENDING

If you are giving advice to the reader, or suggesting products or services, using the "you" ending is often appropriate. In the April 1994 issue of *Car and Driver*, in addition to the Neon test report article, the editors tested five brands of automobile radar detectors. The article, headlined "Lidar Enters the Radar Wars," written by Don Schroeder, ended:

For skinflints torn between these last two detectors in the test, try this advice. If you despise false alarms and are willing to sacrifice laser protection, go with the Cobra. If your car is so loud that you can't hear a falsing detector anyway, go with the Uniden. Make sure you're buying the LRD 9000W-1, not the LRD 9000W, which covers only wideband KA. (Schroeder, 1994, p. 95)

COMBINATION ENDINGS

These categories are part of the vast panorama of endings that writers can use. There are as many variations of endings as there are articles and writers. Can you use a description of an empty racetrack, then a quotation from a driver who won (or lost) a major motorsports race? Surely.

Can you end an article with the "you" ending—talking to your reader—then end with a rhetorical question? Of course.

Can you use an anecdote about a personality, then a description of them? Yes.

Can you contrast two principal subjects at the end of an article?

Can you match a technique used at the end of a feature to the same type of beginning used in the lead?

You are limited only by your imagination—and your knowledge of leads, structures, transitions, and endings. The more you know about writing techniques, the better your material becomes. Count on it.

CHAPTER

7

Writing about Women

In writing about women, writers should not use prefixes indicating marital status. First reference should include a person's title (if any) and given name; later references should include last name only. Use of Mr. and Mrs. is limited to discussions that include a married couple, where the last-name-only rule might cause confusion. Miss and Ms. are not to be used at all. First names alone are also not appropriate for adults. Females over the age of 18, should be referred to as *women*. They are not *girls, gals, ladies, chicks, broads, lovelies,* or *honeys*. Words like *homemaker* and *housewife* are also not synonyms for woman; check carefully for accuracy before they are used. Coed does not mean woman any more than it means man; persons who attend school are *students*.

Gratuitous physical description, uncommon almost to the point of absence in news stories about men, should also be eliminated from such stories about women. If you would not say, "The gray-haired grandfather of three was elected senator," then do not say, "The gray-haired grandmother of three was elected senator." This rule does not apply with equal force to feature writing, especially profiles, in which physical description is often an essential aspect. However, care should be taken to avoid stereotypical descriptions in favour of describing an individual's unique characteristics.

Similar considerations apply to the mention of an individual's spouse and family. In a news story about a man, his wife and family are typically mentioned only in passing and only when relevant; the same practice should apply to news stories about women. See the previous examples. Again, the practice is slightly different for feature stories and profiles, but the test of relevance should always be applied. Most achievements do not need sexual identification; those that do should be so identified for both men and women. If you would not say, "Dan Rather is a male reporter," do not say "Helen Thomas is a female reporter." Instead of "Arthur Ashe is one of the best American tennis players and Billie Jean King is one of the best American women tennis players," say, "Arthur Ashe and Billie Jean King are two of the best American tennis players," or "Arthur Ashe is one of the best American male tennis players and Billie Jean King is one of the best American female tennis players."

Avoid sins of omission as well as those of commission. If, for example, an expert is sought in a given field, or if an example is needed to make a point, women should be used in these cases as a matter of course—not simply as "oddities" or representatives of "a woman's viewpoint." *Man*, used alone and in words like *chairman*, is a sexually exclusive term and should be avoided when possible. "Man-on-the-street," for instance, can easily be changed to "person-on-the-street" or "ordinary person"; "chairman" to "chairperson." The federal government has begun to change its job titles to reflect this problem; persons formerly called "mailmen" are now "mail carriers."

Women's professional qualifications or working experience should always be acknowledged, to forestall the common (and incorrect) expectation that most women are full-time housewives.

Feminist is the correct term to describe a woman committed to equal rights for women. "Women's libber" is an unacceptable pejorative. Headlines seem to be particularly susceptible to the use of stereotypical, simplistic language. As in other areas, play on these stereotypes is to be avoided. When you have completed a story about a woman, go through it and ask yourself whether you would have written about a man in the same style. If not, something may be wrong with the tone or even the conception of your article. Think it through again. Do major publications discriminate against women, consciously or unconsciously? *Houston Post* columnist Bonnie Gangelhoff raised this issue in her February 23, 1994 column headlined:

"Magazine cheats women athletes"

Stabbed. Widowed. Abused. Clubbed. Who are they?

The women on TV miniseries during sweeps week?

Guess again. They are the women in jeopardy on Sports Illustrated magazine covers for the past 12 months. While plowing through Sunday newspapers, an article by Boston broadcaster Lynda Truman Ryan touched a nerve. It seems Ryan's daughter plays baseball and the girl, 10, eagerly awaits Sports Illustrated each week. She likes to read about baseball or anything about girls' sports.

A year ago, Lynda Truman Ryan began to tally how many women attained SI cover status from swimsuit issue to swimsuit issue. What Ryan discovered is surprising. Six Sports Illustrated covers out of 52 featured women. Four of the six women were victims of some sort. The other two *SI* covers featured female models in bikinis. What really disappoints is that the only women athletes to grace SI's cover are ones who have been rendered helpless in some way. Usually tough competitors and fighters, they are caught in a rare moment of victimhood. The four covers:

- Monica Seles, a tough tennis player, wears tennis whites with a knife stuck in her back.
- A picture of the widows of Indian pitchers Steve Olin and Tim Crews, two players killed in a boating accident.
- Tennis player Mary Pierce looking as if she is going to cry. The headline: "Why Mary Pierce Fears For Her Life." The story is about her dad who beats her.
- The most recent cover woman is Nancy Kerrigan. By now we know she's a natural for an *SI* cover. She's been clubbed. "Why me?" rang out the headline.

But we should ask Sports Illustrated "Why them?" Why put women athletes on the cover only at their low points. The magazine sends out a message. This is the way we like our women—beat up (or in a bikini). That some of the best and brightest talents in women's sports get cover play only when they suffer is ridiculous. To wit: Will we see four-time gold medal winner Bonnie Blair on an SI cover? Not unless someone sabotages her skates today as she goes for her fifth gold medal. But Roger Jackson, SI spokesman, says the magazine regularly writes about women's sports. He defends cover choices, saying it's not accurate to call them victims. They are newsmakers, he says: Sports Illustrated is a news magazine that publishes the top news story or newsmaker in the world of sports each week."

So, not one other woman athlete was deemed top newsmaker status for the entire year? Wrong message Sports Illustrated is a magazine read by thousands of kids. Ryan's daughter and others like her who love sports should see some women triumph and honored when they are up, not just down. Somehow the message emerging from such one-note cover choices is bad things happen to women who try to excel. And what about all the boys who read SI? Their opinions are shaped by such images of top women athletes honored only when helpless.

Get a grip, Sports Illustrated. Abuse is no excuse for a cover.

P.S.: Check out the Feb. 21 issue of SI. Sure, we like to read about Tommy Moe and Dan Jansen but there's not one story about a woman athlete on the U.S. Olympic team. The one feature story about a female focuses on a basketball player from Canada. She had a leg amputated. There's a full-page photo of her. It's shot to display her right leg cut off below the knee and posed next to her artificial limb.

Gangelhoff printed letters a few weeks later from readers in response to that column. The readers wrote:

> Dear Bonnie, You whine and bray that only six SI covers featured women. My complaint is, why were there any at all except for the swimsuit issue of course? Ten percent of the covers of SI featured a gender that is basically a non-factor in revenue producing sports. Get it? People who care about women sports are also probably 10 percent of the sports market. Live with it! The only way women will ever be on a par in popularity with men in sports is when they start playing their Sports topless!
> Sincerely, Cowboy
>
> Dear Cowboy,
> I'm really impressed with your enlightened attitudes. By the way, what about the millions of women who watched the Olympics, and made it a windfall for CBS?
>
> Dear Bonnie Gangelhoff,
> How many men have graced the cover of Women's Sports and Fitness over the last year? Or Woman's Day? Or any of the other 2 million publications devoted exclusively to females? Of course, the title of the magazine in question must be Sports Illustrated and not Men's Sports Illustrated despite the fact that male sports account for 99.99999 of all Sports-

generated revenues and garner a like proportion of all sports readers interest.

From R.B.A.

Dear R.B.A.,

If the magazine is for men only, why not call it Sports Illustrated for Men Who Love Women in Bikinis in Exotic Locations? The fact is, boys and girls read this magazine, as do women. SI is missing out on revenue. They might have even more readers if they carried a few more covers and stories about girls and women.

Dear Bonnie,

Thank you for your reaction to the covers of Sports Illustrated. . . If you want to have another reaction, I urge you to look at the Sports TV page at the front of The Post's TV Week. Please note the number of men's basketball games scheduled for televiewing, and the number of women's games likewise.

Sincerely yours, Betty Rudnick

Dear Betty,

I checked it out. Lean.

Can more publications devote more space for more articles about women's sports? Surely. Can we all be more careful in writing about women? Of course.

CHAPTER

8

Advance Story Writing

The advance is an article written prior to a major football game, bowl game, national or international tennis match, championship boxing match, baseball playoffs, World Series, or any other major sporting event. If you are a staff writer on a newspaper, keeping your readers involved with your newspaper (and remember, newspapers are losing readers by the thousands these days) means anticipating coming events and writing about them. There are many guidelines about advances, most based on tradition and common sense. In Modern Sportswriting, authors Louis I. Gelfand and Harry Heath Jr. (1969) suggested 13 key guidelines for writing a substantial advance story. They are:

- Significance of the game.
- The tradition and history of the teams, how their rivalry began, the most exciting games of the past, how they stand in won-lost figures in the series, and the last game.
- Records of the teams or individual competitors during the current season, and comments on the records of

the two teams. Perhaps one has played a tougher schedule than the other, or one team may have scheduled a "weak sister," between tough games, and so on.

- Analysis of comparative scoring records against mutual opponents.
- Squads' condition, both physical and mental.
- Starting lineups and comments on changes in lineups.
- *Weather:* how possible changes may affect the outcome, records of teams in different climates (e.g., northern athletes in the South, track and field athletes in high altitudes, football team on muddy field).
- *System of Play:* Compare them and the advantage one may have over the other; e.g., in tennis, a player's volley attack compared against his opponent's backcourt game.
- *Individual Angle:* In team Sports, the importance of one player.
- *Local Situation:* Atmosphere in the city where the game is to be played.
- *Ticket and Crowd Situation:* Will extra seats be erected? Will there be a television blackout for local fans? Pay-per-view? Is scalping tickets legal or "semi-legal?" Is scalping simply ignored by law enforcement officials? If tickets can be scalped, what are the going prices?
- Statements by coaches.
- *Who is Favoured:* Odds, if available.

It is sometimes, although not always, possible to get quotations from players. Some college and university coaches demand that their players refrain from speaking to the press, especially before a major game. Others don't have such a rule. If it is possible to get good quotations from the players, don't hesitate to do so. If the college or university coach has a rule prohibiting his players from speaking to the press, make sure the coach is interviewed, but beware of pat answers. Gelfand and Heath (1969) also suggested that there are several types of advance articles:

- The standard advance, published the morning or evening before the game.
- The roundup advance.
- The feature advance, which may be a poll advance, in which players, coaches, sports writers, and sometimes even fans give their opinions as to the probable outcome. It may also be the comparison advance, regularly written over the space of a week before a major contest. In it, World Series teams are compared, infield with infield, defence against defence; or bowl football teams are analyzed, tackles against tackles, halfbacks against halfbacks, and so on. It may also be the season's outlook advance, in which a well-informed and observant reporter covers the prospects for an important area team shortly before the season's opening.

The reporter's principal asset, Gelfand and Heath (1969) believed, is the "ability to analyze. The reader wants to know if the event is worthy of his presence. Also, he wants an indication of who will win and why." That sentence is as true today as when it was originally written, but much has changed since the Gelfand and Heath textbook. We now have ESPN; a wide variety of sports channels; CNN News, which carries sports shows; a fourth network, Fox, that outbid CBS for the rights to NFL football; and other venues for sports programming.

To keep your own readers from defecting, these are possibilities to consider:

Graphics. USA Today has been the point publication in the last few years in the use of graphics and colour pages. The Dallas Morning News has won a Pulitzer Prize for graphics-oriented special coverage displays. Given that most major newspapers now employ graphic artists and designers, you may wish to coordinate your advance stories with the graphics department.

- Highlight an advance every day with a special blurb in a "skybox" above the logo or flag on the front page.
- Use a computer-designed box on the front page, as *USA Today* does, to statistically highlight the similarities or differences between two teams.
- Use colour (if possible) with the advances to attract reader interest.
- Ask coaches not connected with the upcoming game to discuss the coaches who are involved.
- Use graphics-designed page layouts to highlight the competition between teams; for example, "When We Have the Ball" diagram the offences and the opponent's defence. "When They Have the Ball" diagram their offences and "our" defence.

How can a major newspaper use advances?

The Dallas Cowboys went to the Super Bowl twice in 2 years (Super Bowls XXVII and XXVIII, 1993 and 1994).

In the last six issues before the 1994 Super Bowl, *The Dallas Morning News* covered the upcoming game this way:

On Tuesday, there were two stories on page 1 under a head "Set for Success". One story was about Atlanta, the site of the game, under the head "Dallas looks to Atlanta as a model". The second article on page one was "Just the ticket" with a subhead "Air fare, Super Bowl seats available, but getting back could be tricky". Both articles were jumped to page A14. On that page the *Dallas Morning News* also ran a two-column by 9 1/2-inch graphic, statistically comparing Dallas and Atlanta in terms of population, race, age, sex, crime rate, weather, airport size, real estate, transportation, and other factors.

That day *The Dallas Morning News* began a special Super Bowl section, titled "Super Bowl XXVIII". It contained eight pages all devoted to the Cowboys.

The articles on page B17 were headlined "Aikman recalls little of NFC title game" (he received a concussion), "Wizard of Odds" (what Las Vegas says), "Proving the line wrong", and "Jerry Jones' deep-pocket moves corrected early chaos."

Page B18 contained "Fan's View", "No matter who's playing people watch Super Bowl", "Fewer tickets in 1995", "Formula deserves 2nd shot", "Cowboys dominate area ratings" (in a box), and "Q & A with Chris Berman" (ESPN's commentator). A full-page article, "Can't Kick the Habit", about kicker Ed Murray appeared on page B19. *"It's another Super Bowl rout for mighty Cowboys vs. Bills,"* Bills enter Atlanta prepared for questions about futility, and "No bye week leaves less time for hype", all appeared on page B20.

Miscellaneous stats and two photos were on the next page. "Failure to win back-to-back titles haunts former Cowboys" was on page B21, and some jump material from the first section page on page B22. Page B23 included " Atlanta's top tables are taken", "Air service plentiful to Atlanta", and "Cowboys were an easy pick" (in a box), plus the point spreads for all past Super Bowl games. The last page contained match-ups: *The Cowboys' centre versus the Buffalo centre,* and the *Cowboys' Emmitt Smith versus the Bills' Thurman Thomas,* plus colour photos. There were a total of 21 major stories in the special section on Tuesday. On Wednesday, *The Dallas Morning News* ran one article on the front page, "Cowboys lineman just wants to be Lett alone" (about Leon Lett). The special section was again eight pages. Page B13 included four articles: "Cowboy cornerback talks the talk", "Head coach Jimmy Johnson gets the picture", "Photo Day is mostly flash", and "Sans prediction headache, Aikman's mind at ease".

"Fan's view", "Atlanta hotel manager compares city to Dallas", "Magic required to get into this party" (by a *Morning News* society writer), "Long says his Raiders match Dallas well" about L.A. Raider Howie Long, and "When members of the media gather, can inane questions be far behind?" were on page B14.

"Oddsmakers expect 100 million wagers", a box headlined "Do You Have a Gambling Problem?", and (Martin Luther) "King home anchors large historic district" appeared on page B15. Two major articles appeared on page B16: "Johnson's confidence is reflection of his coaching", and "Family ties can put you in a bind at Super Bowl", plus two jumps from the first section page. Page B17 was more than 75% advertising, but two small articles were run on that page: "Smith shines only because Newton doesn't play defence", and "Cowboys try to get acclimated". Pages B18 and B19 were the inside pages of the section, which means *The Dallas Morning News* could design through the inside gutters. There was a Q & A column with coach Jimmy Johnson, an analysis article with owner Jerry Jones, "Inside the Locker Room", "Stopping Thomas means stopping Bills", and a complete stats box from the entire season for the Cowboys and Bills.

Page B20 was full of miscellaneous quotations and two photos, plus profiles of Cowboys players Scott Galbreith and John Jett, and Bills players Russell Copeland and Jim Kelley. Page B21 contained three articles: "In case of emergency..." (about backup players), "Haley limited but won't back off" about Cowboys' defensive end Charles Haley, and "Johnson's comments don't affect Bills". The end page of the section carried three articles: "Corner's sentence: Stop end zone exclamations" about *Alvin Harper versus Mickey Washington,* one article about the Cowboys' Tony Tolbert and the Bills' Bruce Smith. There were 24 major stories in the special section on Wednesday. The Thursday issue carried two front page articles— "'93 parade causes upset authorities" about violence in the Dallas parade after the 1993 Super Bowl win, and "Jerry Jones buys Collin tract for luxury-home development"—and colour photos of the Atlanta stadium crew readying the stadium.

The front page of the "Texas and Southwest" section carried an article about Cowboys' fans having cowboys cut into their hair and females who were having Dallas Cowboys insets in their fingernails. The special section first page carried four major stories: one article about the regular season game between the Cowboys and the Bills, which Buffalo won 13-10; a second article about the prior Super Bowl, which Dallas won 52-17; a third article headlined "Peach of an idea", about sports business in Atlanta, and "Under (assistant coach Butch) Davis, Cowboys defence 'gets after people".'

The second page of the Thursday section contained articles about former Atlanta coach Jerry Glanville; one headlined "Hey, maybe opposites do attract" about one couple, she for the Cowboys, he for the Bills; "Mouthy ex-coach getting paid to talk" about an ex-Bills coach; and "In event of Super blowout, Enberg, Trumpy ready to fill in the blanks". The next page contained two major articles: "Message pad", about seat cushions with the GTE emblem on them; and " NFL cities compete in good taste".

The next page (page B22) contained a column by Frank Luksa; an opinion piece by NFL quarterback Babe Laufenberg; short quotations from Edwin Pope of the *Miami Herald,* Vic Ziegel of the *New York Daily News,* Art Thiel of the *Seattle Post-Intelligencer,* and Ron Rapoport of the *Los Angeles Daily News;* and one article, "Bills don't qualify as lovable losers". Page B23 was more than 75% advertisements, but did contain one article, " Jimmy Johnson's staff a laboratory for future NFL head coaches". Page B24 contained four articles: "Apple spot at core of Super ads", "Taking it all in stride" (about Emmitt Smith), "Navigating city without car", and "Cowboys star in Atlanta's late show". (Page B25 was an advertising page.)

Page B26 contained three articles—"Life on the dark side of the boom" (about players who didn't perform well in the last Super Bowl), "Thomas' temperature rises under media glare", and "Dallas' chance to land Super Bowl remains slim"-plus two stories jumped from the first page of the special section. Page B27 was a page of miscellaneous quotations, briefs, and photos. Page B28 also matched the last page of the previous day's sections: match-ups between Darren Woodson and Pete Metzelaars and Kevin Williams versus Russell Copeland. There were 24 major articles in the special section on Thursday.

On Friday, the front page of *The Dallas Morning News* carried one article, "Scalpers' heaven". The first page of the special section (Section 14) carried only one article—"Dynasty in the Making"—under a colour photo of a Cowboys kickoff, but the section itself was 16 pages. Page H2 carried the Fan's Views column, and two society-related stories, "Ice sculptures hot items for Super parties", and "Fear not: Security chief Rathburn is aseer". There was also "Coke's new formula: Cable programming instead of commercials", plus one article about Atlanta, "Atlanta develops habit of drawing big events". (H3 was an advertising page.)

Page H4 contained columns by Blackie Sherrod and Frank Luksa, plus "Nate's World", a diary by Cowboy player Nate Newton. Page H5 was almost all ads, except for one article "Handyman finally will get Sunday Cowboy fix", about a Tim Allen-type TV handyman. Page H6 was a Q & A with Atlanta native Billy Payne, credited with bringing the Olympics to Atlanta. Page H7 was a full-page electronics chain ad. Page H8 contained opinion pieces by NFL coaches Dave Wannstedt and Wade Phillips, plus ads. Page H9 was a lumberyard chain ad. Page H10 contained brief profiles of Cowboy players Daryl Johnston and John Gesek, Bills players Henry Jones and Steve Christie, plus briefs and ads. Page H11 and H12 were full-page advertisements. The top third of page H13 was about the halftime entertainment scheduled for the Super Bowl, and page 14 was the jump-page from page 1. Pages H14 and H15 contained 75% ads. Page H15 held one story ("Cowboys have ingredients to be among NFL's all-time best") and Page H16 was a full-page ad. There were a total of 17 major stories in the special section on Friday.

Saturday's front page contained two Super Bowl-related stories: "Buffalo's a city with a complex", and "Mexican fans are travelling to game, planning parties". The special section (section B) was 12 pages; page B1 contained three stories plus a box. The three stories were " Aikman keeps fortunes in perspective" (he had signed a contract with Dallas for 8 years for $50 million), "Jones is confident Cowboys can prosper under salary cap", and "Bills still Buffaloed by Super Circus: Bet Cowboys" by columnist Randy Galloway. The box on the page was a list of Cowboy players who were "keepers" for the next season.

Page B2 contained the Fan's View feature, two society-type articles and a miscellaneous column about people in the NFL and their plans for the Super Bowl, and one column about players in (or not in) the NFL Hall of Fame.

Page B3 contained two articles—work still to be done at the Super Bowl site and a "think" article: "Some media may protest flying of Confederate flag" (in Georgia).

Page B4 contained three major articles on who would officiate at the Super Bowl (plus a box showing where the officials are on the field), the sounds of music in Atlanta bars and lounges, and the commercials expected to be shown during the Super Bowl.

Page B5 contained two articles, one about NFL commissioner Paul Tagliabue and another about whether Cowboy Bill Bates would retire (no), plus a three-quarter-page sporting goods store chain ad.

Page B6 contained three major articles: "Cowboys tackle on guard for weight challenge", about the Cowboys defence, and profiles of Thomas Everett and Henry Jones.

Page B7 contained two articles, one about Super Bowl parties and one about Dallas-area Bills fans.

Page B8 contained two major articles, "Fans gaining appreciation for underdog Bills, players say" and " Aikman to skip Pro Bowl", plus jumps from page 1 of the section.

Page B9 contained briefs and statistics, plus about one-third page of ads.

Page B10 was all statistics.

Page B11 contained three major stories: "Boom towns" about how the Dallas and Buffalo economies rise when the teams get to the Super Bowl; "On the surface, Georgia Dome field not a major factor" with a graphic of the Georgia Dome, and "Player security at a premium after recent attacks on athletes".

Page B12 contained columns by Frank Luksa, Babe Laufenberg, and Edwin Pope of *The Miami Herald*, plus a colour cartoon of Jimmy Johnson. On Saturday, there were 28 major articles in the special section. On Sunday, Super Bowl day, *The Dallas Morning News* carried two major stories on page 1, plus a colour photo at the fold. The articles were headlined "Super Bowl carries lore of the rings" and "Profit-driven Jones builds fiscal champs". The rings reference was to Super Bowl rings given to the winning team.

The special section (section B) was 16 pages, with three stories on the first page: "Date with Destiny: Cowboys look to join elite group of repeat champs", "Threepiece outfit" (about Aikman, Irvin, and Smith), and "All things considered, Cowboys will beat Bills".

Page B2 contained the Fan's Views column, two society-type articles, and two Super Bowl media articles.

Page B3 contained one article that occupied the top third of the page: "Artificial turf gives groundskeepers a new set of worries".

Page B4 contained opinion articles by Jerry Sullivan from Buffalo ("History likely will judge Levy too much too harshly"), Dave Wannstedt, and Wade Phillips; one piece by Edwin Pope of *The Miami Herald*, and the jump of one page 1 story.

Page B5 was 75% ads, but it did contain one article ("Nate Newton's Diary") and a short piece indicating that coach Jimmy Johnson might consider offers from other NFL clubs.

Page B6 was all statistics.

Page B7 was the jump page for the "Cowboys can join elite by beating Bills" story. It also had a graphic on the top third of the page: "When the Cowboys have the Ball" and

"When the Bills have the ball".

Page B8was the jump page for the "Trio" story, and also contained two major articles: "Official business", about NFL referees and "Cowboys confidence not a sign of arrogance". Page B9 contained 75% ads and one article ("Potent mixture") about offensive coach Norv Turner.

Page B10 contained three articles: "One goal for Buffalo linebackers: Catch 22" (meaning catch number 22—Emmitt Smith), and two articles under one head ("Stand and Deliver"), profiles of quarterbacks Troy Aikman and Jim Kelley.

Page B11 contained ads and one small article "Sanders gives charities 'Prime Time' week", about Deion Sanders.

Page B12 was statistics and predictions by celebrities.

Page B13 contained ads and one article: "Frito-Lay entertains clients at Super Bowl" (Frito-Lay is headquartered in the Dallas area).

Page B14 had one article ("To Levy's credit, Bills come to coach's defence") plus three quarters of a page of statistics.

Page B15 was a "house ad" by *The Dallas Morning News,* with a guest cartoon by Tom Toles of *The Buffalo News*. Readers of *The Buffalo News* saw a cartoon by *Dallas Morning News* cartoonist Bill DeOre.

Page B16 contained a colour photo feature: "How the Cowboys move 6,000 pounds of equipment to the Super Bowl".

There were 26 major articles in the special section for Sunday, and a total of 140 from Tuesday through Sunday. 140 articles! The reason why *The Dallas Morning News* published those special sections day after day is obvious: *The Dallas Morning News* is not only the "home paper" for the Cowboys, the event is broadcast worldwide and if *The Dallas Morning News* didn't make the effort to cover the Cowboys with such special sections, readers (and advertisers) would turn elsewhere. *The Dallas Morning News* could not afford the loss of readers or the loss of advertisers.

CHAPTER

9

Sports Feature

FEATURE STORY

A feature story (also known as a feature article) is an article in a newspaper, a magazine, or a news website that is not meant to report breaking news, but to take an in-depth look at a subject. While there are no precise guidelines on the differentiation between features and news stories, features are often significantly longer than news articles, are more likely to be written from a personal perspective, and unlike news stories do not always deal with the events of the immediate past.

Features are generally written in a different fashion from news stories, sometimes taking several paragraphs to arrive at the main story while trying to engage the reader and keep them reading by employing narrative hooks. Feature stories often delve deeper into their subjects, expanding on the details rather than trying to concentrate on a few important key points. The writing style of the articles can be more colourful and employ a more complex narrative structure, sometimes resembling the style of a nonfiction book more than a news report. As the print media faces ever stiffer competition from other sources of news, feature stories are becoming more common as they can be more engaging to read. At many newspapers, news stories are sometimes written in "feature style," adopting some of the conventions of feature writing while still covering breaking events. Wire services such as the Associated Press, which previously made a point of distributing only news, now also include feature stories.

The Pulitzer Prize for Feature Writing is awarded annually for a distinguished example of feature writing in an American newspaper or magazine, giving prime consideration to high literary quality and originality. Feature writers have the time and space to develop a topic in more depth than news writers do. And their subjects are usually much less urgent—they could normally be delayed a day or week without serious difficulty. In fact, many feature subjects (travel to a foreign land, a conversation with a famous person, *etc.*) are not really "news" at all. And if they concern serious subjects, they are usually of a background nature rather than a report of breaking news.

This leads to a very different style of writing from news writing. Feature stories, like those found in the *Outlook* section of the *Bangkok Post* on weekdays and Friday's *Real Time Magazine*, tend to have a more traditional organization than those found in the news section. They usually have a multi-paragraph introduction, a body containing two or more sections and a conclusion. But feature writers have considerable freedom of expression and their stories are far more varied in style than news stories. While news stories tend to maintain a consistent level of difficulty, feature stories can exhibit a huge range in difficulty and sophistication. Students are often attracted to features because of their entertaining subject matter and the colourful pictures that accompany them. But many students are quickly frustrated when the stories themselves seem far more difficult than news stories. In some cases, their perceptions are correct, but in many others it is more a case of inexperience.

The story's difficulty may be confined to the introduction where the writer attempts to attract readers with clever techniques that may go over the head of non-native speakers. Or, inexperienced readers may not realise that a long story may actually be organized into a series of relatively easy-to-read shorter sections. And they may fail to take advantage of the many aids which accompany a story (blurbs, picture captions, headings) and provide clues to its main focus. All are fruitful areas for teacher intervention.

Introducing Feature Stories

1. Compare one or more feature stories with a news story. Help your students see how much faster you catch the main ideas in the news story. They should see that the main idea in a feature story may be delayed for several paragraphs as the writer tries to attract the reader's attention. And note also how the feature story generally becomes much easier to read once the writer begins developing the main topic.

   It is also useful to consider the subject matter of your feature story. Is the subject "news"? Is it necessary to publish the story today or could it be delayed? Could the news story be delayed?
2. We try to point out that feature writers spend a great deal of time and effort collecting and organizing their information. Many feature writers work on a freelance basis and they *must* be interesting to sell their stories. Have your students skim and scan feature stories to determine their organizations and plan their reading strategies.

3. It may be necessary to give special help with introductions. If possible, try techniques which help students "discover" the meaning by themselves, but at times it may be necessary to explain them directly.
4. Make sure students know how to take advantage of layout aids such as *blurbs* (key sentences extracted from the story and set in large type), pictures and their captions, and any headings the story may contain. This should be an important part of any exercises aimed at finding a story's organization.

   Features are not meant to deliver the news firsthand. They do contain elements of news, but their main function is to humanize, to add colour, to educate, to entertain, to illuminate. They often recap major news that was reported in a previous news cycle. Features often:

- Profile people who make the news
- Explain events that move or shape the news
- Analyze what is happening in the world, nation or community
- Teach an audience how to do something
- Suggest better ways to live
- Examine trends
- Entertain.

Hard News and Soft News

A news story can be hard, chronicling as concisely as possible the who, what, where, when, why and how of an event. Or it can be soft, standing back to examine the people, places and things that shape the world, nation or community. Hard news events—such as the death of a famous public figure or the plans of city council to raise taxes—affect many people, and the primary job of the media is to report them as they happen. Soft news, such as the widespread popularity of tattooing among athletes or the resurgence of interest in perennial gardening, is also reported by the media. Feature stories are often written on these soft news events.

There is no firm line between a news story and a feature, particularly in contemporary media when many news stories are "featurized." For instance, the results of an Olympic competition may be hard news: "Canadian diver Anne Montmigny claimed her second medal in synchronized diving today." A featurized story might begin: "As a girl jumping off a log into the stream running behind her house, Anne Montmigny never dreamed she would leap into the spotlight of Olympic diving competition." One approach emphasizes the facts of the event, while the feature displaces the facts to accommodate the human interest of the story. Most news broadcasts or publications combine the two to reach a wider audience.

Today's media use many factors to determine what events they will report, including:

- Timeliness
- Proximity
- Consequence
- The perceived interest of the audience
- Competition
- Editorial goals
- And the influence of advertisers.

All these factors put pressure on the media to give their audiences both news and features. In a version of featurizing, pressure from advertisers or lobbyists often result in writing that appears at first blush to be news when it is, in fact, promotion for a product, idea, or policy. When a hard news story breaks—for example, the sinking of a ferry in the Greek islands—it should be reported with a hard news lead. Soft leads and stories are more appropriate when a major news event is not being reported for the first time: a profile of the Canadian couple who had their vacation cut short when the Greek ferry struck a reef and sunk while the crew was watching television. Some editors dispute the emphasis on soft writing and refer to it as jell-o journalism.

Feature writing can stand alone, or it can be a sidebar to the main story, the mainbar. A sidebar runs next to the main story or elsewhere in the same edition, providing an audience with additional information on the same topic.

Types of Features

Personality Profiles: A personality profile is written to bring an audience closer to a person in or out of the news. Interviews and observations, as well as creative writing, are used to paint a vivid picture of the person. The CBC's recent profile of Pierre Elliot Trudeau is a classic example of the genre and makes use of archival film footage, interviews, testimonials, and fair degree of editorializing by the voice-over commentary.

Human Interest Stories: A human interest story is written to show a subject's oddity or its practical, emotional, or entertainment value.

Trend Stories: A trend story examines people, things or organizations that are having an impact on society. Trend stories are popular because people are excited to read or hear about the latest fads.

In-depth Stories: Through extensive research and interviews, in-depth stories provide a detailed account well beyond a basic news story or feature.

Backgrounders: A backgrounder—also called an analysis piec—adds meaning to current issues in the news by explaining them further. These articles bring an audience up-to-date, explaining how this country, this organization, this person happens to be where it is now.

Writing and Organizing Feature Stories

Feature writers seldom use the inverted-pyramid form. Instead, they may write a chronology that builds to a climax at the end, a narrative, a first-person article about one of their own experiences or a combination of these. Their stories are held together by a thread, and they often end where the lead started, with a single person or event. Here are the steps typically followed in organizing a feature story:

Choose the theme: The theme is similar to the thesis of a scholarly paper and provides unity and coherence to the piece. It should not be too broad or too narrow. Several factors come into play when choosing a theme: Has the story been done before? Is the story of interest to the audience? Does the story have holding power (emotional appeal)? What makes the story worthy of being reported? The theme answers the question, "So what?"

Write a Lead that Invites an Audience into the Story: A summary may not be the best lead for a feature. A lead block of one or two paragraphs often begins a feature. Rather than put the news elements of the story in the lead, the feature writer uses the first two or three paragraphs to set a mood, to arouse readers, to invite them inside. Then the news peg or the significance of the story is provided in the third or fourth paragraph, the nut graph. Because it explains the reason the story is being written, the nut graph—also called the "so what" graph—is a vital paragraph in every feature. The nut graph should be high in the story. Do not make readers wait until the 10th or 11th paragraph before telling them what the story is about. The body provides vital information while it educates, entertains, and emotionally ties an audience to the subject. The ending will wrap up the story and come back to the lead, often with a quotation or a surprising climax. Important components of the body of a feature story are background information, the thread of the story, transition, dialogue, and voice.

Provide Vital Background Information: If appropriate, a paragraph or two of background should be placed high in the story to bring the audience up to date.

Write Clear, Concise Sentences: Sprinkle direct quotations, observations and additional background throughout the story. Paragraphs can be written chronologically or in order of importance.

Use a Thread: Connect the beginning, body and conclusion of the story. Because a feature generally runs longer than a news story, it is effective to weave a thread throughout the story, which connects the lead to the body and to the conclusion. This thread can be a single person, an event or a thing, and it usually highlights the theme.

Use Transition: Connect paragraphs with transitional words, paraphrases, and direct quotations. Transition is particularly important in a long feature examining several people or events because it is the tool writers use to move subtly from one person or topic to the next. Transition keeps readers from being jarred by the writing.

Use Dialogue when Possible: Feature writers, like fiction writers, often use dialogue to keep a story moving. Of course, feature writers cannot make up dialogue; they listen for it during the reporting process. Good dialogue is like good observation in a story; it gives readers strong mental images and keeps them attached to the writing and to the story's key players.

Establish a Voice: Another key element that holds a feature together is voice, the "signature" or personal style of each writer. Voice is the personality of the writer and can be used to inject colour, tone, and subtle emotional commentary into the story. Voice should be used subtly (unless you're able to make a fetish of it like Hunter S. Thompson!). The blatant intrusion of a distinctive voice into news writing has been called gonzo journalism—an irresponsible, if entertaining, trend in contemporary writing according to traditionalists.

Conclude with a Quotation or Another Part of the Thread: A feature can trail off like a news story or it can be concluded with a climax. Often, a feature ends where the lead started, with a single person or event. A good writer can often develop a good feature from a news event. Many good features can be developed from these areas, including trends in sports, or other topics in sports. An example of a trend in sports might be the latest in exercise techniques. A topic story might be baseball card trading. Equally important is the significance of human events. How can this be applied?

On October 30, 1993, Wisconsin defeated Michigan 13-10 at Madison. At game's end, hundreds of Badger fans rushed the field; many were crushed against chain link fences. By the thinnest margin, no one was killed. Dozens were rushed to area hospitals. Here is Pete Dougherty's story, filed on the *Gannett News* wire. This is how the news story appeared the next day, in *The Houston Post*.

75 injured in Badger stampede

By Pete Dougherty

Gannett News Service

MADISON, Wis.: Jo Ellen Amato was lucky enough to hop the fence just before things got really bad.

The 18-year-old was at the front of a mob of students trying to rush onto the field Saturday to celebrate after Wisconsin had defeated Michigan 13-10 at Camp Randall Stadium. Hundreds of Wisconsin students were about to get wedged into the fence and railings designed to keep fans from the football players. She barely escaped onto the field before the mass squeezed against the chain-link fence. The fence bent and swayed and part eventually broke, but not until nearly squeezing the life out of several young people, their faces becoming blue, or even worse, ashen.

"I sat and watched people get crushed and there was nothing I could do," Amato said. University of Wisconsin security chief Susan Riseling said about 75 people were injured when approximately 12,000 spectators scrambled out of five student sections. Reports from the city's three hospitals about three hours later showed 64 people were examined or treated. Seven victims were considered in critical condition. The inclined tunnel that leads the players in and out of Camp Randall has metal railings in cement that don't move. The

10-foot wide track between the the stands and the field was temporarily blocked; the swinging gates, meant to keep the fans from the players, were fastened back so the teams could leave. But that's right where the Wisconsin students sit, and they wanted on the field to celebrate the Badgers' big victory. The ones who made it were fine, and there were hundreds of them, hugging players and each other, reveling in the win. The ones who didn't, the couple hundred tucked in the corners around the tunnel, were in trouble. They got wedged between the fence, the railings, and the thousands of people pushing towards the field. "I said, 'Open the gate, let them out—they're going to die,'" Amato said. "(The guard) said, 'I can't, there's football players coming.' I said, 'Would you rather have people die?'"

By the time the gate was opened, a couple minutes later, it was too late for many. Many in the first five or 10 rows were too wedged and tangled to move. "They were trampled on top of each other and bent over the stands," said lineman Joe Panos, who helped clear the pile. "I thought they were gone." "One girl just about died in his arms," teammate Yusef Burgess said. "A lot of people were seeing things they've never seen before. Seeing people's faces turn blue, that's not a sight you want to remember." How can a feature story be developed from this news story? By *understanding the significance of human events*.

By November 2, Ed Sherman of the *Chicago Tribune* completed a follow-up story on that disaster. He focused on Michael Brin, a sophomore walk-on quarterback player for the Badgers. Brin was so far down the Wisconsin depth chart "he didn't even have his own number."

Sherman's story was published in the *Houston Chronicle* under the headline:

No. 3 in the programme and No. 1 in her heart

—By Ed Sherman, *Chicago Tribune*

MADISON, Wis.—Michael Brin was the unlikeliest of heroes Saturday.

Brin, a wide receiver from Highland Park, Ill., is so far down on Wisconsin's depth chart that last week's programme listed him as a quarterback. A sophomore walk-on, Brin doesn't even have his own number. Most Badgers fans know No. 3 as starting cornerback Kenny Gales. Brin, though, also wears No. 3, and that was the only number that mattered to Aimee Jansen. Jansen found herself pinned up against a fence Saturday in the terrifying aftermath of Wisconsin's game with Michigan. She was caught in the crush of fans who tried to storm the field, and it got to the point where she couldn't breathe.

Then she saw "a No. 3" in a Badgers uniform who pulled her by the pant leg and hoisted her over the fence to safety. Monday, Jansen had to find No. 3. "I just wanted to say thank you, thank you very much," said Jansen, a sophomore from Antigo, Wis. "He saved my life." Brin didn't get into one play Saturday in Wisconsin's 13-10 victory over Michigan, but no Badger shined more. Brin's quick actions also are being credited with helping revive two other students who stopped breathing, one of whom he gave mouth-to-mouth resuscitation.

On Monday Brin suddenly finding himself in the spotlight, being called a hero. "The only reason why they're saying I'm a hero is because I was wearing pads. I don't feel like a hero;" Brin said. "I feel like a guy who did the normal thing and reacted when he saw trouble." Authorities are crediting the actions of Brin and others with helping to avert a full-blown tragedy. An estimated 69 people were injured when 12,000 Wisconsin students cascaded from the stands towards the field. Seven people initially were listed in critical condition, but as of Monday evening, eight people remained hospitalized, five in good condition and three in fair. Those figures are remarkable considering what the scene looked like Monday. The northeast corner of Camp Randall Stadium was strewn with twisted pieces of fence and railings. The weight of the people was enough to lift 6-inch bolts out of the concrete. Witnesses described students being buried as much as 10 people deep. The injuries included broken limbs and extreme loss of oxygen.

"We're lucky, because it could have been much worse," Wisconsin Chancellor David Ward said. "We're fortunate we had so many people step up and help out." Brin said he normally is one of the first players in the locker room, but he lingered on the field. As he walked towards the tunnel, he noticed a huge surge. "That's when I saw the girl," Brin said. "She was folded over a fence." Brin pulled out Jansen, and then he noticed a couple of girls weren't breathing. He quickly went over to one of them and started to apply mouth-to-mouth. He did it only briefly, "but it got her breathing." Brin, a premed student, isn't certified in cardiopulmonary resuscitation, but he applied the lessons he learned in a high school health class. As for the other girl, he helped move her over to a bench and assisted in stabilizing her. "It was a shock," Brin said. "Nobody expected it. You just acted on instinct."

One of the women who stopped breathing also tried to get in touch with Brin Monday. Brin wasn't sure of her name, but the memory of her face on Saturday hadn't left him. He desperately wanted to see the woman again. "When I saw her, she was blue in the face," Brin said. "I have to see her cheeks all rosy red. I have to see it for myself." Brin said he spent a depressing Saturday night, but his spirits brightened Sunday when he learned all the injured people were improving. "It's a great feeling knowing a girl might be breathing because of me," he said.

He isn't likely to get close to the field for Saturday's game against Ohio State. He has been in only one play all season. However, Brin's football skills didn't matter Saturday. He always will be remembered for what he did after the game. "I haven't changed," Brin said. "I'm not a hero. I'm just Mike Brin."

CHAPTER 10

Investigative Sports Article

There are only a dozen or so major newspapers throughout the United States that have reporters working on special projects in sports. Some of the papers that have special projects people are *The Los Angeles Times; The Des Moines Register*; the Newhouse newspapers in Syracuse, NY, which have been tracking problems in the athletic programmes at Syracuse University; the *Houston Chronicle;* and papers in Pittsburgh and Phoenix. Doug Bedell of *The Dallas Morning News* is such a reporter. Bedell is a native of Houston, Texas. He attended Northwestern University, in Evanston, Illinois, for 4½12 years as a pre-med major, then decided to "do anything different." He transferred to Baylor University, in Waco, Texas and graduated in journalism.

He was then hired by *The Beaumont, Texas Enterprise* as Assistant State Editor, then moved into bureau work in Lake Charles, Louisiana, then Port Arthur and Orange, Texas. In the mid-1970s, he moved to *The Dallas Times Herald* as a general assignments reporter. From 1980 to 1984, he worked for *The Louisville Courier Journal* as a court system reporter.

He returned to Texas in 1984 as a general assignments reporter for *The Dallas Morning News*. In 1986, he was assigned special projects in sports, where he does nontraditional sports stories, which have included steroid use, rules infractions, and other similar stories. His assignments came directly from the recent status of the Southwest Conference (SWC), which was then Texas, Texas A & M, Texas Tech, Baylor, Arkansas, Rice Houston, Southern Methodist, and Texas Christian University. The SWC is now defunct: Texas, Texas A & M, Texas Tech, and Baylor have joined the Big Eight; TCU, SMU, and Rice have joined the Western Athletic Conference. As this is written the University of Houston has not yet affiliated with any other league.

Because of major football violations, Southern Methodist University received the NCAA "death penalty" (no football for 2 years) and almost all of the other SWC conference schools received NCAA warnings or probation in the recent past for sports rules violations. Because *The Dallas Morning News* circulates into Oklahoma, it has also covered violations of the athletic programmes at the University of Oklahoma. During 1994, *The Dallas Morning News* published a series of articles about excesses in the athletic programmes at Texas A & M University, in College Station, Texas. Reporter Olive Talley and others at *The Dallas Morning News* also contributed to this series.

"These stories encompassed, in part, how Texas A & M behaved when they had a 'windfall' of money from football victories. "We ended up with documents a foot high—literally several thousands of pages," Bedell said (personal communication, June 1, 1994). "We received them from several avenues: we got purchase records, vouchers and travel documents from the university; some (records) we received through Open Records Acts (requests). We also sued Texas A & M University and finally obtained an out-of-court settlement. Their response regarding documents has improved, although there has been some foot-dragging. "We at least have an 'improved dialogue' with them about records."

Bedell worked at least 2 weeks on a story about how Texas A & M University squandered thousands and thousands of dollars for gifts, liquor, and other items given to players and university officials going to four recent postseason football bowls. The amount? Over $440,000 in 4 years. In Bedell's lead, he writes, "Expenditures on these items are roughly enough to cover the annual scholarships for all 163 students in the women's athletic programme, which consistently operates at a loss" (Bedell, 1994, p. 1). "We compared their figures with figures from other schools. We put these (the A & M figures) into a database and used a (computer) spreadsheet programme to see what we had.

"It's not uncommon for a university to behave like this. Universities use athletic championships as justification to reward those in all dimensions of the programmes-athletes and staff alike. "The public doesn't understand—and I didn't understand—the allowances given to athletes. The (automobile) mileage—the very generous mileage—given to each athlete as if they were individually driving to a bowl game. It gives you the impression it's just a hemorrhage of greenbacks at that time. "Most sports departments are reticent to run these stories. But these times make it necessary to understand the finances of such programmes. The financial changes going on are baffling unless you know what's behind the numbers. "Many members of the public don't want to hear such things about sports programmes. But it's mandatory that we tell our public what we understand about (sports) economic issues."

Later Texas A & M University president William Mobley called *The Dallas Morning News* to complain about (or correct) a small item about alcohol policy; that other funds—from

Texas A & M alumni and others—were used for liquor purchases. But Bedell said that documents obtained from Texas A & M University did not reveal that and the documents they supplied were "all we had to work on" (personal communication, June 1, 1994). Here then, is Doug Bedell's article, begun on "The Dallas Morning News" front page on Sunday, May 1, 1994. Note: Ross Margraves, Jr., cited towards the end of Bedell's article, resigned as a member of the Texas A & M Board of Regents.

> A&M bowl funds go to purchase gifts Athletic director says policy reflects traditional reward for success.—By Doug Bedell, *Staff Writer of The Dallas Morning News*

COLLEGE STATION— Texas A&M University, whose football success has led it to five bowl appearances since 1990, has spent more than $440,000 during that period on complimentary tickets, souvenirs and merchandise for regents, administrators and prominent boosters. The university's administration spent $161,955 on complimentary tickets and more than $260,000 on extra watches and other items given away, according to the school's financial records. For the 1993 Cotton Bowl, A&M hosted a banquet that cost $44,453, records show. While bowl sponsors provide football players with complimentary watches, warmups and other memorabilia, the university routinely has purchased the same items for its dignitaries.

Expenditures on those items are roughly enough to cover the annual scholarships for all 163 students in the women's athletic programme, which consistently operates at a loss. A&M's financial records show that the bowl appearances grossed the university more than $10.7 million. Of that amount, the school netted about $1 million after deducting travel and hotel expenses, paying shares to Southwest Conference teams and covering other incidental expenses, including the merchandise and complimentary tickets and hotel expenses for VIPs. Athletic director Wally Groff said bowl appearances are considered rewards for successful seasons, not for-profit enterprises. "Absolutely," Mr. Groff said. "We view it that way, and that's why our policies are prepared the way they are." Texas A&M athletics, meanwhile, are facing NCAA sanctions that will lop off an estimated $2 million in bowl and television revenue. Similar practices of university-paid souvenirs for boosters, administrators and regents have sparked criticism at schools from the University of Texas to the University of Nebraska and University of Virginia. Beyond the bowl expenditures, A&M athletic department documents also reveal several areas that have drawn the attention of the Texas Rangers and FBI in their ongoing inquiry into the conduct of A&M officials:

Improper athletic department purchases of alcohol may have been illegally disguised on vouchers as food, ice and soft drinks. Internal university auditors identified the practice as a major athletic trouble spot.

- The athletic department has spent more than $21,000 to send board of regents chairmen and their wives to attend football banquets in New York City.

Source of Controversy

Traditionally, bowl receipts have been liberally lavished on collegiate athletic entourages. After the University of Texas last attended a Cotton Bowl in 1991, it wound up netting about $162,000 out of its initial receipt of $3 million. More than $80,000 was spent on purchases of jewelry and other items distributed among administrators and boosters, said Ed Goble, UT's assistant athletic director for business affairs. "Texas, I think, has a philosophy regarding the Cotton Bowl," said Mr. Goble. "It is regarded not so much as a money-making proposition, but as a reward."

Criticism of bowl spending practices has cropped up throughout the country. More than 70 percent of major college athletic departments now record deficit budgets. And athletic departments have come under increasing pressure to spend more for women's sports scholarships and development. At the 1992 Orange Bowl, for example, University of Nebraska administrators outspent their $1 million allotment by more than $100,000. The next year, the administration cut back the size of the school's entourage, scaled down the length of hotel stays paid for by the university and banned the practice of giving nonathletic administrators souvenir rings, watches or other gifts. After the 1990 season, University of Virginia officials were criticized over their decision to spend more than one-third of the school's nearly $2 million Sugar Bowl allotment on an entourage of 457 officials and guests.

Player 'awards'

Texas A&M's spending practices for players appear to adhere to a strict $300 NCAA cap on the value of bowl "awards." At the 1993 Cotton Bowl, players received $293 in merchandise—a $109 watch, $40 plaque, $45 camera and $99 warm-up suit. Under the school's interpretation of regulations, players also received a minimum of $93 in gas mileage money—figured as if each player had driven to the Cotton Bowl from College Station or his hometown—even if he were from Dallas. More cash ($100) was handed out for "unitemized expenses." A total of $416 went to each player as a food allowance. Gifts for the 95 scholarship athletes are often given to the school by bowl sponsors. A&M regulations, however, permit the athletic director to purchase additional items from bowl receipts.

At the 1990 Holiday Bowl in San Diego, for example, A&M officials ordered 155 watches for $15,190, 207 sweat suits for $11,832, 220 shaving kits for $3,827 and 166 plaques for $5,740—all beyond the complimentary gifts given to players. At the 1992 Cotton Bowl, the Aggies brought 170 extra men's watches for $21,250 and 45 extra women's watches for $5,625. At this year's Cotton Bowl, awards for football players and VIPs totaled $85,813, including extra golf shirts, Sony Walkman units, plaques, ladies and men's watches and warm-ups.

Traditional Spending

Mr. Groff, A&M's athletic director, said such spending is traditional. The gifts go to university administrators, some booster club officials and staff, and selected vendors. A list of recipients is drawn up by the athletic director, head coach and the associate athletic director for business, Mr. Groff said. "It's a difficult decision to know where you draw the line," said Mr. Groff, who was associate athletic director for business until his appointment to head the department. "It's pretty much ultimately the athletic director's decision." Those honored with awards are "university-oriented," including members of the faculty athletic council, regents, top university administrators, the president and staff members of the 12th Man Foundation and, up until this year, car dealers who donated autos for athletic department use.

"It's people that basically work with the football programme and travel to the football games," Mr. Groff said. For the 1990 Holiday Bowl, 1992 Disneyland Pigskin Classic and the school's past three Cotton Bowls, the A&M athletic department spent $172,833 on complimentary tickets that were distributed among faculty, administration officials, regents and prominent boosters. Mr. Groff said those tickets were handed out just like the awards. And, he added, so were free admission gifts to entertainment events held in conjunction with bowl appearances. Party expenses are also deducted from the bottom line. This year A&M spent $37,400 for more than 600 extra admission tickets for entertainment events held from Dec. 26 through New Year's Day.

At the 1990 Holiday Bowl, A&M spent $4,261 on a hosted bar at the instructions of then-President William Mobley. The school also paid a total of $225 in hotel-room bars for A&M vice president Robert Smith, and regents Wayne Showers, Raul Fernandez, Doug DeCluitt, Ross Margraves Jr., John Mobley and Royce Wisenbaker. A year later, the 72nd Legislature expressly banned alcohol purchases with public money. Accountants in an internal audit for the period from Sept. 1, 1991, through March 31, 1992, included a "major finding" that alcohol purchases are not permitted under administrative policies and prohibited by state law when using athletic department funds.

Alcohol Purchases

Mr. Groff said that within the past three weeks, FBI agents and Texas Rangers investigators have questioned him concerning athletic department purchases of alcohol. In February, a Brazos County grand jury indicted two A&M regents' staffers on felony charges of altering expense records to cover up purchases of alcohol for the board of regents. A prosecutor has said more indictments are likely. Current university policy allows open purchase of alcohol with gift money only. More than 33 departments and the board of regents' office spent more than $47,000 over the past six years to purchase items from a College Station liquor store owned by J.J. Ruffino, according to the A&M controller's office. Athletic department records show a similar pattern.

Invoices and vouchers obtained by *The News* show $808 worth of merchandise was purchased from Ruffino Catering from 1990 to 1993. About $500 worth of invoices were paid after internal university auditors cited the athletic department for improperly using athletic funds for alcohol. Mr. Groff said some of the vouchers were for single bottles of wine used by the athletic dormitory chef. Others, he said, were alcoholic beverages for parties and other social functions. "The only way you got anything paid for was to do it that way," Mr. Groff said. Asked how athletic accountants learned to submit the misleading vouchers, Mr. Groff replied, "Just like everybody else, I guess. We probably had it sent back. I don't remember exactly. It's been so long ago."

Mr. Groff said the federal and state investigators interviewed him concerning about $450 worth of bills from Mr. Ruffino paid over the past two years. Since 1990, the athletic department has also spent more than $21,000 to send former board chairman William McKenzie and Ross Margraves Jr. and their wives to attend the National Football Foundation Hall of Fame banquets each December at the Waldorf Astoria in New York City. Mr. McKenzie's trips in 1990 and 1991 totaled $6,496, while Mr. Margraves' trips from 1990 through 1993 cost $14,794. Travel expense reports justified attendance by the wives "to promote public relations and represent Texas A&M University." "I think these types of events are important to our university and in this particular instance, important to the success of or athletic programme," Mr. Margraves wrote in a letter thanking athletic director Groff for the trip.

"I was pleased to see the strong A&M contingent that was in attendance. I know it did not go by you unnoticed that all of the other major universities in America had delegations in attendance, including the University of Texas and Rice from our own conference." The Margraves' expenses for this past year's five-night trip included a $605 dinner at the Tribeca Grill for six couples, including Mr. Groff, head football coach R.C. Slocum and Arno Krebs, a Houston lawyer who has represented the school in internal investigations of possible sports rules infractions.

Trips' Purpose

"The purpose of them going is to represent Texas A&M at the programme," Mr. Groff said. "You have parties with

ABC and ESPN. It's a public relations deal primarily, plus you meet the other schools. All of the big schools are represented." Tips and charges to hotel bars were included in expense reports submitted by both Mr. Margraves and Mr. McKenzie, although auditors have pointed out that neither category is reimbursable under state regulations. During the football season, regents, politicians and other dignitaries are invited to attend each Aggie football game. And, along with the president and chancellor's staff, the board members are given 16 seats on air charter for out-of-town games that require flying, Mr. Groff said.

During the 1992 Cotton Bowl, the athletic department picked up several days' room charges for regents Dough DeCluitt, Alison Brisco, Billy Clayton, Ross Margraves, Wayne Showers, Royce Wisenbaker, board administrator Vickie Running and their spouses. Seven regents, Ms. Running and their spouses also attended the Disneyland Pigskin Classic in Anaheim, Calif., in August 1992 at a cost of more than $2,688 in hotel accommodations and chartered air fare at a cost of $400 apiece. At the 1990 Holiday Bowl, records show, regents' rooms were stocked with liquor and costs were paid by the athletic department.

CHAPTER 11

Editorials, Opinion Articles and Columns

In the daily newspaper or monthly magazine, a sports writer or editor has the opportunity to express himself or herself on sports personalities and issues in the news. Usually the editorial, opinion piece, or column is limited only in length (the length of the newspaper column or the magazine page); the writer can usually write about whatever subjects he or she thinks appropriate. Along with the right to use the newspaper or magazine space, the writer has the responsibility to use the space wisely. Editorials and opinion pieces on sports subjects are usually indicated with a subhead labelled "Editorial" or "Commentary." Novice writers attempting to write a sports editorial or opinion piece may find the three-part format helpful. If the writer plans the article with these three key parts, the article may well be successful:

- ***Premise:*** What is the idea behind the article? If you can state the idea in one simple declarative sentence, the topic is workable (e.g., "University athletes should be paid like professional players because they bring in millions of dollars of revenue to a major university").

- *Evidence:* Prove your argument with facts, statistics, quotations, and other material.
- *Conclusion:* Wrap up your argument for your reader so there is no mistaking your conclusion.

In a column format, however, the writer has several choices of methods for presenting his or her material. How many types or styles of columns are there? In general, there are at least six types of columns. The editorial column, in which an opinion is presented with the weight of the newspaper or magazine behind the idea, in the same style as the editorial page of an average major metropolitan newspaper.

- The "my say" column, perhaps the most popular type of column and perhaps the hardest to write on a regular basis. This type of column is usually given to the staffer with the most seniority, so he or she may draw on previous experience for the material in the column. But even the most senior writer may find himself or herself eventually running out of material and ideas for the space. This is the personal opinion of the writer on a variety of sports issues often used with a mug shot of the writer.
- "Ask the expert." Some newspapers run interpretations of game rules and regulations, often prompted by questions from readers. This may well require the writer to possess a library of sports information books, major league rule books, sports almanacs, and the like.
- ***The Sports Trivia Column:*** This may also require a personal library of reference books.
- ***Readers Write-editors Respond:*** This is a dialogue column in which readers write in comments, opinions, thoughts, biases, and complaints and the editors

respond. This is the newspaper or magazine equivalent of the radio sports call-in show. Car & Driver magazine, for instance, carries on this spirited dialogue with sports car enthusiasts who write in to the magazine.

- *The "Irish stew" Column:* This is a little of everything—some opinion, some second guessing, some name dropping, some editorial material, some guest commentary and quotations, some trivia, some response to readers, some humour, and perhaps even a sports obituary on occasion. To keep a column fresh every issue, the columnist may develop an Irish stew or potpourri approach.

The following are editorial and commentary articles that are exceptional examples of this type of sports writing.

Roy S. Johnson, senior editor of Sports Illustrated, writing in Sports Illustrated for April 20, 1992, discusses the Arthur Ashe case, in the end-of-the-magazine column titled "Point After". Johnson's commentary carried the headline and subhead:

None of Our Business Arthur Ashe is a public figure, but the media had no right to make his illness a public matter.

The first telephone call came to my office in early September. Another call came two months later, just days after Magic Johnson had stood at a podium in L os Angeles and delivered the shocking news that he was infected with the AIDS virus. Both callers were credible members of the tennis community, and both had the same message:

"You know about Arthur Ashe. He's got AIDS." Maybe I should have reacted to this disturbing information strictly as a journalist. After all, I'll wave the First Amendment flag until my arm falls off. And I'll defend until my last breath the public's right to know practically everything about anyone who falls into the category of "public figure."

But now my journalistic instincts were overcome by compassion and concern. I had been well acquainted with

Ashe personally and professionally for more than a decade. Long before that, I had admired his athletic skill—and, more important, his dignity. My admiration for him had grown even stronger in recent years as I watched him fight racism, apartheid, and inequities in college athletics, and as he shared with me some of the insights and convictions that made him a respected champion of human rights throughout the world.

So that's why I said nothing. Not to the managing editor of this magazine. Not to my friends. Not even to Arthur. I could have picked up the telephone and asked him. But I didn't. I could have broached the subject during one of the many conversations we had since I received the first tip about him. But I didn't. In November, soon after Magic's announcement, Arthur and I spoke on the phone about AIDS and the backlash that Magic would surely face because of his promiscuous life-style. The questions were on the tip of my tongue: Were my sources right? And, if so, did Arthur feel any compulsion to join Magic as a spokesman in the fight against AIDS? But I didn't ask. I couldn't.

Last month Ashe was my guest at the United Negro College Fund's annual dinner in New York. Magic was one of the honorees. At one point the discussion at our table turned to Johnson's efforts to promote AIDS education and awareness, but by then I had just about put the calls about Arthur out of my mind. I had decided that if he wanted me to know about his condition, he would tell me. Otherwise, it wasn't my business. I had placed his privacy ahead of any desire to break the story in SI—and it wasn't a tough decision. Last week the editors at *USA Today* weighed the same options and decided differently. They pursued a tip similar to the one I had received, and *USA Today* tennis writer Doug Smith confronted Ashe. Though Ashe neither confirmed nor denied having AIDS, he concluded he could no longer keep his condition secret. The next day, he reluctantly went public.

Right away the role played by *USA Today* ignited a debate. (Why couldn't all this energy have been channeled towards *fighting* the disease?) While the editors of many other papers said that they, too, would have pursued—and, if they could have confirmed it, published—the story, a rising tide of voices expressed outrage that Ashe's privacy had been violated. "It's like the press has given up a touch of humanity," said Chris Evert. "It just kills his spirit." "If the man dies one day earlier because of [stress caused by] this story . . . then [it] is not worth it," said Mike Clark, reader advocate of *The Florida Times-Union*. Terming Ashe's illness "a significant news story," *USA Today* managing editor for sports Gene Policinski noted that the newspaper pursued the story as it would have had Ashe had cancer or some other life-threatening ailment. "We don't have a special zone for AIDS," he said.

Well, it's time we created one. Overwhelming public ignorance remains one of the disease's greatest allies. People with the AIDS virus often are stigmatized by those who either stubbornly refuse to accept that the disease cannot be transmitted through casual contact, or who believe that people afflicted with AIDS somehow deserve their fate. Until these misconceptions are overcome, the media should offer most AIDS sufferers the same consideration it gives rape victims, who are ordinarily not identified in news stories. Admittedly, the line that separates the news value of a public figure's medical condition from his right to privacy isn't always clearly defined. Should the public be alerted that a high-ranking government official has contracted AIDS? By all means. Do we need to know that a health-care worker has been infected? Yes. An athlete who's still active? Probably, because the state of his health is relevant to his profession. The CEO of a publicly held corporation? I guess so; his illness could have an impact on employees and shareholders.

And what if the person isn't as well respected as Ashe? Or doesn't have as good a relationship with the media? Nowadays rumours about the private lives of public figures surface almost daily, forcing reporters and editors to make all sorts of judgments about what is newsworthy. There are no hard rules, no easy answers. Undoubtedly there are thousands of AIDS sufferers who might be considered public figures but who should be allowed to combat the incurable disease without enduring the added stress of public scrutiny and, all too often, condemnation. Arthur Ashe was one of them. Sam Smith of the *Chicago Tribune* wrote a commentary about Michael Jordan and the death of his father. This piece appeared in August 1993.

Reality intrudes on Jordan's charmed world

Commentary —By Sam Smith *Chicago Tribune*

Everyone finds it out eventually. Michael Jordan did last week. The climate's not always perfect in Camelot. For Jordan, the discovery of the tragic death of his father, James Jordan, last week in South Carolina allowed life to intrude, as it inevitably does, on all royal families. And the Jordans, indeed, were our version of royalty: rich, successful, beautiful. We celebrated their triumphs and peered through the keyholes at their excesses and embarrassments. But we always cheered. One might suggest the Jordans, especially Michael, have endured more than their share of long, cloudy winters. There was the supposed Olympic snub of Isiah Thomas, Jordan's failure to attend the White House celebration with his teammates, the publishing of *The Jordan Rules*, the licensing dispute with the NBA that kept Jordan's likeness off All-Star Game T-shirts and then the reprimand from NBA commissioner David Stern for gambling with convicted drug dealer Slim Bouler.

And then there was the reluctant trip to the Olympics, where Jordan draped himself in an American flag so he wouldn't be seen wearing a rival sponsor's logo at the gold-medal ceremony. He opened the season with a court appearance at the Bouler trial during which he admitted he had been lying for a year that his payments to Bouler were a loan—not gambling payments.

Then there were accusations in a book that he had lost more than $1 million gambling and refused to pay his debt, more gambling questions when he went to Atlantic City to gamble before a key playoff game and a self-imposed boycott of the media for two weeks during the playoffs. But the truth is little had changed in the life of Michael Jordan. For it was still Camelot, with perhaps the July and August of his life merely becoming a little too hot. Jordan's fame grew only greater, as did his bank account. The Bulls won an almost unprecedented third straight NBA title, and if Jordan's smile didn't radiate as brightly as always, his star certainly did.

The life of Michael Jordan certainly was a pretty picture. But one doesn't make a picture without a negative. The unexpected death of a parent is difficult for anyone, so it is that much harder when, as in Jordan's case, his father's death was from a gunshot, the body found floating in a stream, violence marking every bit of the end. President John F. Kennedy's administration was known as Camelot in the early 1960s, perhaps our nation's last era of innocence. Someone wrote after Kennedy's assassination that we will laugh again, but we'll never be young again. Michael Jordan will laugh again, but he'll never be the same. That's because James Jordan was more than a father. He had the rarest of relationships with his son, Michael: He was a friend.

Like many boys, Jordan admired his dad, and credited him for his famous trademark, the hanging tongue, which Michael said he developed from watching his father work on the family car. Jordan was quick to credit James, as in the 1992 playoffs against the Knicks, when Michael said he went not to a teammate or a coach for advice before the pivotal Game 7, but to his father. How should he approach the game?

Aggressive, dad replied. Jordan was. James was there, speaking for Michael this year when Michael's gambling came into question and Michael wasn't talking to the media. James, instead, convened a few of his press briefings to defend his beleaguered son.

The questions, beside what happened and how, and perhaps why, figure to be answered someday. But the inevitable answers will only come after some shocks. Undoubtedly, Jordan will consider the wisdom passed onto him from his father. It was once said that the only cure for grief is action. When Michael was most troubled in recent years, James told him to play basketball, to bury his rage and doubt in his childhood and the kids' game that he rode to adulthood. For so many years, Michael Jordan was sheltered from the real world by his talent, his money, his fame and his position. He mistook annoyance for adversity.

But Michael Jordan finally plunged down that magical stalk into the real world, where pain really does hurt, and where loss leaves a well of emptiness. He'll eventually climb out, but he'll never be a boy again. Mitch Albom of the *Detroit Free Press* discusses the quarterback merry-go-round in Detroit in an opinion piece published in September 1993.

Fontes losing hearts of QBs Lions' coach alienates all three Opinion —By Mitch Albom

They don't resent each other, and they don't resent the media. They resent the coach. Let's get that straight. Andre Ware, Rodney Peete and Erik Kramer, the three quarterbacks on this odd little merry-go-round in silver and blue stretch uniforms. Point the finger at one man: Wayne Fontes.

In this way, they are no different than most American workers. They blame the boss. And, like most workers, they have to bite their tongue and keep it to themselves. Andre Ware played all day Sunday in the win over Phoenix at the Silverdome. He was not bad, but not great. He missed a lot of reads for a starting NFL quarterback, and he got away with some truly dangerous passes. And you wish he would hit more receivers in stride instead of making them jump. But he did throw a nice touchdown pass—two if you count the one that was called back—and in a couple of critical situations he looked off the first receiver, found the second and drilled it. On third down late in the game, he took a crushing hit from linebacker David Braxton—who nearly separated Ware's upper and lower intestines—and still delivered a first-down strike to Herman Moore. You mature on plays like that.

But when the game was over and the Lions had won, Fontes deliberately hedged on next week's starter, saying, "Talk to me Wednesday," then joked, "It'll give you guys something to write about."

And when Ware came in and heard that, he snarled, "What are you gonna do, have a quarterback tryout every week?" Apparently, yes. That's the way Fontes wants it. Ware would, at times, like to bite Fontes' head off, and so would Rodney Peete, the former starter, who dressed quickly in the locker room Sunday after being demoted to "third quarterback" status, which means you only play if the Serbs and the Croats shake hands.

"Are you healthy?" Peete was asked.

"I'm fine. I could have played," he said.

"What do you think will happen next?"

He rolled his eyes. "Around here? I have no idea. I have absolutely no idea." So that's two angry quarterbacks. The third, Erik Kramer, is still trying to get over the mistaken message left on his answering machine last week by William Clay Ford, the Lions' owner. Ford thought he was calling Ware when he left these words: "Andre, give me a call, I've got good news." What was that all about? Kramer, by the way, is the voice on his own machine, and believe me, he sounds nothing like Ware. Which only goes to show you how out in left field the owner is when it comes to personnel on his team. "He thought he was dialing 1-800-QUARTERBACK," Kramer said. That's kind of how it works, isn't it? This week-by-week thing might be Fontes' idea of what's best—I have stopped trying to figure out Wayne, who is a wonderfully nice man, but has this boomerang way of coaching; if you stand still long enough he'll come back to the same idea all over again—and yet, he's losing his quarterbacks. They gripe about him. They roll their eyes. All in private, of course. But the result is little confidence between the two most critical positions in the franchise, coach and quarterback. Paul Daugherty of *The Cincinnati Post*, uses the "I" form lead to begin a column about Lenny Dykstra. This piece was published early in October 1993.

Dykstra harks back to tougher era

—By Paul Daugherty

ATLANTA: I like a ballplayer whose chaw slosh stains his uniform top. This is the plain truth. There is a certain something about a man who stuffs a hamster-sized chunk of chewing tobacco into his left cheek before a game. Lenny Dykstra does this. He plays enter field for the Philadelphia Phillies. On the whole, he plays it with the sort of maniacal verve reserved for the foolish, the desperate and the guys who were majorleaguers 30 years ago. This summer, Dykstra led the National League in runs, hits and walks, while playing in 161 games. The only game Dykstra missed was No. 158. It was the game after the Phillies clinched the National League East. Dykstra was temporarily incapacitated, due to, um, extreme celebration. This is how we like our ballplayers. We have seen quite enough of players with multiple agents and players who play hard when the mood hits. We're dizzy with players carrying briefcases. Nothing good can come from a game played by men carrying briefcases.

The Phillies are not yet this way. "We are," brags relief pitcher Larry Andersen, "a bunch of degenerates." The

Phillies are baseball's version of "Boys Night Out." At a time when ballplayers are as touchable as Alpha Centauri, the Phillies are our Everymen. Or at least as close as we're going to get.

Put it this way: The Phils are millionaires. But they belch just like you do. And Dykstra, as much as anyone, is the Phillies. "We're very interesting," he says. It is 5 p.m. on Thursday. Dykstra has emerged from the Phillies' dugout for batting practice. He is in a "Not now, dude" mode with the media. But you know Dykstra is around. He marks his territory with chunks of used cud. The telling brown flotsam leads straight to his feet. "We give everybody their money's worth," he says. Well, yes. The Phillies won the NL East by playing the kind of ball we remembered watching as kids. And stripped to its bones, baseball used to look a lot like Lenny Dykstra. Full-bore full of itself. A working man who was a little loose around the edges. Tug McGraw, the ex-Phillies reliever-turned TV guy, says of Dykstra: "Somehow, Lenny wound up with Pete Rose DNA in his genes."

What's the word here? Ferocity? Dykstra plays that way. It's the sort of calculated recklessness that allows him to lead the league in walks and face-first slams into the centre-field padding. He won't win the Most Valuable Player Award in the National League this year, or any year. But he'll finish top five in the voting. And if the Phillies are to end the Atlanta Braves' two-year run as the league's best, they'll do it hanging on to Dykstra's vapour trail. "Keeping Lenny Dykstra off base is a much bigger key for the Braves than keeping (Otis) Nixon off is for the Phillies," CBS analyst Tim McCarver says. "If Lenny has a big series, the Phillies can win." It's pretty simple with Dykstra. When Dykstra plays, his teams win. He was a catalyst in 1986, when the Mets won 108 games and a World Series. When the Mets traded him to Philadelphia, in June 1989, they started a slow decline. Over the past three seasons, the Phillies are 38 games over .500 with Dykstra, and 33 under without him.

They list him as 5-10, but Dykstra is a few inches short of that. At 185 pounds, he looks compacted. He has no neck. At some previous point in time, he was 6-2 and 170. Norman Braman, owner of the Philadelphia Eagles, was standing at the batting cage before Thursday's game, checking out Dykstra. The self-described "Dude" looks like a refrigerator with a head. Braman wondered aloud if Dykstra could play defensive back. As you might expect, Dykstra's record is as spotty as his jersey. We don't ask our throwbacks to be perfect; we only ask them to be throwbacks. Dykstra has had his share of rough and tumble. He was involved in a serious auto accident in May 1991, in which he broke ribs, collarbone and a cheek. He pleaded guilty to an alcohol-related driving charge from that mishap. That same year, major-league baseball handed him a one-year probation for admitting to illegal, high-stakes gambling.

"The public gets this impression that I'm a wild kind of person," Dykstra says. "That's not true. I think I'm a very mental player. I always have a plan." Dykstra rolls the tobacco in his mouth, side to side like a tennis ball in a paint can. Frequently, he lets go with a stream of brown goo. Snuff remains popular with baseball players; loaded cheeks of extra-strength Red Man are just about obsolete. Then again, so is Dykstra's way of playing the game. "Walks are an underrated statistic," he says. "You not only get on base, but you might make the pitcher throw eight to 10 pitches before you get on. It's a very important stat. By the way, who led the league in walks this year?" Dykstra spits and walks away. "OK, dude?" he says. At our feet is a mound of used-up cud.

Shannon Tompkins published this evocative piece about duck hunting in the *Houston Chronicle* on November 25, 1993. The title and subtitles were: Of dawn, ducks and memories "I could go back and pull the diaries and calendars that begin in 1968 and count the hunts, but there's really no reason. They all flood back, every hunt, in one way or another."

In his transcendental novel, "The River Why?", author David James Duncan lead character is a young adult man consumed by fishing and trying to come to grips with it. The character, Gus, comes to understand that some people don't share his commitment, but can live happy lives nonetheless. But Gus also understands that *his* life is and almost certainly always will be defined by fishing, both in the physical and metaphysical sense. That epiphany hits him when he realizes he can remember every one of the hundreds of fishing experiences he's had. And that, he sees, is not so much a sign of his cognitive ability as it is a manifestation of fishing's hold on his soul. "It's not an ability to remember," Gus says to himself. "It's an inability to forget."

A couple of hours before dawn Saturday morning, with the stars of Orion the Hunter hanging in the cold sky overhead, I stood in the coastal marsh I've hunted for almost 25 years and felt a lot like Gus. How many duck hunts? Three hundred? Four hundred? At least. There were those years in the '70s when I hunted 40 or 50 times in a 65-day season. Even last year, with a 39-day season, I made half the open days. I could go back and pull the diaries and calendars that begin in 1968 and count the hunts, but there's really no reason. They all flood back, every hunt, in one way or another. Maybe not every detail of every day afield, but pieces of all of them flash in my mind from time to time. In the darkness ahead of Opening Morning, with the decoys on the pond and nothing left to do but wait and watch and feel, memories came in a torrent. "Listen!" brother Les said, breaking the spell.

The sky, slowly turning deep pink and purple in the east, was alive with the sound of wings and whistles, quacks and honks. There were splashes in the shallow pond—unseen ducks alighting. "This is the best time of the morning," Les said, his face pointed at the stars as he squatted next to the clump of cord grass he'd use as a blind. He's right. Those are magic moments, those several minutes before legal shooting time, when birds begin flying, the sky pinks and you're flushed with adrenaline and anticipation. All things are possible. This could be the best day of your life. Duck hunting, to me, is a lot like life. You're stupid if you spend it with people whose company you don't enjoy. And success depends on your ability, skills, and determination. Luck—chance—plays a role, too.

There are some things you can't control—the abundance of ducks, the weather, your own physical limitations. So you roll the bones, hoping for the best. And right before shooting time, when the dice are bouncing on the table, there's always the chance they'll come up "seven." My idea of a rolling a "seven" has changed over the past couple of decades. It's had too. I've watched fewer ducks come to this marsh over the years. Where 20 years ago, the sky was constantly dotted with skeins and clumps of ducks, now most days produce maybe half the ducks we'd see in, say, 1973. The decline of duck populations gets driven home when you've watched it from the same spot for 20 years or more. Same goes for the number of duck hunters. When limits and season lengths were cut during the drought-plagued 1980s, a lot of people abandoned the marshes. A *lot*.

The number of waterfowl hunters in Texas dropped from 110,500 in 1980 to barely 55,000 in 1992. That 50 percent decline is, to me, embarrassing evidence of how many so-called hunters were interested not in the duck hunting experience but in the number of times they could pull the trigger. Maybe the marsh is better off without them. If enough ducks are in the air for me to take a limit of three "big" ducks, then I'm tickled. Most times, that happens. But some mornings, even in this prime marsh, it's a struggle to get the opportunity to take a three-duck bag of gadwall, wigeon, pintail, mallard or mottled duck. If you don't shoot teal, shovelers, ringnecks or scaup, you just might not shoot much.

Some recent opening days have been tough, so there was no guarantee that Les and I would see a lot of ducks. But the number of birds in the air ahead of shooting time Saturday certainly was encouraging. When it was show time, we scrunched down in thick mottes of cordgrass, a gusty north-northeast wind at our backs. And the ducks came. They came in waves. Clumps of gadwall. Pairs and trios of mottled ducks. Big squadrons of green-winged teal. They swept downwind of the decoys, turned into the blustery wind and aimed for the opening we left for them among the decoys. It was almost like the old days. We watched, giggling to ourselves, for maybe 20 minutes without shooting. Then Les got down to business. One shot, and a drake gadwall splashed, webs up, into the pond. My turn. The ducks just kept coming. I made a decision to pass everything and wait for the really big ducks—pintails, mallards, mottled ducks—and let everything else slide.

It took maybe five minutes of being bombarded by teal and spoonbills and gadwall before we heard that distinctive thin, reedy, drawn-out "quuuuuack." I hit the call with three quick notes, and saw the bird swing around the east side of the pond, wings locked and silhouetted against the burnished sky. It called again. No doubt about what it was. When the bird was right over the decoys, I struggled to my feet, lifted the gun and fired the first shot of a new season. The drake mallard dropped nearly at my feet. A gift from the gods. It just got better. Ducks kept coming, swinging over the pond in the stiff wind and coming right to where we wanted them. We could have taken our limits no more than 20 minutes into the season, but we wanted this to last.

Les and I agreed to trade opportunities, vowing to shoot only at prime big ducks that were right over the decoys. The only time that vow was broken was when a drake bufflehead, a rare bird in this marsh, came out of nowhere. Les took the gorgeous little "spirit duck" for a place of honor on his wall.

We ended up with a beautiful string of ducks: two greenheads, the drake gadwall and bufflehead, a drake mottled duck and a drake pintail. We shucked the duck loads from our pumps, replacing them with "T" shot in case some geese wandered too close, and sat back to enjoy the show. For the next hour or so, we watched and photographed dozens of ducks piling into the pond, everything from a flock of Mexican squealers (fulvous whistling ducks) to a single wood duck. It was a beautiful thing, just sitting there, watching and talking. Ducks were still hovering over the pond even after we'd collected the decoys and were preparing to leave. Gadwalls and shovelers, ringnecks and greenwings. Mallards and pintails. "We're gonna remember this day for a long time," Les smiled and said as another bunch of gadwalls pitched over the empty marsh pothole. Yeah. At least for the rest of our lives. We don't have a choice.

In this ingenious column, Dave Anderson of *The New York Times* speculates what might happen if Kenesaw Mountain Landis was alive today and applying for the job as baseball commissioner.

This was published February 20, 1994.

Keney M. Applies for Commissioner

—By Dave Anderson

"Please sit down. On behalf of the baseball search committee interviewing candidates for commissioner, we're delighted you're here. You certainly have the look we're looking for. Your name again?"

"Keney M."

"Keney M. what?"

"Keney M."

"That's certainly a different name."

"Hey, it's the '90s."

"That's your real name?"

"No, in my first life my real name was Kenesaw Mountain Landis, but nobody has a name like that anymore. So in my reincarnation I decided to go by Keney M." "In your first life you were Kenesaw Mountain Landis, baseball's first commissioner?"

"The very same. And when I heard people saying, 'If only Kenesaw Mountain Landis were alive today,' I thought I'd apply for the job."

"But you don't understand."

"What don't I understand?"

"The job has changed. Your flowing white mane and your firm chin project the image we want but we don't want a commissioner to have the power that you had when you were named baseball's first commissioner in 1920 after the Black Sox scandal. We don't even want a commissioner to have the power that Fay Vincent had when he resigned in 1992."

"You mean when Fay, for all practical purposes, was fired by the club owners because he believed in 'the best interests of baseball.'"

"Please, we don't use that phrase in baseball anymore. We prefer to think that a commissioner should be more of an office boy . . . I mean, more of an officer. . . . Yes, more of an officer and a gentleman."

Owners' interests all that matter

"But what's a commissioner without the power of the 'best interests of baseball' clause?"

"To use your words, Keney M., hey, it's the '90s. You'll have authority. If there's another strike by the players, you'll have the authority to negotiate the daily meal money."

"Meal money? The players are making millions and they still get meal money? No wonder so many clubs are losing money."

"We're not really losing money. That's just creative accounting. If we were losing money, we wouldn't be paying Bud Selig $1 million a year as the interim commissioner even though Bud really doesn't want the job."

"I don't understand. Bud doesn't want the job, but as long as nobody else gets the job, Bud keeps making $1 million a year."

"Your job, Keney M., is not to understand. Your job is to sit in an office on Park Avenue and wait for a phone call from some of the owners to tell you what to say and do."

"Suppose there's another Black Sox scandal? What's my authority if that happens?"

"You must remember that the Chicago club known as the White Sox is owned by Jerry Reinsdorf now, not Charles Comiskey as it was in your first life. Fay Vincent would be the first to tell you that Jerry certainly wouldn't appreciate eight of his players being banned from baseball. Now that I think of it, Jerry wouldn't even appreciate Michael Jordan being banned from spring training."

"Suppose there's another George Steinbrenner-Howard Spira scandal? Could I sus- pend George like Fay Vincent did?"

"I don't see why not. George might even like the idea. If he were suspended, he wouldn't be able to go to Yankee Stadium, and a game there without George would be a game with one less spectator. With all of George's complaints about Yankee Stadium, one less spectator is important. Yes, you probably could suspend George—as long as he agreed."

Just smile and do what you're told

"Is there any authority I would have?"

"Well, since the commissioner is in charge of the umpires during the World Series, you would have the authority to settle any dispute about the interpretation of the infield-fly rule if a controversy were to develop during a World Series game."

"What about removing a player from a World Series game? I did that in 1934 when the Detroit fans threw all those tomatoes at Joe Medwick of the Cardinals."

"If another Medwick scene developed, you must remember that in our new television venture with the NBC and ABC networks, we're hoping to land a big tomato-soup commercial. We wouldn't want to do anything that might antagonize a sponsor."

"But what's a commissioner without authority?"

"He's a commissioner we can tell what to do."

"In my first life, I told the owners what to do."

"Kenny M., you still don't seem to understand that it's the '90s, that baseball wants a commissioner who would put the mustard on the hot dogs for the club owners whenever he attends a game, who would choose the honorary batboys and batgirls for the All-Star Game, who would be the ticket-taker at the Hall of Fame induction ceremonies at Cooperstown."

"That's it?"

"If you do a good job at those tasks, maybe we'll let you throw out the first ball at the World Series some day."

"For the first game?" "No, only if there's an eighth game."

On January 1, 1994, the Anchorage Daily News republished an I form column by Bill Conlin, sports columnist of the *Philadelphia Daily News*:

How it would be in one man's perfect world—By Bill Conlin

PHILADELPHIA: When I'm King of the World . . .

There will be a baseball salary cap. Also a baseball thinking cap. What are the new San Francisco Giants owners smoking, ground-up $1,000 bills? The five-year contract that will pay third baseman Matt Williams $30.75 million means the small-market ballclub now has committed $92.5 million to just four players—Barry Bonds, Robby Thompson, Mark Portugal and Williams—over the next five years. No wonder senior general partner Walter Shorenstein, the No. 2 guy in the limited partnership that saved the Giants a year ago, has thrown in his hand. Shorenstein, whose wealth has been estimated at $400 million, resigned before the Williams signing, saying he disagreed with the direction the club was heading. Safeway supermarket mogul Peter Magowan better reread those headlines. That was the NFL, not major league baseball, that just signed new TV contracts worth more than $4 billion with Fox, NBC, ESPN and TNT.

The way it works now, Walt, your guys signed a scaled-down contract with ESPN this year and entered into a risky, profit-sharing deal with NBC and ABC whereby everybody's profits will depend on how much advertising you can sell. With one of the smaller local TV and radio incomes and attendance traditionally wired to club success, it would appear the Giants are terribly overextended through the end of the century . . .

When I'm King of the World . . .

Minor league prospects will be able to refuse instructional league assignments only for medical reasons. . . . The Yankees signed high school lefthander Brien Taylor for $1.55 million in 1991. The signing shattered the existing amateur bonus structure after acrimonious negotiations that didn't end until after the kid had squandered his first season of professional ball. For an extra $500,000, Taylor lost a year at the end of his career, a time when he could have been earning $6 million or more. I wonder if agent Scott Boras flew that concept by the kid. Which is another reason why owners would rather suck the heads off a bottle of tapeworms than do business with Boras.

The agent completed a hat trick of sorts Tuesday when Taylor had his pitching shoulder rebuilt by Dr. Frank Jobe. Taylor will not pitch again before the 1995 season, if ever, after suffering a tom capsule and labrum in a bar fight near his Beaufort, S.C., home. Boras informed the Yankees, "It's nothing serious." You might remember Taylor's mother, Bettie, going on "60 Minutes" in '91, proud she had not permitted the Yankees to insult her boy with a mere $1 million offer. Taylor had a decent 1993 season in Double A, but he's sushi-raw. The Yankees asked him to go to the instructional league to work on his pickoff move, his deficient fielding and maybe develop another pitch. Taylor refused. Now, he's got what's left of the $1.55 million. He's got police charges to deal with in the wake of a fight in which he says he was defending his brother. Best of all, Brien Taylor still has Scott Boras. And, somehow, I have a feeling they deserve each other.

I had been meaning to update "Mondo Cane," the dog crisis that has shattered the security-monitored calm of Indian Creek, the 44-resident beighbourhood near North Miami Beach where Eagles owner Norman Braman hangs his overnight bag and Eagles Stadium blueprints. In case you missed the saga of rich man's inhumanity to rich man's dog, the Indian Creek council has arbitrarily outlawed six feisty breeds—American Staffordshire terriers, Staffordshire bull terriers, German shepherds, Doberman pinschers, Rottweilers and American pit bull terriers. Why such an eclectic mix? It turns out the ban was aimed at the noisy, foliage-soiling Rottweilers of our old friend Prince Turki bin Abdul Aziz, Norman's next-door beighbour. Aziz is a Saudi who showed up during the Persian Gulf War and spends about as much time on the island as Braman spends in Philly.

Among the projected canine casualties of war was Natacha, an 8-year-old Rottweiler belonging to filthy-rich auto dealer Gus Machado. But Natacha was grandfathered into the ordinance, which was a slap in Aziz's fez. Just between you and me, all this rich-people bluster sounds unconstitutional as hell. I mean, how do we implement this law, Norm, a house-to-house search? . . .

When I'm King of the World . . .

If you're taller than 7-foot, you've got to position yourself inside the foul line, or it's an illegal-offences violation, then a technical. . . . I've got my early assessment of Shawn Bradley down to six words: Wilt Was Better—In Eighth Grade. No doubt in my mind that the Mormon mission the Sixers centre served in Australia was good for the inner man. And if he had chosen a life in the pulpit—I know, I know, every Mormon adult male is a minister—prayer in Perth would have been perfect. But you watch his court demeanour and realize that, in the absence of growing up tough in some urban hellhole, Marine boot camp would have been better.

Nor am I convinced that two more seasons in the Western Athletic Conference would have done much more to prepare a young man with minimal basketball instincts for the NBA. Right now, two monolithic, related, obstacles stand between Bradley and anything close to stardom: 1. He is unable to prevent all but the most marginal NBA centres from posting him up. 2. He is just as unable to post up enemy centres. Until he can master those elemental facets, you'll see his height and enormous wingspan wasted 18 feet from the basket, doing stuff the stiffs of the NBA world can do $4 million a year cheaper. Ray Buck, columnist of *The Houston Post*, remembers "Jimmy V," Jim Valvano, in his column of February 28, 1994: *Valvano's words remain truthful.*

It doesn't seem like a year has passed since Jim Valvano made us laugh and think and cry during one of the most moving 10 minutes in sports television history. Racked by cancer, the former North Carolina State coach and ESPN analyst slowly and painfully climbed the seven steps leading to a podium at the inaugural ESPYs to accept the Arthur

Ashe Courage Award. It would be Jimmy V's last public appearance. Two months later, he was dead at 47.

"Three things we all should do every day," he told us. "No. 1 is laugh. You should laugh every day. No. 2 is think. You should spend some time in thought. And No. 3, you should have your emotions moved to tears . . . could be (tears of) happiness. "Think about it. If you laugh and you think and you cry, that's a full day." Well, I saved those 10 minutes of videotape—and I'm glad I did. Watching them again Sunday gave me a full day.

'Don't ever give up'

I listened again to what Valvano had to say about dreams and hugs and family and goals and enthusiasm and his now-famous motto: "Don't give up, don't ever give up." I saw again the part where he broke off in mid-sentence less than seven minutes into his speech: "The screen is flashing 30 seconds. Like I care about that screen right now, huh? I got tumors all over my body. I'm worried about some guy in back going 30 seconds?" I heard him again say how the funding for AIDS research is "10 times" greater than the funding for cancer research—"and the amount of money pouring into AIDS is not enough," he clarified.

I cringed again at his grim statistics: Half a million people will die of cancer this year. One in every four of us will be afflicted with this dreaded disease. Since Valvano's death on April 28, golf's Heather Farr has died of cancer and Paul Azinger has been diagnosed with lymphoma in his right shoulder blade. Mario Lemieux amazingly still plays hockey for Pittsburgh despite his ongoing bout with Hodgkin's disease, a form of cancer.

Sports, Real World Alike

The sports world is not unlike the real world, so we're reminded every now and then. Tonight at 8, ESPN will air the second annual ESPYs—a.k.a., American Sports Awards. Keep a box of Kleenex handy, just in case.

Honored for his courage this time will be former American League umpire Steve Palermo, who was shot and paralyzed while trying to break up a robbery attempt outside a Dallas restaurant in July 1991. Palermo had just worked a Texas Rangers game. He was enjoying dinner when came a cry of help that two waitresses were being robbed and assaulted by three thugs in the parking lot. Palermo immediately joined several others from the restaurant in chasing down—on foot—one of the three suspects. The other two fled in a car, only to circle back and carry out their cowardly attack by firing a .32-caliber pistol into the small group of captors.

Palermo carries on

Three shots hit former Southern Methodist football player Terence Mann, who since has recovered from his wounds. One shot hit Palermo, who was not so lucky. "I felt like somebody was pouring hot water on my legs," he later described. The bullet grazed his spinal column—but it could've been worse. He isn't bound to a wheelchair, he didn't bleed to death. An umpire normally isn't a sympathetic figure. Or a hero. But this one's story is about to touch us all.

I wanted so much for Jimmy V to be able to keep his promise and be there tonight to present the Arthur Ashe Courage Award. On second thought, he is. Almost a month later— March 18, 1994—Buck devoted a column to Bobby Knight.

Knight no help to sports' image

Seeing Bob Knight featured on ESPN and NBC this week only proves that if you're a big enough jerk in this country, the networks will fight to get you on. Knight routinely stiffs reporters after Indiana U. basketball games. He is vulgar, insensitive and boorish. But because he's bigger than the game he coaches, he has his own set of rules. Temple's John Chaney loses it and gets suspended one game. Knight loses it—nothing. Everybody is afraid of Bob Knight, that's the way he wants it. He's a control freak. When approached by ESPN and NBC, Knight chose Beano Cook and Bob Costas (must be an initials thing) to do the honours. Costas' interview had some teeth, although I still want to know who dresses Knight in those red sweaters two sizes too small. It examined the complexity of a man whose record, community service and ideals are distorted only by his madness.

Read between the lines

He is a man with two sides.

Bob Knight says: "The absolute essence of coaching is to teach."

His Eminence Really Means: "The absolute essence of coaching is to browbeat 19- and 20-year-olds."

Bob Knight says: "I don't think I'm a horse's ass. I think I'm a pretty good guy."

His Eminence Really Means: "Moe Iba was a pretty good guy."

Bob Knight says (on head-butting freshman Sherron Wilkerson): "We apparently collided heads. I didn't notice anything more about it at the time than two guys, in close quarters, one of 'em bending over, one of 'em leaning forward..."

His Eminence Really Means: "I went too far—but I can't say that. I'm Bob Knight."

Bob Knight says (on the chair-throwing incident earlier in his career): "Am I the only coach in history who's ever thrown a chair? A coat? A clipboard? A water cooler? I may be the most infamous chair-thrower—but certainly not the only one."

His Eminence Really Means: "I can do better than that. I bet I can toss Damon Bailey above the backboard. Wanna see?"

Wait 'til Father's Day

Bob Knight says (on kicking his player-son Patrick earlier this season): "Patrick knows there's no one on the face of the earth that I love more than him. He understands that."

His Eminence Really Means: "Patrick understands he made a really careless, bad, blind pass out on top." Oops, he did say that.

Bob Knight says: "We don't get there with milk and cookies. These (three national championship) banners would not be hanging above my head if that's the way I coached."

His Eminence Really Means: "Help! Maybe I'm losin' it. I haven't won a national championship since Woody Hayes died in 1987. Is that how *my* career is going to end? Like Woody's? Am I going to punch some kid from the other team and get myself fired? (Pause) Wait a minute, what am I thinking? They can't fire me at Indiana. I *own* Indiana."

A loose cannon

I asked UH's Alvin Brooks of and Rice's Willis Wilson—members of the "new breed" of that grew up with March Madness and the media explosion—what they thought of Knight.

They pretty much agreed: Great coach, loose cannon.

"He sends a signal that reinforces a lot of negative notions that people have about college coaches," Wilson said. "That's a little bit troubling."

Said Brooks: "He wins, fills his building and graduates most of his kids . . . he just doesn't always conduct himself in a manner conducive to leading young men."

Imagine if Knight—whose team plays Ohio U. late tonight in the first round of the NCAA tournament—could do all of those things?

"Then," said Brooks, "you'd have Dean Smith."

Touché.

After the tawdry Tonya Harding-Nancy Kerrigan affair, *Associated* Press sports writer Jim Litke wrote a column about Harding. This appeared in the Huntsville, Texas, *Item* on March 18, 1994.

Tonya got what she deserved

—By Jim Litke, AP Sports Writer

For everyone who thought this day would never come, Tonya Harding finally ran out of shoelaces to break. She finally ran out of costumes that would come undone, out of doctor's notes and court orders, out of flip answers and tearful excuses. And she finally ran into a judge who said no more do-overs. Some people still argue that fining her heavily and forcing her out of competitive skating is just a slap on the wrist. But justice in this instance was served and not, like so many other times in the past 10 weeks, swerved around.

No, she is not going to jail. But she is not going to Disney World, either. At least not until she gets permission from her probation officer first, cashes in the frequent-flyer miles from the Norway trip and ponies up the admission fee. Even then, Mickey Mouse will not be greeting her at the gate as he did Nancy Kerrigan, with a smile on his face and fistfuls of money overflowing his mitts. Under the plea-bargain agreement, she had to surrender the one thing that defined her, the oasis where she could hide and forget all the other harsh, hurtful places in her life. She kept holding out for one more chance to make everything right, and now even Harding must realize that is gone for good.

For the foreseeable future, her life will consist of suffering through a series of small humiliations and cutting costly deals so they don't become large ones. The only character, real or imagined, who is willing to pay her Mickey Mouse dollars right now is a Japanese wrestling promoter. And while Harding could probably use the $2 million, and while she has worn sillier costumers of her own choosing, the opportunity sounds too grubby—even for her. A stint with the ice shows, or selling the rights for a made-for-TV movie are options that could keep her solvent for some time, at least. But as with the offer to wrestle, the only way Harding gets paid now is by playing the tough, clumsy villain.

And frankly, it's hard to think of a sentence more fitting than that. Because what probably made Harding fall in love with skating as a young girl, what kept her there and made her fight so long and so hard to stay there, was the chance to play a role different than the one life kept pushing her into. For those who still feel that the punishment didn't fit the crime—whatever Harding's real involvement was—there will be more.

While the controversy roiled, Harding made the people from the U.S. Figure Skating Association and the U.S. Olympic Committee appear timid and inept. But now that the skate is on the other foot, they are eager to been seen as neither. They have lawyers, too, and more money to boot. And all the time it seemed she and her legal team were skating circles around them, these people were only sharpening their blades. With her admission of guilt, the USFSA can now initiate proceedings to strip Harding of the national championship she won last December in Detroit.

Maybe this whole affair was best summed up by what Harding's replacement, 16-year-old Nicole Bobek, told reporters of how she was informed that she was going to the world championships in Japan:

"I was told she was sick and would not be able to compete."

Harding is sick, all right, heart sick.

She should be.

Dan Barreiro, of the *Minneapolis-St. Paul Star Tribune* wrote a commentary piece about rough play in the NBA. This article was published the first week in May 1994.

Rough play in NBA not new or outrageous, Commentary

—By Dan Barreiro, Minneapolis, Star Tribune

After a bloody week in the NBA playoffs, the awful bleating has begun from the tea-and-crumpet set. Call the cops, the pacifists say. They're killing the game. They're turning the NBA into the National Brawling Association.

Did you see the full-court riot that broke out in Atlanta? All the other spats that have turned physical? And when are they going to do something about all those utterly dreadful 87-83 games?

Here's a little advice to the pacifists: Relax. Lighten up. Read a Fabio romance novel. Take up shuffleboard. You say you loved the Suns' wide-open, free-wheeling 140-133 victory over the Warriors on the West Coast on Wednesday night. Defence was optional. I say I loved the Knicks' scratch-and-claw, nothing-comes-easy 90-81 victory over the Nets on the East Coast on Sunday. Offence was optional.

You say you loved Charles Barkley scoring 56 points and doing a tap dance on a big kid named Chris Webber. I say I loved the way the Knicks refused to wither and played suffocating defence with Patrick Ewing thrown out of the game in the second quarter. You'll take Dan Majerle bombing in another 3-pointer. I'll take Charles Oakley hurtling himself out of bounds to get an offensive rebound. You say the Phoenix-Golden State game is what pro basketball should be all about. I say an occasional effort to play defence is helpful. But there is room in pro basketball for both styles, and the contrast between the two makes the NBA all the more compelling, especially when those styles meet on the court. Which they have been doing for a long, long time.

Do people really have memories this short? Do they really believe this debate is new?

More than 10 years ago, the Celtics and Lakers met in the NBA Finals in two straight playoffs. Do the tea-and-crumpeters forget some of those battles, some of those brawls? The Celtics, remember, were the physical team whose game was to play defence and wear down an opponent. The Lakers were the elegant team that wanted to frolic in the open court and play a game called Showtime. Pat Riley complained the Celtics were thugs. The Celtics complained the Lakers were prima donnas. The matchups were historic. And if you think there have been some hard takedowns in this year's playoffs, what about Kevin McHale's infamous mauling of Kurt Rambis under the basket on a breakaway? You think the Celtics won two titles in three years by being sweet and polite?

The past two years, the Bulls and Knicks provided the contrast. The Bulls were an outstanding defensive team, but with Michael Jordan, were about grace and athleticism. The Knicks were about heavy lifting. Phil Jackson complained the Knicks were thugs. Riley, in a new role, complained the Bulls were prima donnas. The matchups were semi-epic. No NBA playoff would be authentic without a little spilled blood. The fact is, there is no one team today as singularly bent on the destruction of its opponents as the Pistons were when they won their back-to-back titles.

And even the Pistons actually were less offensive by the time they won their second title. Certainly, there are individuals who must be muzzled, and not surprisingly, Public Enemy No. 1 is a former Piston, Dennis Rodman. When Rodman sticks to running and jumping and rebounding and defending, he remains one of the most intriguing players in the league. When he resorts to the indefensible tactics he tried on the Jazz last weekend, Rodman is an on-court hoodlum who must be punished. And the league did, taking him out of the pivotal Game 3 of the Spurs' series with Utah. The frightening thing now is that Rodman sees himself as a martyr, and martyrs have been known to do desperate things. This guy needs a good doctor.

Nobody would defend the disgraceful acts of cowardice that took place during Game 2 of the Hawks-Heat series. On the street, Keith Askins gets jail time for the sucker punch he threw at Doug Edwards. The pacifists say those incidents have helped create a climate in which it is impossible for offences to flourish. Nonsense. Those incidents have nothing to do with taking offence out of the game. Offence is hurting in the NBA for two reasons. The first is that few players want to do anything but dunk anymore because the dunkers make all the highlight reels and shoe commercials. What should worry the purists is that too many players refuse to develop and refine other offensive skills. The other is that more teams are paying some attention to playing defence. There is great irony in all the praise for the Phoenix-Golden State point-o-rama, in which both teams were entertaining, but nobody guarded anyone.

Once upon a time, many games were ending with 137-134 scores, and do you know what people were saying about the league? They were whining that teams met so little resistance on the offensive end that all the scoring lost its meaning. Now, there are a number of teams—the Knicks, Bulls, Hawks, Sonics and Rockets among them—that are actually attempting to play more than token defence. Pacers coach Larry Brown even has Reggie Miller taking charges. There is one thoroughly alarming NBA trend that is well worth hammering. It is simply this: A young player now makes three good plays in a row and he wants the action stopped and a monument erected in his honor. Latrell Sprewell nails a slam dunk and then gets in the face of Charles Barkley. Isaiah Rider nails a slam and then gets in the face of Hakeem Olajuwon. Sprewell and Rider are talented young players, but what have they really done in this league?

There is far too much yapping going on from players who don't have the credentials to do it. "It's changed a lot," Magic Johnson says of younger players in general. "Everybody cares about me. Where's my minutes? Where's my shots? What's wrong with my game? It's a lot of that now, and I don't like that side of it." It's an obnoxious side to the game, and the league should find a way to deal with it. And nobody's suggesting that the pro game be turned into roller derby. Brawls like the one in Atlanta should be dealt with severely. As for all the ranting and raving that pro basketball is being ruined by those 87-85 games, key down. Pro basketball? To steal a slogan that McHale would endorse, it ain't croquet, baby.

CHAPTER

12

Tips on Writing Editorials, Opinion Articles and Columns

1. If you can state the idea to yourself in a short, declarative sentence, it's probably a workable idea. If you cannot state the idea in a clear, concise way, you have not yet clarified the idea into a workable form.
2. Your material may be easily written if you remember three topics: premise, evidence, and conclusion. State the idea, provide evidence to prove and buttress your case, and conclude the editorial or column.

Note that if you do not use the "I" form early in the editorial or column, don't use the "I" of the author abruptly towards the end of the material. Perceptive readers may wonder why you have changed the style and tone of the material needlessly.

COMMON STYLISTIC ERRORS SPORTS WRITERS SHOULD AVOID

Sports writing is often the best and worst writing in a newspaper—and often these best and worst examples can be found on the same sports page. Errors of style can be corrected on an editor's screen, but the best solution to sports writing style errors is not to let them appear on the reporter's screen in the first place. The following are seven common stylistic errors that should be avoided in the reporter's original copy.

The One-sentence Paragraph

If your writing becomes predictable, no matter what the subject, a perceptive reader may simply turn the story off because of observed sameness of style. One-sentence paragraphs are important and dramatic. One of the most dramatic passages in the Bible is: "Jesus wept." Quoted material is often one-sentence replies because people often speak in one-sentence replies. Veteran reporters hear their own words and sentences as they create articles; they listen for cadence and rhythm and style. They want a story to sing.

Novice reporters often simply hammer out words on a computer screen and save the story when they are finished, without listening to the sound of their words and sentences on their screen. Here is a key: If you read your story to yourself and the story has awkward gaps, misplaced emphases, and illogical sentences, it must be rewritten. If, on the other hand, you can read the story with style and grace, if the pauses appear where they should appear, if the sentences and paragraphs have a flow and a meter and a cadence to them, then you have written your story well. Good writing includes not only one-sentence paragraphs, but multisentence paragraphs as well.

The Excessive Example

In Sports in America, his thorough analysis of sports and our society, James Michener (1976) wrote:

> My affection for John Kiernan and Red Smith is considerable; they have added luster to the sports page. Many of my friends believe Jim Murray of the

Los Angeles Times to be their inheritor, and he has been named sports writer of the year numerous times by a restricted group of experts who always choose Chris Schenkel as the television pundit.

Murray is one of the funniest men alive, and a short, quick collection of his best lines would rate high: "This club has a chance to go all the way. So did the *Titanic*. But Murray has a bad habit which his young imitators work into the ground. He takes one subject, usually worthy of comment, then beats it to death, with crack after crack, belabouring the idea long after the dullest reader must have tired. Of Luis Rodriguez, the Cuban welterweight, he says: "This face is old, yet young. The eyes are merry, yet sad. It is not a fighter's face. It is a clown's face. Fernandel in burnt cork. Grimaldi without bells. Durante in boxing shorts." This habit of excessive citation can be seen at its most flamboyant in his introduction to his book about football. In short, descriptive phrases do not have to be used in triplicate to be effective.

The Blind Attribution

A story about golf champion Arnold Palmer might read like this:

Palmer was noted for "Arnie's Army," his devoted followers who watched him play every hole in every major tournament. The native of Latrobe, Pa., often said, "______."

Was Palmer a native of Latrobe, Pennsylvania? He was, but don't make your story a sports trivia challenge. Perhaps the reference to Latrobe had never been cited in the article prior to that reference. If it was not, you lead your reader through a guessing game.

Again:

Nolan Ryan was one of the most durable pitchers in modern baseball.

The native of Alvin, Texas, once said, of his fame, "______."

Was Ryan a native of Alvin, Texas? Again, yes, but these two references could most easily be phrased this way:

Palmer was noted for "Arnie's Army," his devoted followers who watched him play every hole of every tournament.

Palmer, a native of Latrobe, Pa., often said " ______."

And:

Nolan Ryan was one of the most durable pitchers in modern baseball.

Ryan, a native of Alvin, Texas, once said, of his fame, " ______."

Writers must, however, scroll up through their copy to make sure there aren't too many paragraphs beginning:

Palmer ______.

Palmer ______.

Palmer ______.

Or:

Ryan ______.

Ryan ______.

Ryan ______.

Equally vexing is the sports writer who refers to an athlete, let's say a football player: "Joe Jock says he will ______." A paragraph later or, worse, several paragraphs later, the writer uses this phrase: "This six foot, three inch fullback ______." Does he still mean Joe Jock? We assume so, but may not know.

Don't needlessly confuse your readers. Don't play guessing games with your readers and don't make them mentally sort through the most obscure of sports trivia to identify subjects in your articles.

Excessive Adjective and Adverb Usage

If a major league baseball player has a .185 average, avoid temptation to write "a meager .185 average" or an "anemic .185 average." If a football player runs a 40-year dash in record time, avoid the temptation to write "a blistering 40-yard time." Just as the continual use of the one-sentence paragraph robs the reader of any real involvement in the article, so excessive use of adjectives and adverbs also robs the readers of any decision-making thought processes in reading the article. Was the .185 average "meager" or "anemic?" Let the reader decide. Was the time "blistering?" Perhaps, but let the reader make the judgment. Offer factual evidence to support your claim that the time was fast, but let the reader mentally add that sort of qualification.

If the time was the fastest ever in the 40-yard dash, let the reader mentally add "*Holy Smoke!*" or whatever else he or she wants to think about the achievement. If you make all the decisions for the reader in the article, if you qualify all the achievements and times, then you leave the reader very little room to be involved in the article. You leave the reader very little reason to care about your article. Ultimately, you leave the reader very little reason to continue reading your piece.

The Q&A Format

Unless you are requested to do so, avoid the pure question-and-answer format, as used in the *Playboy* "Interview of the Month" and in other magazines.

The format is simply this:

Question: "Don't you think that . . . ?"

Jock: "Yep, you bet . . . I think that. . . ."

Question: "On subject B, do you believe . . . ?"

Jock: "Nope, I think. . . ."

Playboy interviewers and editors spend week after week during the interviewing stages of a *Playboy* interview, then week after week cutting, trimming, and rearranging the interview questions and answers to make the interview seem as spontaneous as possible. Yet even the best interviews may leave readers glassy-eyed with fatigue and disinterest. Try to read more than one lengthy *Playboy* interview—say two at one time—and then decide how fresh this format is. The Q & A story, at its best, leaves little involvement for the reader. The Qs and As march down the page; There is little change of pace, except for the length of the answers, there is no literary style, and little to delight or enchant the reader. It's stenographic journalism, and no one ever won a Pulitzer Prize for stenography.

Cliches

No one past the fifth grade would use a phrase like "quiet as a mouse," yet sports writers use sports cliches in articles frequently:

- "We play 'em one game at a time . . ."
- It's a physical game . . ."
- "Blazing speed . . ."
- "Grid classic . . ."
- "Archrival . . ."
- "He went to the well once too often . . ."
- "That win is the icing on the cake . . ."
- "He gave 110 percent . . ."

And a hideous new phrase, which I believe came from Monday Night Football, "His athleticism . . ."

Avoid every cliche. Every one. To use any cliche (except in a direct quotation) is to signal to your readers that you are sloppy, mediocre, and unimaginative. Strive for fresh phrases, new images, and bright writing. In his book, On Writing Well. An Informal Guide to Writing Nonfiction, William Zinsser (1985) stated: "What keeps the average writer from writing good is, first, the misapprehension that he shouldn't be trying to. He has been reared on so much jargon, so many cliches, that he thinks they are the required tools of the trade".

Unfathomable Numbers

Sports fans are traditionally numbers fans. Some are statistics junkies. Sports writers are often tempted to chain statistics together, assuming the chain must mean something; assuming that it is important to pile numbers, averages, and statistics together. Statistics may be more important to a ballplayer's career than they logically would be in any article. Zinsser (1985) also wrote:

True, every sports addict lives with a head full of statistics, cross-filed for ready access, and many a baseball fan who once flunked simple arithmetic can perform prodigies of instant calculation in the ball park on a summer afternoon. Still, some statistics are more important than others. If a pitcher wins his twentieth game, if a golfer shoots a 61, if a runner runs the mile in 3:48, please mention it. But don't get carried away.

ENDNOTE: "FOOTBALL MINUS FRILLS-AND DRILLS"

In the Introduction to this book, we wrote "sports writing isn't just scores and standings. These days, sports is more ethics and anguish, more front page than back section."

Do you ever wish that sports could be pure and simple and clean again (if it ever was)? Did you ever wish you could cover a coach and a programme that was nearly perfect?

Consider football coach John Gagliardi; he coaches at Minnesota's St. John's University, in Collegeville. If you ever wished to cover a perfect coach and a perfect programme, John Gagliardi is such a coach and he runs that kind of programme. So, for an upbeat end to this book, here is Richard Vega's article, "Football minus frills—and drills." It appeared in *USA Weekend* magazine (published by USA Today), for October 29-31, 1992. The article carries the subhead: "A Minnesota college coach's winning strategy: no slogans, no whistles, no problems."

After a tentative knock on the door, a 215-pound defensive end pops his head into the coach's office. He's flustered; he needs to get something off his chest. The coach invites him in warmly. The player's problem? Well, gosh, he was wondering if he could captain the St. John's football team in the upcoming game against Gustavus Adolphus College. Turns out his best friend is their captain. No problem, the coach says. He whips out a folder and pens in the senior player as captain. The deal is done.

That's pretty much how coach John Gagliardi, 66, conducts business at St. John's University in tiny Collegeville, Minn. Real loosey-goosey. The team's captains rotate weekly. There are no film sessions or playbooks, no blocking sleds or wind sprints. No player gets cut; everyone plays. Gagliardi doesn't even carry a whistle. Somehow, though, this relaxed regimen has led to three national championships, including the 1976 NCAA Division III title, and 18 conference championships. "I'm always amazed how well it works," says Gagliardi, who insists on being called "John," not "Coach." He is soft-spoken; his eyes are in a perpetual Mr. Magoo-like squint—hardly the kind of drill sergeant qualities associated with football. He expects his players to keep fit on their own time without baby-sitting.

Ken Roering, 51, a former All-American player for Gagliardi, calls him "a marvelous teacher" who keeps plays simple at first, then adds them till the team has memorized a playbook. "He gives students small doses they can absorb." Gagliardi began his career at 16 at a Catholic high school in Colorado. When the football coach left to fight in World War II, Gagliardi took over, making revolutionary changes: no calisthenics, no scrimmages and, most unbelievable, thirsty players actually could drink water. "We were near the coal mines, and we'd see mules coming out," Gagliardi says. "First thing they gave them was a drink." He figured what was good enough for mules was good enough for his team.

At season's end, the team won the league championship. The coach likens that team to kids home alone goofing off. Fifty years later, the same can be said of the 1993 Johnnies.

At 4:15 during a recent afternoon practice, it's calisthenics time . . . sort of. The seven captains (seniors rotate) face the team. "Three jumping jacks!" one captain barks. The players perform dutifully, then pat themselves on the back with loud cheers. "Nice Day Drill!" another captain shouts. The players flop onto their backs like sea lions, joyfully yelling: "What a nice day!," "The football gods are out!" and "Seinfeld's on tonight!"

"You're relearning the game," says Ryan Murray, a senior. "It turns from physical to mental."

By game day, the Johnnies have transformed the mental aspect of the game into old-fashioned, hard-hitting football. They stuff running backs, sack the opposing QBs and make spectacular touchdown passes. The players are Gagliardi's extended family. (His wife and their four kids all are football buffs, too.) After one practice, Gagliardi treats his seniors and starters to dinner at an all-you-can-eat establishment in nearby St. Cloud. There they load up on biscuits and country gravy, chicken wings and frozen yogurt. The mashed potatoes disappear in seconds. As the players stroll out, laughing, jostling, full to the point of bursting, they shake hands with their coach. "Thanks, John," they say. Gagliardi gets a little kick asking each if they had enough to eat. His face beams; his eyes squint. What a nice day!

CHAPTER 13

Glossary of Newspaper and Magazine Terms

Advance: A sports story about an event, written prior to the event.

Angle: The point-of-view, focus or emphasis in an article.

Annual: Yearly special or extra issue devoted to seasonal subject, such as a Christmas annual (issue).

Art: Illustrations, drawings, diagrams, or other non-print material that accompanies an article; common name for all non-textual material.

Assignment: Any specific task given to an individual; for example, a commissioned article assignment to a freelancer by a magazine.

ATT: The *As Told To* story. An athlete's autobiography that is prepared for publication by a writer, the writer shares the byline credit, such as, *"My Life in Football"* by Joe Jock, As Told To Writer Charley Someone.

Author's Alterations (AAs): Changes or corrections made by the writer in textual material (usually in galley proof form) before the material is printed.

Back Issue: Any issue of a magaize or newspaper printed prior to the current-date (newsstand) issue.

Back-of-the-Book: Secondary articles, columns, and other material literally or figuratively printed behind the primary articles.

Back Shop: Composing room area of a newspaper.

Bingo Card: Postage-paid insert in a magazine, that readers can complete and return to begin a magazine subscription. So called because they are often the size of bingo playing cards.

Bleed: To run an illustration past the margins to the edges of a page.

Blue-Pencil: Slang for editing corrections. Sonamed because blue pencil or ink can't be photographed by photo-offset cameras.

Blurb: Short description of an article or subject.

Body (of the article): The core of an article; that is, material following the lead segment.

Book: Industry slang for *magazine*. So named (perhaps) because some monthly dummies are the sizes of books.

Byline: A line of type printed before or after an article, identifying the author.

Camera-Ready: Material that has been corrected and is ready to be photographed for photo-offset printing.

Caption: Material that explains the contents of a photograph or illustration. Sometimes called *art lines* or *cut lines*.

Centre Spread: The two facing pages at the exact centre of a magazine.

Circulation: The number of copies of a magazine or newspaper printed, distributed, or sold during a specific period.

Clean Copy: Pristine text, unmarred by many editing symbols. Opposite of *dirty copy*.

Close (Closing date): The deadline for all material for a newspaper or magazine to be on the press.

Cold Type: Material prepared for printing without old-fashioned hot metal; that is, without Linotype machines.

Commission: Same as *to assign an article.*

Contents Page: Page usually near the front of a magazine that lists the contents of the issue.

Copy: All written material in manuscript form that will eventually be considered for publication.

Copyeditor: Person who reads and corrects all copy prior to publication.

Copyright: The legal ownership of a manuscript.

Cover (noun): The outside front page, inside front page, inside rear page, and outside rear page of a magazine or *to cover* (verb): To gather all the facts necessary for an article.

Crop: To mark unwanted sections of a photograph or illustration.

Cut (noun): A metal engraving of an illustration. Or *to cut* (verb): To edit material.

Cutlines: Same as caption or art lines.

Dateline: Line on an article, giving the location and date that the article originated; such as, Washington, Feb. 23.

Dead: Material that has been *killed*; that is, material that will not be printed.

Deadline: Time when all material to be published must be written, copyedited, and ready for the press.

Department: Specific section of a magazine or newspaper, involving special features or area of interest.

Dirty Copy: Material that has been heavily copyedited, such that it is illegible. Opposite of *clean copy.*

Double-Spread: Two facing pages treated as one unit.

Dummy: Planning or proof pages for an issue that has not yet been printed; a checking copy to make sure changes and corrections have been made to a particular issue.

Edition: Same as *issue.*

Editor: Person who reads, changes, or verifies all material and makes it ready for publication, in a newspaper or magazine.

Editorial Content: All nonadvertising material in a newspaper or magazine; the literary contents of a publication.

Editorialize: To express a position or opinion on behalf of the publication, as in an editorial or publisher's or editor's column.

Editor's Note: Material that helps explain an article or author or a position that a publication has taken on an issue.

Engraving: Same as *cut*.

Feature (noun): A human-interest article, or *to feature* (verb): To emphasize or give permanence to.

Filler: Incidental (usually short) material that is used to complete columns or pages.

Flag: The name of a newspaper or magazine recognizable not only by name, but also by design; for example, the Gothic flag of *The New York Times*.

Format: The size, design, and appearance of a magazine.

Four-Colour: Pages that are printed in the colours of red, yellow, blue, and black inks.

Free Lance: Person who contributes articles, photographs, or any other material without the security of a staff salary.

Front-of-the-Book: Articles of primary importance literally or figuratively printed at the front of the magazine.

Galley Proof: Vertical column of material typeset for checking purposes.

Gatefold: A page in a magazine, that is larger than the normal page and that must be folded to fit inside the magazine; for example, the *Playboy* Playmate-of-the-Month pages.

General Magazine: Any magazine edited and published for a wide reading audience, all ages, interests, religions, and so on. Life and The Saturday Evening Post are examples. Opposite of special-interest magazine.

Ghost Writer: Person who writes material that will eventually be published under the name of another person.

Graf (or Graph): Short for *paragraph.*

Gutter: The inside margins of pages.

Handout: Publicity release.

Head: Headline.

Horizontal Magazine: Same as *general magazine.*

Hot Type: Material prepared with hot metal; that is, Linotype machines. Opposite of *cold type* or photo-offset composition.

House Ad: Advertisement that promotes the same newspaper or magazine that published it.

House Organ: Publication issued by a commercial firm to promote interest in the firm by employees, stockholders, or the public.

HTK: *Head to Come;* headline not yet ready.

Human Interest: Feature article with emotional appeal to the reader; different than straight news, which is presumably toneless in content.

Insert: Material that has to be added to the inside of a previously completed article, or a specially prepared advertising supplement to a newspaper or magazine.

Inventory: Material on hand in a magazine or newspaper office, that may be used at any time.

Issue: Same as *edition.*

Italic: Script type that slants to the right, like handwriting. Italic type is often used to emphasize or highlight material.

Jump: To continue a story from one page to another or from one section to another.

Jump Head: Headline over the second or continued part of a story.

Keep Standing: Material that is held in a newspaper or magazine's inventory. Opposite of *kill.*

Kill: To delete material set for publication.

Kill Fee (Kill Rate): Payment made to a writer after an article is assigned, completed, then killed by a magazine. The kill rate or kill fee is usually a percentage of the fee paid for a published article. The writer usually retains legal rights to material killed by a publication.

Layout: The design of a page including textual material, or art that will later be published.

Lead: Beginning segment of an article.

Libel: A defamatory statement or representation published without just cause, expressed in print or by pictures, that exposes the subject to public hatred, contempt, or ridicule.

Linotype: Trade name for a keyboard-operated typesetting machine that produces a line of type in the form of a metal slug.

Little Magazine: Small circulation magazines, often less than 8½″ × 11", that contain poetry, fiction, or avant garde material. Because of lack of advertising or subscription base, little magazines often die quickly. They are the publishing equivalent of the Mayfly.

Localize: To stress the local angle of a story.

Logo: Same as flag or masthead.

Magazine: Regularly issued publication that contains fiction, nonfiction, and art, and that is aimed at a specific reading public. Carries the original definition of powder magazine, that is, storehouse.

Makeup: The consistent design of a total publication.

Mark up: To edit copy and make corrections on galley proofs.

Market: The audience for a magazine or publication.

Masthead: Material usually printed towards the front of a magazine, that lists title, editors and staff members, address, and subscription rates.

More: Used at the bottom of a page, often in parentheses, to indicate that there are additional pages to the article.

Morgue: Newspaper or magazine library or files.

Ms.: Manuscript.

Must: Material so marked has a high priority and should be printed.

Nameplate: Same as *flag* or *logo*.

Nonfiction: Material based on facts; not fiction.

Obit: Obituary; biography of recently deceased person.

Offset: Printing process in which an inked impression is made on a rubber "blanket" and then transferred or "offset" to paper.

OK for Press: Notation meaning "Can now be printed."

Op-Ed Page: The right-hand page opposite, or facing, the editorial page. Many metropolitan newspapers use the Op-Ed page as a continuation of editorials, essays, letters-to-the-editor, and other allied material.

On-Sale Date: Date on which a particular issue is available for sale throughout the publication's circulation area.

One-Shot Book: Magazine that has only one planned issue. One-shot books are often published after the death of a president, the Pope, or other famous or notorious people. There were a variety of one-shot books published after the death of Elvis Presley.

On Spec (On speculation): Any material written and submitted for publication without prior financial agreements with a magazine.

Outline: Topic-by-topic skeleton of an article.

Overset: Material that has been set in type but not used by a newspaper or magazine.

Over-the-Transom: Unsolicited material that is submitted to a magazine, that must be sorted, read, bought, or returned. (Some magazines will not read over-the-transom material because of the costs of staff member's time to read and reply to it.) Over-the-transom material becomes part of the magazine's *slush pile.*

Pack Journalism: The tendency of journalists to deliberately or accidentally write like each other. The press that covers Washington, DC has been accused of pack journalism, as have many sports writers.

Pad: To lengthen with additional materials.

Periodical: Publication issued at regular intervals longer than one day; that is, for example, magazines, not newspapers.

Personality Piece: Biography on a person in magazine form.

Pics or Pix: Pictures.

Piece: Slang for article.

Play up: To emphasize.

Policy: Official viewpoint of a magazine as stated in editorial columns or other features; such as "The Playboy Philosophy", a series in *Playboy* written by publisher Hugh Hefner.

Profile: Personality article.

Promotion: Active campaign to enhance the acceptance and sale of a newspaper or magazine.

Proof: Copy of material used for checking and correction purposes.

Proofread: To check such material prior to publication.

Pulp: Magazines printed on cheap newsprint; often carries the connotation of sensational material.

Put to Bed: To put on press; to close an issue.

Query Letter: Letter from a freelance writer outlining an article idea and asking for an acceptance from a publication on the idea.

Quote: Quotation.

Readability: The ease with which a story can be read; visually, pertains to legibility and design of article or layout.

Readership: Surveyed or estimated audience of a magazine; not the same as circulation.

Regional Advertisements: Advertisements that appear in issues of a magazine for a particular region.

Rejection Slip: Small letter sent to freelancers with articles that a publication has decided not to buy.

Reprint: Article printed separately and sent to readers or advertisers after the article has first appeared in print. Scholarly magazines often sell reprints to authors for their own distribution. Or, an article that had appeared previously in another publication.

Researcher: Editorial staff member who supplies facts necessary for an article or who verifies facts in an article. Slang term for researcher is *checker*, in news magazines.

Résumé: Summary of education and experience, sent by individual to prospective employers.

Rewrite: To write manuscript again.

Rim: Edge of copy desk, where editors check material.

Rough: Full-size sketch of layout.

Roundup: Article that is largely summary in nature.

Running Head: Headline that gives magazine title, date, volume, and page, printed at the top of magazine pages.

Running Story: Story that is continuing and that may demand follow-up articles on a day-to-day or week-to-week basis.

SASE: *Self-addressed stamped envelope*. Many magazines require a writer to enclose a SASE to receive an answer to a query. The writer pays the return postage.

Scoop (noun): Exclusive material, or *to scoop* (verb): To beat the competition.

Seasonal Story: An article emphasizing a season, holiday, or celebration. Must be prepared well in advance, sometimes as much as a halfyear in advance for monthly magazines.

Shelter Books: Magazines related to the home.

SID: Sports Information Director. The promotion-and-publicity arm of a college or university's athletic department.

Sidebar: A short feature that accompanies a longer article. The sidebar usually focuses on one aspect of the larger article; an aspect that the larger article may have only touched on.

Sister Publications: Magazines that are published by the same firm: Time, Life, Fortune, Money, People, and Sports Illustrated are all sister publications, published by Time, Inc.

Slant: To emphasize a particular aspect of a story.

Slick: A magazine printed on high-gloss heavy paper. Common industry term for mass circulation consumer magazines.

Slug: Abbreviated headline used to identify each story. In hot metal composition, a line of type.

Slush Pile: Unsolicited manuscripts that arrive at magazine editorial offices and that must be sorted, read, and accepted or returned.

Solicit: To commission an article, photographs, or other material from contributors.

Special-Interest Books: Magazines that are edited for a special subsection of the population; those interested in a hobby, craft, or other particular subject.

Split Run: A press run that is stopped to change an advertisement.

Staffer: Magazine staff member, writer, researcher, editor, and so on.

Style: A writer's individual expression through the special use of grammar, spelling, punctuation, and point of view.

Summary Lead: A lead that generally covers most of the "5 W's and the H": Who, What, When, Where, Why, and How.

Syndicate: Organization that sells photographs or textual material to a variety of publications. A journalism wholesaler.

Taboo: Words, phrases, or subjects that cannot be published for moral or legal reasons.

Take: One page of copy. As more and more publications are written and edited on computers, *take* is likely to fade from writers' vocabularies. Originated (perhaps) in earlier years when a fast-breaking story was *taken* page by page from the writer to the backshop.

Tear Sheet: Articles or advertisements torn from a published newspaper or magazine and sent to writers or advertisers to verify that the material (article, ad) was published.

Teaser: Headline or blurb printed on the front cover of a magazine to interest readers in the magazine's content.

Think Piece: Interpretative article or essay slanted to make a reader think about the subject. Sometimes condescending term referring to such issues as oil production, taxes, and other hard-to-explain subjects.

Thirty (30): Used on the last page of an article to indicate the end.

Tight: Issue that has little room for any additional material.

Title: Same as headline.

TK: Indicates material to *come*; not yet ready.

Typo: Typesetting mistake.

VDT: Video Display Terminal. Typewriter keyboard and television-type screen that allows a writer to compose his story on the keyboard, view it on the screen, edit it, and enter it into a computer for storage and retrieval. Electronic storage and publication is said to constitute the third stage of communications, from mechanical to electric to electronic.

Vertical Magazine: Same as special interest magazine; not necessarily a magazine that is vertically designed.

White Space: Blank spaces on a page, left blank for design purposes.

Work-for-Hire: Writing that is assumed by a magazine to be done as staff work. Freelancers who sell material on a "work-for-hire" basis generally lose all other further legal rights to the work.

XXX: Used in copy to indicate facts to come (or needed); "There are XXX automobiles in Russia this year." News magazine usage.

CHAPTER

14

Glossary of Sports Terms

ARCHERY

American Round: 30 arrows from 60 yards, 50 yards, and 40 yards each.

Anchor Point: Point on the archer's face to which the bowstring or arrow nock is brought for each shot.

Archery Golf: Game similar to golf in which archers shoot for the target—that is, a small ball—and count the number of arrows required.

Arm Guard: Protective cover made of leather or other material that protects the forearm from the bowstring as the arrow is released.

Arrow Plate: Material set in a small ledge in the bow to protect the bow as the arrow slides across it.

Arrow Rest: The ledge on the bow that the arrow sits on prior to release. The arrow slides across it upon release.

Back: Side of the bow away from the string.

Backed Bow: Bow in which the back and belly are made of different material.

Belly: Side of the bow nearest the string.

Brace: To string the bow.

Broadhead: Arrow with large, flat point used in hunting.

Butt: Target backing, usually made of a bale of straw.

Cast: The distance a bow can shoot.

Cock Feather: Feather of a different colour than the rest, which is set at right angles to the arrow head.

***Columbia Round*:** For women: 24 arrows shot at 50, 40, and 30 yards each.

Composite Bow: Bow that has pulleys at the top and bottom ends, which lessen the pull as the string is drawn back. State-of-the-art in archery.

Creeping: Letting the hand slowly inch forward momentarily before the arrow is shot. Will likely ruin the accuracy of the shot.

Double Round: Round shot twice.

Drift: Inaccurate shot because of crosswinds between the archer and the target.

Fletching Jig: Small mechanical machine to attach feathers to arrow.

Fletchings: Feathers attached to arrow to help it "fly" smoothly and accurately through the air.

Flight Arrow: Used for long-distance accuracy shooting; has small feathers.

Flight Shooting: Competition to shoot flight arrows the farthest.

Follow: Tendency of some bows to "warp" to their strung shape.

Form: The archer's stance and technique.

Full Draw: A bow is said to be at full draw when the archer pulls the arrow back completely, just before releasing.

Handle: Midsection of the bow, which the archer grips.

Hen Feathers: Feathers other than the cock feather.

Holding: Keeping the arrow at full bowdraw momentarily before shooting.

Limbs: Upper and lower parts of the bow, with the handle in between.

Loose: To release tension on the bow; to shoot the arrow.

National Round: For women: 48 arrows shot at 60 yards, 24 at 50 yards.

Nock: Groove in the end of the arrow opposite the point; the bow string is inserted in the nock.

Nocking Point: Point on the bow string where the nock is placed. Usually marked by archer.

Overbowed: Using a bow that has a pull too strong for the archer.

Point Blank: Target distance so short that there is no allowance for trajectory of the arrow.

Quiver: Receptacle for holding arrows, usually leather, often decorated.

Range Finder: Mechanical device used to determine distance to target.

Reflex Box: Bow whose tips curve towards bow back when unstrung.

Round: Shooting a determined number of arrows at a target at a specific distance.

Shaft: Main part of the arrow.

Shooting Glove: Glove that protects the two fingers that hold the arrow nock on the bowstring.

Spine: The relative stiffness of an arrow.

Tackle: Archery equipment. Similar in usage to fishing tackle.

Target Face: Front of a target.

Trajectory: Path of an arrow in flight towards the target.

Underbowed: When a bow is too weak for the archer.

Vane: The feather of an arrow.

Weight: The pull of a bow in pounds or the weight of an arrow in grams.

Wide: Arrow that misses the target on either side.

Windage: Effect of wind on the arrow in flight.

BADMINTON

Backhand: Stroke made with the back of the hand towards the opponent's end of the court. Usually cross-body stroke.

Bird: See shuttlecock.

Clear: High shot that falls near the back line.

Cross-Body Stroke: A shot, in which the player's arm crosses in front of the torso.

Cross-Court Shot: Any shot that crosses the net on a diagonal path.

Drive: Hard shot that crosses the net horizontally.

Driven Clear: Any drive that goes to the back court, but not high enough for the opponent to kill.

Drop: A shot that falls close to the net.

Fault: A violation of the rules that involves the loss of a point or the loss of a serve.

Forehand: A shot made with the palm of the hand facing the opponent; a shot that is not a cross-body shot.

Hand-Out: The loss of a serve.

Let: A shot that hits the top of the net, but falls on the opponent's side of the court.

Over-Head Stroke: Shot made over the player's head.

Rally: To return the shuttlecock several times without scoring a point.

Receiver: Player who receives a serve.

Server: Player who puts the shuttlecock in play.

Setting the Game: Deciding how many further points will win the game, when it is tied.

Short Serve: Serve that barely clears the net, but lands in the opponent's court.

Shuttlecock: Feathered object—now usually plastic—that is batted back and forth across a net in the game.

Smash: Powerful overhead stroke that sends the shuttlecock over the net and in a downward arc.

Toss Serve: To throw the shuttlecock into the air so it comes down to be served across the net. Similar to a tennis serve.

BASEBALL

Aboard: On base when the side is retired.

Advance: To move to the next base.

All-Pro: Player elected to a team of exceptional players. (Also appropriate in basketball, football, and other sports.)

All-Star: Same as All-Pro.

All-Time: The best who ever played a game at that particular position. (Appropriate for almost all team sports.)

Alley: Imaginary line or lane between outfielders playing in their normal positions.

American League: One of two major professional major leagues, now split into two divisions. In the Eastern Division are: Baltimore, Boston, Cleveland, Detroit, Milwaukee, New York, and Toronto. In the Western Division are: California, Chicago, Kansas City, Minnesota, Oakland, Seattle, and Texas. Abbreviated AL.

Artificial Turf: Synthetic grass substitute, sold under a variety of brand names. Also called *carpet*.

Assist: Credited to a player who throws to a base to aid in an out.

Babe Ruth Baseball: Non profit organization that sponsors summer baseball for youth aged 9-18.

Backstop: A screen that protects spectators behind the plate from pitches that might get away from the catcher.

Bad Hop: Awkward bounce that allows a ball to get away from a fielder.

Balk: Illegal act by the pitcher that allows all runners on base to advance one base. A balk is technically a pause during the normal pitching motion.

Baseball Annie: Woman attracted to baseball players.

Basket Catch: Catch made with the glove held at waist level with the palm up.

Battery: The pitcher and catcher as a team.

Battery-Mates: Same as *battery*.

Batting Average: Number of hits divided by the number of times at bat.

Batting Helmet: Protective hatlike helmet now required of all professional teams, to prevent injury to the head by a pitched ball. Protective helmets were first used in 1941 by the Brooklyn Dodgers.

Bean Ball: Ball thrown to deliberately hit (or just barely miss) a batter's head. In 1920, a ball thrown by Carl Mayes of the Yankees hit and killed Ray Chapman, of the Cleveland Indians, which has been baseball's only fatality. Also called brushback and knockdown pitch.

Bench Jockey: A player who seldom plays. He "rides the bench."

Big League: Either or both professional leagues.

Bleachers: Seats in the outfield area, usually cheap seats, in an area of a stadium without a roof.

Bottom of an Inning: The last half of an inning.

Box Score: A condensed report of a game that shows the lineups for both teams, runs batted in, score, and so on. The baseball equivalent of shorthand reporting.

Breaking Ball: A ball that curves in or out as it crosses the plate area.

Bronx Cheer: A "razzberry" sound made by a spectator. Usually made in contempt.

Bullpen: Area behind the outer fences of a baseball field where relief pitchers warm up and wait for their possible entry into the game.

Bunt: A ball that is not swung at. The batter holds the bat horizontally and taps the ball into the infield.

Bush League: Minor leagues. Carries the connotation of amateurish, unprofessional, not yet top-flight.

Cactus League: Spring training league that plays in the Southwest.

Cellar: The lowest team statistically in a league's standings is said to be "in the cellar."

Charley Horse: A slight muscle pull or strain, usually in the leg muscles. Also appropriate in football, track and field, and other sports.

(To) Choke Up: To be unable to play to the best of a player's ability because of fear or tension.

To Choke up on a Bar: To hold it higher than the normal grip position.

Clean-Up: The fourth position in the batting order.

Clothesline: Baseball hit in such a straight line that clothes could be hung on the level.

Contact Hitter: A player known for an ability to hit the ball regularly for base hits, although probably unspectacular ones.

Count: The number of balls and strikes a player has when he is batting.

Cup of Coffee: A brief visit to the major leagues by a minor league player. He is said to have visited the majors just "long enough for a cup of coffee."

Curve: A ball thrown in such a way that it curves in flight towards the batter's box.

Cy Young Award: An award made annually to the pitcher who has made an outstanding record that year. Voted by the Baseball Writer's Association.

Designated Hitter: A player who comes to bat for a team, but who does not field. Allowed in the American league, but not in the National League. Allowed once every other year in the World Series. Abbreviated DH.

Diamond: The infield part of a baseball field.

Disabled List: A player who is injured and can not play is placed on the disabled list. Also appropriate in football.

Doctor: To secretly treat a baseball to gain an advantage.

Doctored Bat: To treat a bat so it is not of regulation weight, for an advantage to the batter. A doctored bat is usually made lighter by drilling a hole in the bat and covering the hole so the doctored area cannot be seen.

Double-Dip: Two games played in one day, a double-header.

Double Play: Two consecutive outs during the same play.

Downtown: A home-run ball that clears the outfield fences and flies into the seats is said to have gone downtown.

Dugout: An area where team benches are located, usually slightly lower than the spectator's seats so as not to block the view of the field. One is located on the first base side of the field, the other on the third base side.

Earned Run: Run that scores as a result of base hits, stolen bases, sacrifice hits, walks, hit batter, wild pitches, or balks and before fielders have had a chance to retire the side.

Error: Is charged against a player when a misplay (ball that is dropped, etc.) causes the play to continue, when without the error, the play would have been over.

Extra Innings: A game that goes beyond the normal nine innings to break a tie.

Fair Ball: A hit ball that remains inside the playing area of the field.

Farm Team: A minor league team associated with a major league team is said to be a farm team because that's where major league players are "grown" or developed.

Fast Ball: A baseball thrown at 100 mph or more.

Fielder's Choice: When a defensive player chooses to retire a base runner previously on base, rather than the batter who hit the ball.

Fielding Average: Put-outs, assists, and errors, divided into put-outs and assists.

Fireman: A relief pitcher who wins games in the late innings by putting out the opposition's "fire."

Flake: A psychologically unreliable ball player.

Foul Ball: Ball that rolls off the field of play before reaching first base or third base, or lands off the field of play past first or third base.

Foul Tip: A batted ball that fields directly into the catcher's mit and is caught by the catcher. This is a fair ball.

Frame: An inning.

Free Agent: A player not under contract to any club and who can negotiate a contract with any club in the league.

Fungo Bat: Lightweight bat used for batting practice.

Gamer: A player who plays with an injury.

Goat: Nickname for a player who loses a crucial game.

Go Down Looking: To take a called third strike for an out without swinging.

Go Down Swinging: To swing and miss at a third strike and be called out.

Golden Glove Award: An award made every year to the fielders with the best performance at each position.

Grand Slam: A home run hit with the bases loaded, thus scoring four runs.

Grapefruit League: Spring training league, played largely in Florida.

Hit: Ball hit in such a way that the batter may reach base safely or preceding base runners may reach an additional base or bases safely.

Hook Slide: To slide into second or third base or home plate while avoiding a player's tag, but while keeping one foot pointed towards the base.

Hot Corner: Third base.

Iceman: A relief pitcher who can "ice" an opponent's "hot streak." Same as *fireman.*

Iron Mike: Pitching machine that is used during batting practice.

Infield Fly: Fly ball with runners on first and second, or on first, second, and third, that is hit into the infield and that can be handled by the infielders for an out.

In the Hole: Unfavourable position for the batter. If the batter has two strikes against him and no balls called, he is said to be in the hole.

Junk Pitch: An unorthodox pitch or slower than normal pitch.

Junk Man: Pitcher who relies on junk pitches for effectiveness.

Knockdown Pitch: A pitch deliberately thrown at the batter's head or thrown so close to the batter that he must fall to the ground to avoid being hit by the pitch. Same as *bean ball.*

K: Indicates a strikeout in a baseball box score. A backward K indicates a swinging strikeout.

Lead: A few steps away from a base taken by a runner towards the next base.

Line Drive: A ball hit in a straight line.

Lineup Card: Card given by the manager to the umpire that lists all the players to be used during a game by their position in the batting order.

Little League: A minor league for youngsters that plays on a field that is one third smaller than normal. Now headquartered in Williamsport, PA, the Little League plays a World Series every year.

Load the Bases: To have runners on first, second, and third base at the same time.

Long Reliever: Relief pitcher who can pitch five innings or more.

Magic Number: The number of games that a particular team must win to win a divisional race and thus qualify for playoffs leading to the World Series.

Major League: Refers to either or both the National League or the American League.

Minor League: Any league other than the two major leagues.

MVP: Most Valuable Player. Award given to the outstanding player in each league each year. Awarded by the Baseball Writers Association.

National League: One of two professional major leagues, now divided into two divisions. In the Eastern Division are: St. Louis, Montreal, Philadelphia, Pittsburgh, New York, Florida, and Chicago. In the Western Division are: Los Angeles, Cincinnati, Atlanta, San Francisco, Colorado, Houston, and San Diego. Abbreviated NL.

Nightcap: Second game of a doubleheader, often played at night.

No-hitter: A game in which a pitcher does not allow any base hits by the opposing team.

Off-Speed Pitch: Slower than normal pitch.

On Deck: Player waiting to bat next.

Outfield: That part of a baseball field beyond the base paths that connect first, second, and third bases.

Out In Front Of: To swing too early at a pitch.

Passed Ball: Is charged against the catcher when he drops the ball or loses possession of it and that loss causes a runner to advance a base or bases. Called an error if the catcher drops a called third strike; the player is allowed to advance to first base.

Pennant: A league divisional champion team. So called because the team is allowed to fly the league flag or pennant during the next season.

Perfect Game: A game in which a pitcher allows no opposing players to safely reach base.

Pick Off: To throw a runner out with a quick throw to a fielder who tags the runner out, off base.

Pinch Hit: To hit in place of another player, to substitute for.

Pinch Run: To run in place of another player.

Pitcher of Record: The pitcher who is officially charged with winning or losing a game.

Pitcher's Duel: A close game in which opposing pitchers have both performed well.

Pitcher's Mound: A slightly elevated part of a playing field that the pitcher throws from. Generally elevated 10 inches higher than normal ground level.

Pitch Out: A pitch that is thrown wide of the plate so a catcher can throw to put out a runner who is off base.

Play-by-Play: A running account of a game in progress.

Playoff: Games conducted at the end of a season to determine a league championship.

Pop Fly: A high fly ball.

Portsider: Same as *southpaw.*

Put-Out: Credited to fielder who handles a ball in a play that results in an out for a baserunner.

Rabbit Ball: A ball that bounces or hops in a lively manner.

Rain Check: A ticket stub that can be used again if a game is rained out and replayed later.

Rain Out: To rain hard enough to cause a game to be postponed.

Ribbie: Abbreviation for Runs Batted In. Important offensive statistic for ball players.

Relief Pitcher: A pitcher who does not start a game, but who comes in to relieve the starting pitcher in late innings.

Retire the Side: To put out three batters to end an opposing team's turn at bat.

Rhubarb: A noisy argument.

Rookie: An inexperienced player, a novice.

Rookie of the Year: An award made by the Baseball Writers of America to the outstanding first-year players in the American and National Leagues.

Rosin Bag: A bag that contains powdered rosin. This is handled by the pitcher between pitches to allow him to keep a firm grip on the ball.

Rotation: The regular order in which pitchers are used by a team.

Run Batted In: A run that scores because of a hit by another player.

Run Down: To chase a runner between bases and tag him for an out.

Running Squeeze: Runner on third base begins running towards home plate, as the ball is pitched, hoping that the batter will bunt safely and allow him to score.

Sack: The first, second, and third bases.

Sacrifice Bunt: Batter bunts the ball to advance a baserunner and is called out while the baserunner advances safely.

Sacrifice Fly: Ball hit to the outfield that results in an out for the batter, but a successful advance for a runner on base.

Safety Squeeze: Runner on third heads for home plate when the ball is bunted. Slightly different than *running squeeze.*

Sandlot Ball: School yard baseball, or any other informally organized game.

Save: When a relief pitcher wins a game begun by a starting pitcher, he is said to have saved the game.

Set Down: Same as *retire the side.*

Seventh-Inning Stretch: Spectators' tradition of standing and stretching before the home team comes to bat in the seventh inning. Spectators usually go to the restrooms, get a beer, or otherwise take a break.

Shake Off a Sign: Occurs when a pitcher refuses to pitch a specific type of ball that the catcher signals him to pitch.

Shoestring Catch: Catch of a ball made at the shoe level. Also appropriate in football.

Short Reliever: Relief pitcher used for only a few innings, or a relief pitcher who is effective for only a few innings.

Shut Out: To prevent an opposing team from scoring through an entire game.

Sign: Signal shown to the pitcher by the catchers to indicate what kind of ball to throw next. First base and third base coaches may also signal to runners and batters, and the manager may signal to his team from the dugout.

Sinker: Pitch that drops vertically as it crosses the plate.

Slugger: Hitter known for many hits and runs.

Southpaw: Left-handed player. Usually refers to left-handed pitcher.

Speed Gun: Portable radar unit used to determine the speed of a pitched ball.

Spitball: Illegal pitch caused by the pitcher adding some foreign material, such as spit or vaseline, to the ball.

Spring Training: Time before the start of major league season in which players regain playing abilities lost during the off season. Major leagues also test minor league players during this time. Generally starts in March and ends just prior to the season.

Stand-Up Double: A hit that allows the runner to reach second base without sliding.

Stand-Up Triple: A hit that allows the runner to reach third base without sliding.

Stolen Base: Runner advances successfully without the aid of a base hit, put-out, walk, force-out, fielder's choice, passed ball, wild pitch, or balk.

Strike Zone: The area that the pitcher must throw in to successfully throw strikes. Generally from the hitter's armpits to his knees, when he is in a normal batting position.

Stuff: A pitcher's effectiveness; either he has good stuff or not.

Switch Hitter: Player who bats both right- and left-handed.

Tape-Measure Homer: Long home run that might be measured for a record.

Texas Leaguer: Fly ball hit just over the head of the shortstop or second baseman, just barely into the outfield.

Three and One: Three balls and one strike on the batter.

Tools of Ignorance: Mask, glove, and pads used by a catcher.

Top of the Inning: The first half of an inning.

Top of the Order: The first batter in the batting order.

Triple: A hit that allows the batter to reach third base successfully.

Triple Play: A play in which three baserunners are put out.

Twin Bill: Same as *doubleheader*.

Twilight Doubleheader: A doubleheader with the first game scheduled about twilight.

Unearned Run: Any run that scores on the basis of an error by an opposing player.

Walk: To be awarded first base because of four balls pitched by the pitcher.

Wild Pitch: Pitch thrown so that the catcher cannot control it.

Wind-Up: The motion of a pitcher prior to releasing the ball.

Winter Ball: Organized baseball played during the off season.

World Series: A best-of-seven game series played by the champion teams of the American and National Leagues.

BASKETBALL

Air Ball: Shot that misses the basket and the backboard and hits "only air."

All-Court Press: To closely guard the offence all over the court.

Alley-Oop Shot: Shot made by one player to another player on the same team who is waiting under the basket to instantly tip the ball in for a score.

Assist: A quick pass from one player to another, which results in a quick score.

Backboard: Flat 4- × 6-foot surface, suspended above and perpendicular to the floor, to which the basket rim is attached. In some cases, the backboard may be fan shaped and approximately 35 × 54 inches, with a 29-inch radius. Players may bank the ball off the backboard to score.

Back Court: The half of the court that a team defends.

Ball Control: The ability to maintain possession of the ball through dribbling or passing.

Bank Shot: A shot that bounces off the backboard into the basket.

Basket: An 18-inch metal ring with a suspended cord net. Players attempt to shoot the ball through the ring to score.

Blocking: To impede an opponent. (Blocking is a foul.)

Boxing Out: The position of a defensive player under the basket that does not allow an offensive player a favourable position for a shot or rebound.

Buzzer Shot: Shot that is made as the buzzer goes off, signaling the end of the first half or the end of the game.

Centre: The player responsible for the centre jump and for playing the "pivot position" near the basket. Usually the tallest player on the team.

Charging: Contact against an opponent by a player with the ball. (Charging is a foul.)

Charity Line: Free-throw line.

Charity Shot: Free throw.

Clutch Player: Player who can be depended on to score in a crucial moment.

Cold: A player or team temporarily unable to score.

Collapse: When two defensive players converge on an offensive player the moment he receives the ball.

Conversion: A successful free throw.

Corner Men: Forwards who are key rebounding players.

Defensive Boards: The backboard of a defending team's basket.

Double Dribble: A dribble that is resumed after having once been stopped; this is a rules violation. The ball goes to the opposite team.

Double Figures: To score 10 points or more during a game.

Double Foul: When two players on opposite teams foul each other at the same time.

Double Team: To guard one offensive player with two defensive players at the same time.

Down Court: The end of the court that a team is defending.

Draw a Foul: To behave so as to deliberately be fouled by an opponent.

Dribble: To control the ball by bouncing it repeatedly on the floor.

Drive: Powerful effort towards the basket. Dunk: To jump up and push the ball through the basket from above.

Fade-Away Shot: To shoot while moving away from the basket.

Fast Break: To drive towards the basket before the defensive team has a chance to set up in position to block the drive or the shot.

Follow-in: To follow the progress of the ball to be position for a rebound.

Forward: Player who operates to the side of the offensive back and who is usually a good rebounder.

Foul: Violation of a rule, which results in a free throw by the opposing team. Fouls generally include: blocking, charging, pushing, holding, tripping, illegal substitution, and delaying the game.

Free Throw: Opportunity to score one point unhindered from the foul line as a result of a foul by the opposing team.

Freeze: An attempt to keep possession of the ball by one team, to maintain a lead in the score, or to dribble to kill time on the clock.

Front Court: The half of the court that contains the team's own basket. Opposite of *back court.*

Full-Court Press: Same as *all-court press.*

Garbage Shot: Any easy or uncontested shot.

Give and Go: To pass to a teammate and drive to the basket to await a return pass, which would set up a scoring opportunity.

Goaltending: Any interference with the ball when it is in its downward arc above the rim of the basket, or trapping the ball against the backboard.

Guard: Usually a small player who brings the ball into the forecourt and passes to the forwards or the centre for a shot.

Gunner: Player who shoots obsessively at the basket.

Hardship Case: A college basketball player who enters the professional basketball draft before his college eligibility is used up, pleading that family poverty necessitates an early entry into professional basketball. Also called *poverty case.*

Held Ball: When two opposing players each hold the ball and neither can gain complete possession.

Holding: To prevent an opponent from moving freely. Usually a foul, if caught by the officials.

Hook Shot: High arcing shot made by swinging the arm from behind the back, up over the shoulder.

Hot Hand: Player who temporarily has a high shooting average.

Inside Man: The centre of the team, usually the tallest player, who plays with his back to the basket, then jumps for a rebound.

In Your Face: Player who is guarding his opponent in a close and intimidating manner. Often refers to schoolyard tactics.

Inside Game: Refers to maneuvers close to the basket.

Jump Ball: To put the ball in play by tossing it in the air between two opposing players; the one who can jump up highest for it takes possession.

Lay-Up Shot: A shot made close to the basket that bounces off the backboard into the basket.

Loose Ball: A ball that is in play but not in possession of either team.

Man-to-Man: Defensive play in which each defensive man has a special offensive player to guard.

Multiple Foul: Two or more fouls committed at the same time.

NBA: National Basketball Association.

Net: The mesh sleeve that is attached to the basket rim.

Offensive Boards: The backboard rebounding area of a team's offensive basket.

One-and-One: A rule in college basketball in which a player receives the right to a second foul shot if the first foul shot is successful. This rule is also used in women's and high school basketball.

One-on-One: A situation in which a specific offensive player is guarded by a specific defensive player, or when a specific offensive player challenges a specific defensive player.

Open: A player who is not guarded by an opponent or who has an unguarded path to the basket.

Outlet Pass: Player who grabs a rebound and passes to a teammate to establish a fast break.

Outside Shooter: A player who has the ability to make long shots.

Overhead Shot: A two-handed shot in which the ball is released over the player's head.

Overtime: A 5-minute period of play to decide a game that is tied at the end of regulation time. Abbreviated OT.

Pass: To move to the ball to a player on the same team by throwing it across the court.

Personal Foul: Rules violation when a player contacts an opponent when the ball is in play.

Pivot: To take one or more than one step with one foot, while in possession of the ball. The other foot must remain stationary.

Play for One: To possess the ball and to shoot when there is time for only one shot.

Post: Same as *post man.*

Post Man: Player who stands in a particular position on the court. The high post is near the free-throw line; the low post is close to the basket. He coordinates offensive plays from that position. Also called *pivot man,* because his play is crucial to the play.

Pressing Defence: Defence that attempts to break an offensive drive by closely guarding the ball.

Rebound: To attempt to gain possession of the ball when it has bounced off the basket or the backboard without going through the net.

Rim: Metal hoop, 18 inches wide, through which the ball must fall to score. The net is attached to the rim.

Run-and-Gun: Aggressive type of play in which a team frequently runs the length of the court for a fast break. Also called *run-and-shoot*.

Screen: To protect a teammate in the act of shooting by standing between him and an opponent.

Set Play: A play in which offensive positions are deliberately taken; opposite of run-and-gun play.

Shave Points: To illegally limit the number of points scored, to affect a bet on a basketball game.

Shot Clock: Clock that indicates that the team with the ball has a time limit to take a shot.

Sky Hook: High hook shot that is impossible to block.

Slam Dunk: Hard dunk shot.

Stall: To keep possession of the ball to maintain a lead or to keep the opposing team from gaining control of the ball. Usually occurs when a team is trying to run out the clock.

Technical Foul: Foul committed by a player not in possession of the ball, or a foul committed by a coach, or an unsportsmanlike call while the ball is dead. Often abbreviated T.

Thirty Second Clock: Same as *shot clock*.

Three Point Play: Foul committed during the act of successfully scoring; the player then gets one foul shot after the basket.

Throw In: Act of beginning play by throwing the ball into the court from an out-of-bounds position.

Tip-Off: The jump ball used to begin play.

Toss-Up: A jump ball.

Tower: See *tree*.

Travelling: To take more than the maximum steps allowed while in possession of the ball at the end of a dribble.

Tree: A centre who is so tall and powerful that he cannot be moved or outrebounded.

Trailer: Player who follows behind a player with the ball.

Turnover: To lose the ball to the opposition because of a mistake, a foul, or a stolen ball.

Two Against One: Two offensive players playing against one defensive player, or vice versa.

Two-Time: Same as *double dribble.*

Upcourt: The end of the court that one team is attacking.

Zone: Particular area of the court.

Zone Defence: Type of play in which each player is responsible for a particular part of the court and responsible for the play when the action enters that zone.

Zone Press: Type of play in which a player is responsible for close man-to-man coverage when the action is in his zone.

BOATING & FISHING

Aft: Towards, near, or at the stern a boat.

Back Cast: Drawing the rod back, the first movement in the cast.

Backlash: Line that becomes tangled by rolling over itself in the reel during the cast, because there is too much play in the reel. (Note: Some modern reels have an anti-backlash mechanism built in.).

Bait: Natural or artificial lures to attract fish.

Bait-Casting: Placing a natural or artificial lure in the area of fish by using a rod and reel.

Ballast: Weight, usually metal, placed low in the boat, or externally, on the keel, to provide stability.

Batten: A light wooden or plastic strip inserted into a pocket in a sail to help shape it.

Beam: The width of a boat at its widest.

Berth: A bunk or sleeping place in the cabin of a boat.

Boom: A spar that is used to extend the foot of a sail.

Bow: The forward part of a boat.

Bucktail: A fly used in bass fishing.

Clew: The lower aft corner of a fore-and-aft sail or either corner of a spinnaker.

Cork Arbor: The part of the reel to which the line is attached.

Cowling: A cover over the engine of a boat.

Dry Fly Fishing: Casting a fly so it resembles an insect on the water.

Ferrules: Metal connections between sections of a take-apart rod.

Flies: Artificial lures that resemble insects.

Fly-Casting: Placing a fly in the area of fish by using a rod and reel.

Fore: Towards or at the bow of a boat.

Fore-and-Aft: In line from bow to stern; on, or parallel to, the centreline.

Forward Cast: Forward movement of a rod that places the lure into the water. Final step in back cast-forward cast movement.

Furl: To roll a sail and secure it to its yard or boom.

Gaff: Small hook used to bring fish on board a boat.

Genoa: A larger jib used in light breezes.

Gimbal: A device consisting of a pair of rings pivoted on axes at right angles to each other so that one is free to swing within the other: A ship's compass will keep a horizontal position when suspended in gimbals.

Guides: Small loops on the rod. The line runs through these guides.

Halyard: A rope, wire, or chain by which a sail, flag, or yard is hoisted.

Head: Toilet on board a ship.

Helm: The steering apparatus.

Hooking the Fish: Setting the hook in the fish after it takes the bait or lure.

Hull: The frame or body of a ship, excluding the spars, sails, and rigging.

Inboard: Motor mounted inside the boat or ship.

Jib: A fore-and-aft triangular sail, set forward of the mast.

Keel: The fixed underwater part of a sailing boat used to prevent sideways drift and to provide stability.

Knot: A measure of speed: one nautical mile (6060.2 feet) per hour.

Lanyard: A short line or rope used to attach one object or item to another.

Leader: Material that connects the lure or hook to the line.

Leech: The aftermost edge of a fore-and-aft sail; both side edges of a square sail.

Lures: Artificial or natural bait used to attract fish.

Mast: A pole or system of attached poles, placed vertically on a vessel, used to support the sails.

Net: Mesh device on a metal frame to pull fish out of the water.

Outboard: Motor attached to the stern of a vessel.

Plane: To gain hydrodynamic lift as the boat lifts up on its bow wave.

Port: Left side of a ship when looking forward.

Reel: Mechanical device that winds or unwinds line for fishing.

Reel Set: Part of the rod handle to which the reel is attached.

Rig: The form in which a vessel's mast, spars, and sails are arranged.

Rudder: Movable underwater part of a vessel used for steering and to prevent side-slipping.

Sheet: The line attached to the clew of a sail, used to trim it. When the sheets are brought in and made fast they are said to be sheeted together.

Ship: Vessel large enough to carry its own lifeboat or lifeboats.

Shrouds: Wires that support the mast on either side; part of the standing or permanent rigging.

Spar: Long wooden beam, generally rounded and used for supporting or extending the sails of a ship.

Spinnaker: A lightweight three-cornered sail, set flying from the masthead and controlled by sheets from each clew.

Spinner: Artificial lure that spins as it is drawn through the water.

Spoons: Artificial bait that generally resemble kitchen spoons.

Starboard: The right side of a vessel when looking forward.

Stern: The aftermost part of a vessel.

Still Fishing: Fishing with bait held motionless in the water.

Strike: When a fish grabs the bait or hook.

Tack (noun): The forward lower corner of a fore-and-aft sail. Or *to tack* (verb): To turn the bow of a boat through the wind so that it blows across the opposite side.

Tackle: Fishing gear—rod and reel.

Tip: Smallest end of the rod.

Torque: A force that produces a twisting, rotating, or spinning motion.

Trapeze: A support used by the crew of a racing boat to enable them to move their weight outboard.

Trim: The adjustment of the sails of a vessel.

Trolling: To fish with a moving line.

Winch: A crank with a handle.

Windlass: A device used for hauling or hoisting, usually for sails.

Yacht: Vessel used for private cruising, racing, or other noncommercial purposes.

BOWLING

Alley: Same as *lane.*

Anchor: Last bowler on a team.

Approach: The act of taking 3, 4, or 5 steps, swinging the arm and releasing the ball towards the pins.

Beer Frame: Frame during a bowling game in which the player with the lowest score buys beer for the team.

Box: See *frame.*

Brooklyn: Ball that crosses the lane and hits the 1-2 pins first, instead of the 1-3 pins.

Creeper: A ball that rolls slower than normal.

Double: Two strikes in succession.

Foul: To go beyond the foul line during the approach.

Foul Line: Line that marks the end of the approach and the beginning of the lane. To step over the line during the approach results in a foul.

Frame: Box in which the scores are marked: 10 frames make a game.

Gutter: Channel on each side of a bowling lane in which balls can drop and roll into the pit without touching any pins.

Gutter Ball: Ball that drops into side gutter without hitting any pins.

Handicap: Bonus score or adjustment to an individual's score or team score, based on averages.

Head Pin: #1 pin.

Hook: Ball that breaks to the left for a righthanded bowler.

Kegler: German for bowler.

Lane: Bowling alley: 41 inches wide and 60 feet long from the foul line to the head pin, usually made of wood. An additional 16 feet, consisting of the bowler's approach to the foul line and from the head pin to the end of the lane, is made of maple, the lane of pine. Formerly called *alley*.

Line: Complete game scored on a scoring sheet.

Loft: To loft a ball means the bowler releases it too late; the ball arcs into the air and hits the lane heavily, instead of sliding onto the lane from the bowler's grip.

Mark: A strike or spare in a particular frame.

Pit: Area behind the lane where all pins are scooped for resetting.

Open Frame: Frame in which the bowler has made no strike or spare.

Pocket: Space between the 1 pin and the 2-3 pins.

Sleeper: A standing pin hidden from the bowler's view.

Spare: All pins knocked down on two balls.

Spot: Aiming point on the alley.

Strike: All pins knocked down on the first ball.

Three Hundred (300): Perfect game.

BOXING

Ali Shuffle: Rapid series of front-and-back foot movements made famous by Muhammad Ali. The advantage was said to be tactical—to show his opponent he was in control of the fight and could still move quickly.

Answer the Bell: To get up from a corner to begin fighting when the bell sounds. If a fighter fails to answer the bell, he is declared the loser in that round.

Apron: The floor outside the boxing ring. It is approximately 2 feet wide.

Arm Puncher: A boxer whose strength is only in his arms; lacks the power of his body behind his punches.

Arm Weary: Tired of throwing punches.

Backpedal: To retreat across the ring.

Bang: To punch hard, without finesse.

Beat the Count: To get up before the count is over.

Bell: A bell that is rung to indicate the beginning and the end of a round.

Below the Belt: A punch that lands below the top of the hipbones, generally in the crotch. If a *low blow* is deliberate, a fighter may be disqualified.

Bleeder: A fighter who cuts easily.

Bob and Weave: To move side to side and up and down to evade an opponent.

Body Punch: Blow delivered to the body of an opponent; that is, the abdomen or ribs.

Bolo Punch: Punch that begins in a wide are from below the hips swinging upward. Popularized in the early 1940s by middleweight champion Ceferino Garcia, who described the punch as comparable to the swing of a bolo knife cutting through the jungles. Now thought of as any wildly exaggerated punch that begins low.

Break: To withdraw from a clinch when ordered to do so by the referee.

Bum: Unskilled fighter, often thought of as being *punch-drunk*.

Can't Lay a Glove On: A boxer so clever defensively that his opponent can't hit him.

Canvas: The floor of a boxing ring.

Carry (To Carry a Fight): To hold back from ending a fight to make a weak opponent look better than he is.

Cauliflower Ear: A deformed ear; caused by too many blows to the ear.

Challenger: A fighter who fights a reigning champion.

Class: Same as *division.*

Clean Break: To separate from a clinch.

Clinch: To hold an opponent with both arms so neither fighter can score cleanly.

Club Fighter: A small-time boxer with mediocre skills; a fighter who fights mainly in local clubs.

Coldcock: To knock out an opponent with one blow.

Combination: Two or more punches in rapid succession.

Contender: A fighter good enough to be a challenger. Popularized in a speech by Marlon Brando in the film *On The Waterfront,* "I cudda been a contenda . . ."

Corner: Any of the four corners of a boxing ring, or, the particular corner assigned to each fighter.

Cornerman: One of the assistants allowed to be in a fighter's corner between rounds.

Count: Counting 10 seconds after a fighter has been knocked down. If a fighter does not arise after the 10 count, the opponent wins the fight by a knockout.

Counter: To respond to an opponent's punch by returning a punch.

Counterpuncher: A boxer who prefers to wait for an opponent's punch to deliver a punch.

Cover Up: To protect the body and head from an opponent's punches, with the arms.

Cross: A punch delivered over and above an opponent's lead, such as a right cross.

Cut Man: Assistant in a fighter's corner who is responsible for stopping cuts or bleeding.

Cut Off the Ring: To move sideways across the ring to reduce the room an opponent can maneuver in.

Dance: To use rapid footwork.

Decision: To win a fight based on the number of points scored by judges witnessing a fight, in which there is no *knockdown* or *technical knockdown*.

Distance: The maximum number of rounds in a fight. (*To go the distance*, to fight 12 rounds in a 12-round fight.)

Division: A category of fighters based on weight. In general, these are the professional divisions:

Flyweight	112 lbs.
Bantamweight	118 lbs.
Featherweight	126 lbs.
Junior Lightweight	130 lbs.
Lightweight	135 lbs.
Junior Welterweight	140 lbs.
Welterweight	147 lbs.
Junior Middleweight	154 lbs.
Middleweight	160 lbs.
Light Heavyweight	175 lbs.
Heavyweight	Unlimited

Down and Out: To be knocked down and be unable to rise.

Down for the Count: Same as *down and out*.

Draw: Same as *tie*.

Drop a Guard: To lower the gloves; to leave face or body unprotected.

Elimination Bout: One of a series of matches to determine an eventual champion.

Fight Card: Series of bouts on the same programme.

Five-Point Must System: A method of scoring in which the winner of a round is given five points, the loser, less than five. In the case of a tie round, both fighters are given five points.

Five-Point System: A method of scoring in which the winner of a round is given one to five points and the loser is given fewer, usually less than one point difference. In the case of a tie, neither fighter is awarded any points for the round.

Footwork: The movement of the feet during a fight.

Foul: Any illegal action or blow during a prizefight, usually a blow to the back of the head or neck, a blow below the belt, wrestling or head butting, or punching after the bell.

Go Into the Tank: To intentionally lose a fight.

Golden Gloves: A programme of locally sponsored amateur fights that lead to the National Golden Gloves Tournament.

(To) Guard: To hold the gloves close to the face or body to protect from an opponent's punches.

Gym Fighter: A fighter who looks good in the gym, but bad during a bout.

Handler: Someone who helps train a fighter or acts as a cornerman during a fight.

Haymaker: A knockout punch.

Headgear: Padded headpiece that is used during training to protect the head.

Heavy Bag: Large stuffed canvas bag, approximately 1-1½ feet in diameter and at least 3 feet long, hung from the ceiling of a gym, that a fighter punches to help strength, power and technique.

(To) Hit on the Break: To punch during the break period, as required by a referee.

Hungry: A fighter who financially or professionally desperately needs a win.

Infighter (Infighting): Fighting close to an opponent.

In the Bag: Fight that has been decided before it has begun.

In the Tank: Fighter who deliberately loses a fight.

Jab: Direct punch used to bother an opponent or keep him off balance. Usually not a knockout punch.

Kayo: To Knock Out.

Knockdown: To punch an opponent and cause him to fall onto the canvas. Once a fighter has been knocked down, the referee begins the 10-count.

Lead: The first in a series of punches.

Left: A punch thrown with the left hand.

Long Count: Any count that takes longer than a strict 10 seconds. Usually is a controversial count.

Low Blow: A blow below the hip-line, usually to the crotch and usually a foul.

Main Event: The most important and the last bout during a boxing programme.

Majority Decision: A decision made by two of three boxing judges.

Make the Weight: To gain or lose pounds to enter a specific weight class, for a fight in that class.

Mandatory Eight Count: A rule that indicated that when a fighter has been knocked down, the referee must count to eight before the fight can proceed, to protect the downed fighter.

Measure: To hold a gloved hand against a stunned fighter to guide a knockout blow.

Mouse: A swelling around the eye.

Mouthpiece: Protective rubber guard worn inside the mouth to protect the teeth and lips of a fighter.

Neutral Corner: Either of the two corners of a ring *not assigned* to a particular fighter and his cornermen.

No Contest: An act of ending a fight by a referee because of problems not directly connected to the two fighters, such as a power blackout.

No Knockdown: A rule by a referee during a fight that a fighter who was on the canvas was not there because of a knockdown, but rather a slip or a push.

On the Ropes: Leaning helplessly on the ring ropes; usually means the fighter cannot defend himself.

Out: Knocked out.

(To) Outpoint: To win a fight with the highest number of points awarded by the judges.

Palooka: An unskilled fighter.

Preliminary Bout: One bout on a boxing programme before the main event.

Pugilism: The art of boxing, from the Latin pugunus, fist, and *pugil*, boxer.

(To) Pull a Punch: To land a punch without full force.

Punch-Drunk: To suffer the effects of taking too many punches to the head. A punch-drunk fighter is said to slur his speech and generally give the impression of being drunk on alcohol.

Punched Out: Tired from throwing too many punches.

(To) Put Away: To knock out an opponent.

Quick Count: A count that takes *less* than 10 seconds.

Rabbit Punch: An illegal punch to the back of the opponent's head.

Reach: A measure of arm length. Generally speaking, a boxer with a longer reach than his opponent will have an advantage in the ring.

Referee: The official in the ring who controls the action during a fight, watches for fouls, and separates fighters in a clinch. Sometimes called *the third man*.

Rematch: A bout in which two fighters who have fought each other previously fight again.

Ring: An elevated 18- to 20-foot square area surrounded by three ropes attached to vertical posts at each corner. Sometimes called *the squared circle*.

Ring Savvy: Knowledge of the tricks and techniques of boxing.

Roadwork: Running that is part of a boxer's training and conditioning.

Rope: Ropes that are strung at 2-foot, 3-foot, and 4-foot heights around a boxing ring.

Round: Any 3-minute period during a boxing match.

Saved By the Bell: A boxer who is about to be counted out is said to be saved by the bell when the bell to signal the end of a round is rung before the count is up. No fighter can be saved by the bell during the final round of a bout.

Scorecard: A card on which an official keeps score of rounds won or lost by each fighter.

Second: One man who is allowed in a boxer's corner between rounds to advise him.

Slip: To dodge a punch.

Slug: To punch hard.

Slugger: A fighter with little finesse.

Spar: To box in practice.

Sparring Partner: An opponent during a sparring match.

Speed Bag: Lightweight punching bag used for coordination.

Split Decision: Decision of the judges in which two judges vote for one fighter, and the third judge votes for the opponent.

Standing Eight Count: A count of eight given by the referee when a boxer has been hurt. In professional boxing, this is a knockdown.

Step Back: To separate from a clinch.

Stop a Fight: The act of a referee to end a bout, when one fighter cannot continue.

Straight-Up Fighter: A boxer who does not bob or weave.

The Sweet Science: A famous book on boxing by the late boxing critic A. J. Liebling.

(To) Take a Dive: To deliberately lose a fight.

Take the Count: When a boxer allows himself to be counted out.

Tale of the Tape: A boxer's measurements: reach, chest, weight, and so on.

Technical Draw: Termination of a bout because of an accidental injury to one fighter.

Technical Knockout: The end of the fight as ruled by the referee when one fighter is unable to continue. Abbreviated on fight cards as TKO.

Ten Point Must System: A method of scoring a bout in which the winner of a round is given 10 points and the loser of the round about 2 points less. In the case of a tie, both fighters receive 10 points.

Three Knockdown Rule: If a fighter is knocked down three times in one round, the fight is over and he loses. Not a universal rule.

(To) Throw in the Towel: A fighter's cornermen concede defeat by throwing a towel into the centre of the ring from the corner.

Timekeeper: Official at ringside who keeps track of the time of the rounds and the time between rounds.

Title: Highest level of any weight class.

Twenty Point Must System: A method of scoring in which the winner of each round is awarded 20 points and the loser a lesser number. In the case of a tie, both fighters are awarded 20 points.

Unanimous Decision: A decision in which all judges vote for one boxer.

Undercard: Any bout on a programme prior to the main event.

Warning: A statement by the referee that a boxer has fouled his opponent and points will be subtracted from his score.

WBA: World Boxing Association.

WBC: World Boxing Council.

Weigh-in: Ceremony before a bout to ensure that boxers' weight is within the class designations.

Weight Division: See division.

White Hope: A White boxer who is a contender for a title held by a Black boxer.

Win on Points: To win by a decision.

FENCING

Advance: To move towards the opponent.

Attack: To attempt to hit the opponent by moving the body or the weapon forward.

Attack of Second Intention: An attack that is meant to be defended, so the attacked may score on a counterattack.

Balestra: See jump advance.

Benefit of the Doubt: If two side judges disagree and if the meet director has no opinion, no point is scored.

Blade: Strong: near the guard. Middle: centre section. Weak: tip end.

Bout: Contest between two fencers.

Button: Small pad on the tip of a weapon to prevent injury to an opponent.

Competition: Contest with one type of weapon.

Epee (Dueling sword): Weapon generally similar to the foil, but with a heavier handle and heavier guard.

Fleche: Running attack. Illegal in college fencing, women's fencing, and public school fencing.

Foil (French Foil): Weapon approximately 35 inches long, with a flexible four-sided blade, and cup guard for the hand, weighing about 17.5 ounces. The tip has a small guard or button to prevent injury to the opponent during a bout.

Guard: The standing position when two fencers face each other momentarily prior to the bout.

Invitation: To invite an attack by moving towards an opponent.

Jump Advance: A lunge in which both feet leave the ground at the same time and meet the floor at the same time.

Jury: Usually four judges and a meet director.

Lunge: Key offensive movement in fencing; a long reach with one leg, preceeded by a thrust with the foil. In a successful lunge, the fencer's whole body follows the arm and leg thrust instantly.

Mask: Mesh protector for the competitor's face.

Match: Contests between two teams with one type of weapon.

Meet: Contests between two or more teams in which more than one type of weapon is used.

Pass: A touch that would not inflict a puncture or wound.

Phase: Continuous action during a bout. Similar to a tennis volley.

Pool: Fencers or teams in a round-robin tournament.

Redoubled Attack: A lunge, followed by a second lunge.

Remise: A delayed riposte.

Retreat: To move away from an opponent.

Return (Riposte): To advance after a successful defence.

Sabre: Weapon similar to the foil in size and weight, but with a two-sided blade, instead of the four-sided blade of the foil.

Touch: A hit on the opponent that would inflict a puncture or wound if the tip of the blade was not padded.

Tournament: Series of competitions with one or more types of weapons, organized on an individual or team basis.

FIELD HOCKEY

Advancing: Foul committed when the ball rebounds from a player's body.

Backing Up: Defensive play behind or outside the bully.

Bully: Action to start or restart a game. Two opposing players alternately strike the ground and each other's stick three times before touching the ball.

Circular Tackle: An attempt to take the ball from an opponent on the player's right side.

Covering: To guard the goal—usually refers to a player away from the action on the field.

Defensive Hit: A free hit towards the goal from 15 yards away.

Dodge: To elude an opponent while controlling the ball.

Dribble: Series of strokes used to control the ball while moving it down the field.

Drive: Hard stroke with a backswing to propel the ball downfield.

Fielding: To control an approaching ball before passing it or moving it downfield.

Flick: Stroke with no backswing.

Foul: Violation of the rules.

Free Hit: A play following a violation of the rules. Taken by the team that was fouled.

Goal: Score made when the ball crosses the goal line after being touched by a player inside the striking circle.

Holding the Whistle: When a play continues after a whistle by an official, when, in the opinion of the official, it is better to allow the play to continue than to stop it and award a penalty.

Lunge: Play used to take the ball from an opponent on the opponent's left.

Marking: Defensive position close to an opponent. Similar to guarding in basketball.

Obstruction: To interfere with an opponent by placing any part of the body between the opponent and the ball. A foul results.

Offside: A foul when a player receives the ball while in an illegal position.

Push-Pass: Quick pass without any backswing on the stroke.

Roll-In: Method of putting the ball in play after it has gone out of bounds.

Scoop: Short pass in which the ball is lifted with the front end, or toe, of the stick.

Stick Side: The player's right side.

Sticks: Foul committed when the player raises the stick shoulder high or higher at the beginning or end of a stroke.

Striking Circle: Inside the curved line that is the goal-shooting area.

FOOTBALL

Activate: To move a player from a reserve or injured list to a list of eligible players.

All the Way: To score a touchdown.

Audible: When a quarterback changes the play by the use of a code, at the line of scrimmage, just before the ball is snapped. By calling an audible, the quarterback hopes to fool the defence, which may be ready for a different play.

Backfield (Defence): Consists of four players, two defensive cornerbacks and two safeties or three defensive backs and one safety.

Backfield (Offence): Usually consists of a quarterback, a fullback, a halfback, and a flanker back.

Backfield in Motion: On the offensive team, one player is allowed to run parallel to the line of scrimmage or back away from the line of scrimmage before the ball is snapped. If the back runs towards the line of scrimmage, it is a penalty for backfield in motion or illegal procedure.

Balanced Line: Offensive line in which there are an equal number of linemen on each side of the centre.

Ball Control: To keep possession of the ball by gaining yards until a score is made. To keep gaining yards (and first downs) prevents the opposing team from gaining possession.

Blitz: When a defensive back moves towards the quarterback before the ball is snapped, he is said to be *blitzing*.

Block: Offensive manoeuvre in which a player uses his body to keep a defensive player from the ball carrier.

Blue-Chip: Quality college player to be selected by a professional team.

Bomb: Long arcing pass that may be caught for a touchdown. Also sometimes called a *rainbow*.

Bootleg: A running play in which the quarterback hides the ball from the defence by holding it against his thigh, away from the defensive line. He may or may not run in the direction of the rest of his backfield.

Crackback Block: Run by an offensive player that ends with a block at the back by a defensive player. Like a clip, it too, is potentially very dangerous to the defensive player, who may not be watching or know the offensive player is about to block.

Crawling: To gain added yardage when the play is over by crawling with the ball at the bottom of a pile of tacklers.

Cut Back: Offensive play by a receiver who runs down the side of the field and cuts back towards the centre of the field.

Cup: Same as *in the pocket*.

Dead Ball: After a play is over and when the referee blows his whistle to indicate that the play is over. Any foul after that is a *dead ball foul*.

Delay: To hold a position at the line of scrimmage momentarily to confuse an opposing lineman.

Delay of Game: The offensive team has 30 seconds to begin a play. If the play has not begun in 30 seconds, the referee may call a delay of game penalty.

Depth Chart: A coaching chart showing the #1 player at each position, then #2, then #3, and perhaps even #4 at some positions.

Diamond Defence: Defensive formation with seven men on the line, then one back (fullback) then two backs behind him (halfbacks), then one back (safety) behind them. Called a diamond because from above, the backfield formation would have the shape of a diamond.

Dime Defence: Six defensive players (one more than the nickel, or five-man defence).

Dive Play: Offensive play in which the ball carrier literally dives over the line of scrimmage.

Double Team: Occurs when two offensive players block one defensive player.

Down and In: An offensive play in which a receiver runs down the field and in towards the centre of the field.

Down and Out: An offensive play in which a receiver runs down the field then out, towards the sideline.

Downing the Ball: On a kickoff, a player on the receiving team may catch the ball in the end zone. He may elect not to run the ball out of the end zone. In that case, he downs the ball, by touching one knee to the ground. The next play begins on the offensive team's 20-yard line.

Draft: The act of choosing eligible college players, on a team-by-team basis. The worst team in the professional league has the first chance at eligible college players, to (in theory) equalize the teams in terms of player-by-player ability.

Draw Play: An offensive play in which the quarterback drops back from the line of scrimmage as if he is going to pass, then hands the ball to a runner, who may gain substantial yardage through the defence, which was expecting a pass.

Drop Back: Occurs when a quarterback receives the ball from the centre and moves away from the line of scrimmage to pass, or to hand the ball to a runner.

Dump Pass: To quickly throw the ball to the closest eligible player to avoid a loss in yardage (or an embarrassingly inept play).

(To) Eat the Ball: To down the ball with a loss of yardage, to prevent a more substantial loss of yardage. Usually involves embarrassment to the ball carrier.

End Around: Offensive play in which an end runs in an arc through his own backfield, receives the ball and carries it into the defence at the other end of the field. The end must have superior speed to make much yardage on an end around play.

End Zone: Teams score points by running, passing, or kicking the ball into the end zone. It is 10 yards deep; there is one at each end of the playing field.

Extra Points: Awarded after a touchdown; on a play from scrimmage, two points are awarded if the ball is run or passed successfully over the goal line; one point if the ball is kicked between the goal posts.

Face Mask: Metal cage that prevents injury to the player's face. May be grabbed by an opponent and still cause injury to the player's neck. A penalty results if an official catches a player grabbing or holding another player's face mask.

Fade Back: Occurs when the quarterback takes the ball from the centre and retreats from the line of scrimmage to pass the ball or hand it off to another back.

Fake: Any movement or motion intended to fool the opposing team.

Fair Catch: A player may make a fair catch on a kickoff, return kick, or kick from scrimmage by raising his hand clearly above his head. If he is tackled after a fair catch signal, a penalty results. He may not take more than two steps after catching the ball. The ball is put in play at the point of the catch. If the player drops or fumbles the catch, it is a fair ball and may be recovered by the defence.

Field Goal: A kick over the crossbar and between the goal posts that results in three points for the kicking team.

Films: Films of an opponent's previous games are studied by a coaching staff to prepare a team for an upcoming game.

Fire Out: To move from the line of scrimmage offensively when the ball is snapped.

First Down: An offensive team has four tries to gain 10 yards. If they gain 10 yards within the four tries, they have a first down and are then eligible to gain 10 more yards in another four tries.

Flag: Penalty marker used by officials.

Flag Football: A nontackle form of football in which players wear (usually) two streamers of cloth. The play is stopped when a defensive player grabs one or both flags from an offensive player's waist.

Flak Jacket: Padded protective vest worn under their uniforms by quarterbacks (and occasionally by others) to prevent rib, abdomen, or kidney injury. Named after the similar jackets worn by World War II airmen to prevent injury by anti-aircraft fire.

Flanker: A backfield player who is positioned away from the rest of the linemen.

Flat Pass: A pass thrown parallel to the line of scrimmage and with a flat trajectory.

Flea Flicker Play: An offensive play in which the quarterback fakes a pass, then laterals to an offensive back, who then passes to a third offensive player, a risky play because the ball may be fumbled or the pass intercepted.

Flex Defence: In this defence, as the ball is snapped, the ends drop away from the line and become additional linebackers.

Fly Pattern or Fly Pass: Play in which an end runs ("flies") past the defence and hopes to score by simply outrunning the defence and catching a pass for a touchdown.

Foul: Any violation of the rules.

"Four Yards and a Cloud of Dust": Famous Ohio State techniques, used by coach Woody Hayes, of using a fullback down after down to gain "four yards" (and a cloud of dust) into the line, without passing each down.

Franchise Player: A single player so valuable to a team he is said to be able to "save a franchise," financially, by himself.

Free Ball: A ball that is not in possession of either team.

Free Safety: Defensive backfield player who plays in the deep defensive and has no specific man-to-man responsibilities.

Front Four: The two tackles and two guards on the offensive line.

Fullback: Offensive player who lines up behind the quarterback and who usually has the job of gaining short yardage in tough situations.

Fumble: To lose control or possession of the ball.

Fundamentals: Basic skills that any football player should know. Also applies in other *sports.*

Game Plan: Strategy devised by the coaches to cover general offensive plans and general defensive plans.

Gang Tackle: To tackle the ball carrier by two or more players at the same time.

Gap: Real or imaginary hole between two players in correct position.

Giveaways/Takeaways: The relationship between fumbles lost by Team A and recovered by Team B to fumbles lost by Team B and recovered by Team A; a relatively new NFL statistic.

Goal-Line Defence: Special defence when the offensive is within the 10-yard line and is close to a touchdown. Generally, defensive players will be closer together, as they have less field to cover.

Go Against the Grain: To run away from the traffic flow; for example, if all the offensive backfield is running to the right, the ball carrier runs to the left.

Gridiron: Common name for the football field.

Grind it Out: To make yardage in short gains, as in Woody Hayes' "Four Yards and a Cloud of Dust" system.

Grounding the Ball: If a passer cannot find an eligible receiver, he may throw the ball over the heads of all receivers. This is called *grounding the ball or intentional grounding*. The passing equivalent of *eating the ball*.

Gut Check: A crucial situation; team members pause to check their courage. Do they have enough to win the game? Variations: *gutting it up*, and so on.

Halftime: A 30-minute pause between the second and third quarters of a football game. Allows teams to rest and regroup and allows TV networks a chance for commercials.

Hail MaryPass: Long bomb, usually thrown in a desperate situation. When the pass is in the air, the quarterback (and coach) pray that some offensive player will be under it and catch it for a touchdown. Doug Flutie of Boston College threw a Hail Mary and defeated The University of Miami 47-45 in the last second of the game during the 1984 collegiate season.

Hand-off: An offensive play in which one player (usually the quarterback) hands the ball to a second player.

Hang Time: The seconds of time a kick stays in the air. A longer hang time will allow the kicking team a chance to get downfield and stop the receiving team from advancing the caught ball.

Head Hunter: Player who willfully looks for an opportunity to injure an opponent.

(To) Hear Footsteps: To hear (but not see) an opponent moments before a tackle.

Heisman Trophy: Award given annually to the best collegiate player in the country.

Holding: To illegally impede an opponent by grabbing the uniform, arm, leg, or any other available part of the opponent.

Honey Shot: Shot of cheerleader or other pretty girl during a televised game.

Hot Dog: Player who deliberately shows off for the opposition, audience or TV cameras.

Huddle: Brief meeting before a play. The quarterback announces the play and the count to the rest of the team.

Formation: Offensive backfield formation in which the halfback is behind the quarterback and the fullback is behind the halfback. So called because the backfield formation looks like the letter I.

Impact Player: A player whose presence can make a significant difference to a team's winloss record. Similar to *franchise player*. Ineligible Receiver: Player (usually a lineman) who may not catch the ball.

Interception: Occurs when a defensive player catches a ball intended for an offensive player.

In the Trenches: Offensive and defensive linemen at work doing their jobs at the line of scrimmage when the ball is snapped.

Intentional Grounding: When the quarterback passes the ball during an offensive play, the officials may call intentional grounding if they decide that there was not a receiver near the play and that the quarterback simply threw the ball away to avoid a loss. A penalty results.

Interception: Pass caught by a defensive player, that was intended for an offensive player.

Interference: Penalty for illegally blocking the action of a player or a play.

Jammed: A running play that is stopped at the line of scrimmage is said to have been jammed.

Keys: Movements by certain players, or team formations that signal how a play will develop. Coaches watch previous game films in order to discover keys.

Kicking Tee: Small plastic device that holds the ball in correct position for a kick.

Kicking Unit: Special team used in kicking situations.

Line of Scrimmage: An imaginary line or vertical plane passing through the ball and parallel to the goal lines, marked by the nearest yard number (line of scrimmage, 35-yard line). There is a line of scrimmage for each team and the area between the two is the *neutral zone.* Any player who enters the neutral zone before the ball is snapped is guilty of being offside.

Look In: A pass play in which a receiver runs diagonally down the field and "looks in" (looks back towards the quarterback) for the pass.

Man-to-Man: Defence in which each player is responsible for one specific offensive player.

Messenger: Player who enters the game with a specific play from a coach.

Mid-Field: The 50-yard line.

Misdirection: Play in which the "flow" of the backfield misdirects the defence away from the path of the actual ball carrier.

Momentum: Enthusiasm working for a particular team. Momentum can "flow" from one team to another depending on the game, score, or players.

Mousetrap: Offensive play in which a defensive player is allowed past the line of scrimmage after the ball is snapped, then blocked (mousetrapped) so he may not reach the ball carrier.

Multiple Set: Offensive plays that can't be predicted. A variety of possible plays.

NFL: National Football League.

Nickel Defence: A pass defence in which the coaches insert an extra defensive backfield player—the fifth back; thus the name.

Nose Tackle: Defensive player whose position is in the centre—the nose—of the line.

Numbering System: In football, numbers from 1-89 are assigned to particular positions, in this system:

1-19:	Quarterbacks
20-29 &	
40-49:	Halfbacks
30-39:	Fullbacks
50-59:	Centres and linebackers
60-69:	Guards
70-79:	Tackles
80-89:	Ends and flankers

Nutcrackers: Drills or exercises during training camp in which coaches hope to find the toughest players.

Offside: A penalty when one player—offensive or defensive—moves across the line of scrimmage before the ball is snapped.

Off the Ball: How quickly a lineman can react when the ball is snapped.

On the Same Page: Everyone knowing what to do and going out on the field and doing it; being in sync with the playbook.

One-Back Offence: Formations that involve only one offensive backfield player, other than the quarterback. This back, usually the biggest and the most powerful, is used in running situations.

On-Side Kick: A kick that is deliberately short—10-15 yards, so that the kicking team can recover it immediately if the receiving team fumbles it.

Option: A play in which the quarterback has the choice, depending on the offence and the defence, of keeping the ball or passing it.

(To) Pay the Price: To play while injured as a condition of keeping the job; to receive an injury while playing; a masochistic macho image of a football player who will play while hurt without complaining or without leaving the game. Considered a complimentary term by most players. Also applied to other contact sports.

Penalty: A loss of yards as a result of a foul.

Penetration: Moving into the opponent's part of the field, either defensively or offensively.

Period: A 15-minute segment of a 60-minute football game.

Piling On: Jumping on or tackling the ball carrier after the play is officially ruled ended.

Pit: Offensive and defensive linemen "in the trenches," at or near the line of scrimmage, are said to be "in the pit."

Pitchout: An underhanded toss of the ball from the quarterback to another player.

***Place Kick*:** To kick a football when it is held motionless by a player or when it rests on a kicking tee.

***Playbook*:** A team book of possible plays, offensive and defensive, that team members usually memorize during summer camp. Highly guarded by team coaches, even though most plays are no longer secret.

Plug a Hole: To fill a gap in the line, during a play.

Pocket: Protective screen of players around a quarterback, who is getting ready to pass. A quarterback who is "out of the pocket" has inadvertently outrun or been chased away from his protective cover of players.

Pooch Kick: Short- or medium-range kick, usually soft and high. Similar to an approach shot to the green in golf. A finesse kick. The pooch kicker may not be the same as a field goal kicker or a kick-off specialist.

Post Pattern: A pass pattern in which the receiver runs towards the goalpost.

Power Back (power runner): Offensive back who can gain yardage because of his superior size or speed.

Power Sweep: An offensive play in which the ball carrier runs around the end of the line of scrimmage and has at least two players ahead of him blocking.

Prevent Defence: Defence that will give up small yardage but that will not give up extensive yardage. Often, if time is running out, the defence will go into a prevent defence, willingly giving up small gains by the offence, but not yielding a touchdown.

Pulling Guard: An offensive guard who "pulls" away from the line of scrimmage when the ball is snapped, to help protect the quarterback or ball carrier.

Punt: A kick on fourth down by the offensive team when it cannot get a first down on the next play.

Quarter: Same as period.

Quarterback: Offensive team leader who calls the plays in the huddle, then takes the ball from the centre to begin the play. He either runs with it, passes it, or hands it off to another.

Quarterback Sneak: Short yardage play in which the quarterback takes the ball from the centre and follows the forward motion of the centre, into the line of scrimmage.

Racehorse: Pass receiver with exceptional speed through the defensive backfield.

Read the Defence: To know what defensive men will do in a play because of their positions (or keys) at the line of scrimmage.

Read the Offence: To know what offensive men will do in a play because of their positions (or keys) at the line of scrimmage.

Red Dog: Same as blitz.

Red Shirt: To hold a player out for a season, usually to allow an injury to heal.

Referee: Senior official during a football game. He stands behind the offensive backfield before each play.

Reverse: A running play in which the ball carrier hands the ball to another back, running in the opposite direction.

Retire a Number: To honor a player by holding a ceremony and officially declaring that the number he wore during his playing days will never again be used by the team.

Rookie: Novice member of a football team. A player recently out of college on a professional team.

Roughing the Quarterback (Roughing the Catcher, Roughing the Kicker, etc.): Hitting the player unnecessarily hard, or after the play is over, perhaps with an intent to injure. Calls for a penalty if the officials see the incident.

Run to Daylight: Run to an open part of the field.

Running Back: Offensive ball carrier other than the quarterback.

Rushing: To gain yardage by running with the ball.

Sack: To tackle the quarterback for a loss.

Safety: Is scored when a ball carrier is tackled behind his own goal. A safety scores two points for the defence.

Sarah: Coaching code for a strongside formation or play.

Screen Pass: A pass that is thrown parallel to the line of scrimmage or a pass that is completed behind the line of scrimmage. Or, a pass that is thrown to a receiver who is screened (blocked) from the defensive by another offensive player.

Scrimmage: The line on which a play takes place.

Secondary: Defensive positions behind the line of scrimmage.

Shank a Kick: To miskick a ball so that it travels only a few yards (football equivalent of hooking a golf ball).

Shoestring Catch: To catch a football at the ankle (shoestring) level.

Shoestring Tackle: To tackle a ball carrier below the knees.

Shotgun: Offensive formation in which the quarterback stands to receive the snap a few (5-10) yards behind the centre. This gives the quarterback slightly more time to find his receivers for a pass.

Shovel Pass: Pass that is thrown underhanded to a receiver.

Skirt the End: To run offensively around the defensive end.

Smurf: In the NFL, a "midget," that is, a player under 6 feet tall and under 180 pounds.

Snap: To start a play, the centre throws the ball upwards between his legs to the waiting hands of the quarterback.

Soccer Kicker: To kick the ball with the instep of the foot, instead of with the point of the toe. Soccer kickers are said to have more accuracy than regular kickers. Soccer kickers are often Europeans who learned their technique by playing soccer first, then football.

Spear: To hit an opponent using the top of the helmet as a weapon. It is illegal and calls for a penalty when caught by the officials.

Special Teams: Players assigned to a kickoff team, for instance, or a prevent defence team or a nickel back team.

Spike: To energetically throw the ball down after a touchdown. Many players make a real show of spiking the ball. Too much spiking (or dancing) in the end zone after a touchdown is now a penalty.

Split the Uprights: To accurately kick an extra point or field goal straight through the goalposts.

Squib Kick: A kick that is hard to catch because it is wobbly or bouncing.

Straightarm: A defensive play in which the player uses a locked arm to thrust an opponent away from a tackle.

Strongside: The side of an offensive line having more players than the opposite side of the same line.

Student Body Right or (Student Body Left): A running play in which the entire team, plus coaches, cheerleaders, and trainers seem to be running in the same direction to protect the ball carrier. Established at the University of Southern California.

Stuffed: Same as jammed.

Stunting: Defensive formation in which players are out of their usual place, to fool the offence.

Submarine: To hit a ball carrier low.

Substitute: A player who is not a starter, sent in to play because another player has to leave the game. Also appropriate in other team sports.

Sudden Death: A period after the normal four quarters of play. If the game is tied at the end of regulation play, the game goes into sudden death and the first team to score wins. There is no additional play after a score in sudden death.

Suicide Squads: Kickoff and kickoff return teams in which individual players are assumed to sacrifice themselves for the team. Usually a thankless job, but a position in which a rookie can prove himself worthy of a permanent job on the team.

Super Bowl: The championship game of the National Football League. Played at various locations at the end of the regular season.

Sweep: Running play in which the offensive line swings towards a sideline and the ball carrier follows that protective wall.

Swing Pass: Short pass thrown by the quarterback towards the sideline.

Tackle: To stop a ball carrier and throw him to the ground.

Tailback: Running back in the offensive backfield farthest from the line of scrimmage.

Taxi Squad: Players good enough to keep on the team but not exceptional enough to use regularly. So named because an early professional team owner used them to man his fleet of taxi cabs to give them work and also keep them available for the team. Now used for any group of nonregular players.

T Formation: Offensive formation in which members of the offensive backfield are lined up parallel to the line of scrimmage and behind the quarterback. So called because the backfield formation looks like the letter T.

Three-Point Stance: Stance that the linemen assume before the ball is snapped. They have both feet on the ground, are crouched low to the ground, and have one hand touching the ground.

Throw Into a Crowd: To throw towards more than one receiver. Usually a Hail Mary pass will be thrown towards a crowd.

Throw it Away: When a quarterback deliberately throws a pass over or past a receiver so that he will not risk having the pass intercepted.

Time Out: To stop the clock that marks the 60 minutes of the game.

Touchback: Occurs when a ball is dead off the field behind the goal line in possession of the offence, when the ball was downed or the ball carrier was downed by the defence. Different than a safety: A safety occurs on the field of play behind the goal lines; a touchback occurs *off* the field of play behind the goal line. The ball is put into play at the nearest 20-yard line.

Touchdown: Scores 6 points for the offensive team when the ball is carried or passed over the goal line.

Touch Football: Informal game in which the play is stopped when the ball carrier is touched with two hands of an opponent.

Trap: To allow a defensive player to cross the offensive line, then block him from the ball carrier once he has crossed into offensive territory.

Triple-Threat Player: Player who has the ability to run, pass, and kick the ball well. Because college and professional football is so complex, there are few triple-threat players. Most are happy to specialize in just one aspect of the game.

Turk: Nickname for assistant coach or other member of the coaching staff who has the job of telling players in training camp that they have been cut from the team. So named because of the image of a Turkish fighter with a broad sword.

Turn In: Pass pattern in which the receiver runs downfield then turns towards the middle of the field to catch a pass.

Two-Minute Drill: Special exercises to take advantage of the last 2 minutes before the end of the first half or before the end of the game.

Two-Minute Warning: Special warning given to each coach by the officials that there is 2 minutes left before the end of the first half or before the end of the game.

Two-Way Player: Player who can play offence and defence. Because of the specialization of football, there are as few two-way players as there are triple-threat players.

Umpire: Another key official during a football game.

Unbalanced Line: Offensive line that has an unequal number of players on one side of the centre than on the other side.

Uprights: Vertical poles on the goal posts. Place kickers must kick extra points and field goals between the uprights to score.

Veer Offence: Complicated offence in which the quarterback ran either: (a) run with the ball; (b) give it to the fullback; (c) run towards the sidelines and pitch to a running back; or (d) pass. The veer takes advantage of the fact that the defence may react quickly to one of these options, thus allowing the quarterback to quickly execute another of these four options. How to prevent the success of the veer? Down the quarterback behind the line of scrimmage before he gets a chance to execute the veer.

Wanda: Coaching code for a weakside formation or play.

Weakside: Opposite of strongside. The side of the offensive line with the fewest players from the centre.

Wide Receiver: Formerly known as the split end, a lineman eligible to catch passes, whose position on the line of scrimmage separates him from the rest of the line.

Wild Card: Team eligible for playoffs in the National Football League that did not outright win its division race towards the Super Bowl.

Wishbone: Offensive formation in which the quarterback lines up behind the centre and the three other backs are behind him; seen from well behind the line and from above, the formation looks like a Y or like a chicken wishbone. The quarterback may keep the ball with two of the backs blocking ahead for him, or he may pitch out to one of them; similar in general respects to the option-style play of the veer offence.

X's and 0's: Chalkboard symbols for offensive and defensive players and strategy. It's a compliment to a coach if it is said, "He really knows his X's and 0's."

Zebras: Because of their black-and-white striped jackets, officials are sometimes called zebras (also true in basketball).

GOLF

Ace: Hole in one.

Action: To put spin on the ball.

Address: Correct body position before hitting the ball.

Approach: To hit a short- or medium-length shot to the green, with an iron.

Apron: Area immediately surrounding the green.

Away: Refers to the ball that is furthest from the cup, when more than one golfer is playing a particular hole.

Best Ball Tournament: Tournament in which the better score between members of a twoperson team on each hole is used as the team score.

Birdie: One under par on a particular hole.

Bogey: One over par on a hole.

Bunker: Common name for a sand trap.

Caddy: Person who carries the golfer's clubs.

Can: To sink a putt.

Casual Water: Water on a course after a rainstorm; not part of a permanent hazard such as a pond or lake.

Course Rating: The difficulty of a particular course.

Divot: Ground cut up by the clubhead during a swing.

Dog-Leg: Hole that has a sharp bend to the left or the right from tee to green.

Double Eagle: Three strokes under par for any particular hole.

Driver: No. 1 wood, usually only off the tee.

Eagle: Two under par for a particular hole.

Fairway: Ground between the tee area and the putting green, excluding any hazards.

Flag: Banner on top of a metal pole inserted in the cup, to indicate the hole, to golfers at a distance from the green.

Fore: Signal shouted to indicate to those on the course that a golfer is about to take a stroke.

Foresome: Match in which two players play against two other players, or all four play against each other.

Green: Manicured grass area where each hole is located.

Hazard: In golf, any bunker, water (except casual water), trees, brush, or other natural obstacles.

Head: The part of the club that strikes the ball.

Hole: In golf, the hole is 4 1/4 inches deep and 4 inches in diameter. The hole may be anywhere on any particular green, and may be moved from time to time.

Hole High: An approach shot that is on the green as far as the hole, but to the right or the left.

Hole in One: A drive shot from the tee that hits the hole.

Hole Out: To sink a putt.

Home: The green.

Honor: The first person or the first team to drive from the tee is said to have the honor. Generally, those who have the honor are those who won the previous hole.

Hook: A shot that curves in flight from the right to the left, for a right-handed golfer.

Iron: A golf club with a metal lead, used for medium shots towards the green.

Leader Board: A billboard-size chart, generally located near the clubhouse, that shows the leader of a tournament. Lowest scores (below par) are at the top of the board, followed by par, then above par.

Lie: The position of the ball on the fairway or green.

Match Play: Competition in which the winner is decided by the total number of strokes taken for each hole. A team may win a hole, lose a hole, or halve a hole (take the same number as the opposition).

Medal Play: Competition in which the total number of strokes by a player is used in determining the winner.

Nassau: Another alternate method of scoring: one point for the first 9 holes, one point for the second 9, and one point for the entire 18 holes.

Open: A tournament that allows both amateurs and professional golfers to play.

Par: Average shot for a particular hole.

Penalty Stroke: One stroke added to the total for a violation of the rules.

Pigeon: Easy mark. Victim.

Provisional Ball: Ball played when a previous ball was hit out of bounds or lost.

Pulled Shot: A shot that is straight, but to the right of the green (or hole) for a right-handed golfer.

Push-Shot: A shot that is straight, but to the left of the green (or hole) for a right-handed golfer.

Putt: A delicate stroke on the green to roll the ball towards the hole.

Rough: Weeds or other natural hazards at either side of the fairway.

Shank: To hit the ball with the heel of the club.

Slice: A shot that curves from left to right for a right-handed golfer.

Storke Play: Same as medal play.

Summer Rules: Playing the ball as it lies anywhere on the course.

Tee: Small wooden peg that a ball is placed on before being driven.

Topping: To hit the top of the ball, thus causing it to roll along the ground without any loft.

Trap: A bunker, a sand trap.

Waggle: To wiggle the body, arms, or legs, when the golfer addresses the ball.

Wedge: Heavy club used for hitting out of sand.

Whiff: To miss the ball completely during a swing.

Winter Rules: To drop the ball for an advantage if it is in the rough during play.

Wood: A golf club with a wood head, used to hit distance shots from the tee.

GYMNASTICS

All-Around: Competition in which the gymnast must perform in the floor exercise, side horse, long horse, horizontal bar, parallel bars, still rings, and long horse.

Approach: To walk to the equipment, prior to the gymnastic routine. Similar to the approach in golf.

Balance: To maintain equilibrium during a routine.

Break: To stop to dampen the bounce of a trampoline.

Check: To slow or stop body revolutions during a trampoline routine.

Gainer: A backflip in which the performer lands ahead of the take-off spot.

Perfect Ten: Redundant phrase. Ten is the top score that any gymnast can receive.

Pommels: The curved iron handles of a side horse.

Spotter: Guard who stands beside a trampoline to catch the gymnast if he or she bounces or falls off the trampoline bed.

Vault: A leap or jump aided by the gymnast's hands.

HANDBALL & RACKETBALL

Ace: Serve that is untouched by an opponent; scores a point. Same usage in table tennis, tennis, badminton, and other sports.

Anticipation: The ability that a player has to guess where the opponent's shot will rebound so the player can be in a position to return it.

Avoidable Hinder: Intentional interference of one player by another. Penalty is the loss of a score or the addition of a score by the player who was hindered.

Back Court: The area behind the short line to the rear wall.

Backswing: Beginning motion to hit the ball. Similar usage as in a golf backswing.

Back-Wall Shot: A ball that is hit after it rebounds from the back wall.

Ball: In handball, the ball is 1 7/8 inches in diameter and weighs between 2/10 and 3/10 of an ounce.

Blocking: To hinder an opponent's shot by placing all or part of the body between the opponent and the ball.

Bolo Shot: A shot hit with the fist, underhanded (handball).

Bone Bruise: Deep bruise of the palm of the hand (handball).

Bottom Board: Lowest part of the front wall.

Bye: Tournament in which some favoured players are allowed to progress without playing the first rounds.

Ceiling Serve: A serve that strikes the ceiling after it bounces off the front wall.

Ceiling Shot: A shot that is hit directly to the ceiling, then the front wall, then the floor, and then rebounds to the back wall.

Centre Court Position: The middle of the court about 3 to 5 feet in front of the short line. Ideal position for offensive and defensive play.

Change of Pace Shot: Any shot that changes the tempo of the game, either faster than normal or slower than normal.

Consolation: Round of a tournament in which first-time losers face each other.

Control: The ability to hit a ball to any specific spot.

Court: A standard handball court is 40' by 20' by 20'.

Crosscourt Shot: A shot that is hit diagonally across the court.

Crotch: Any place where two surfaces meet: wall-wall, wall-ceiling, or wall-floor.

Crowding: Playing too close to the opponent.

Cutthroat: A game for three players in which two play against the server.

Dead Ball: Ball that is not in play.

Die: A ball that hits the front wall without much bounce.

Dig: To return a low shot before it reaches the floor.

Doubles: A game in which two players oppose two other players.

Error: The inability to return a playable ball.

Fault: Illegally served ball. Generally similar usage as in tennis.

Floater: A ball that travels so slowly that the opponent has time to set up a return shot.

Fly Shot: A shot that is returned before it hits the floor.

Forehand: Shot made from the same side of the body as the playing hand.

Front-and-Back: Doubles play in which one partner covers the front court and the other partner covers the back court.

Game: When 21 points are scored by one player or team.

Game Point: Point that will win the game for a player or team, if it is won.

Half-and-Half: Same as *side-by-side* play.

Hinder: To accidentally interfere with an opponent.

Hop: To put spin on the ball by snapping the wrist (handball).

IRA: International Racketball Association.

Inning: One complete round of play in which each player or each team has the opportunity to gain or lose the serve.

Kill Shot: A shot that strikes the front wall so low that it is unreturnable.

Lob: Ball that hits the front wall high then rebounds in a high arc towards the back wall

Masters: In singles competition, players must be over 40 years of age; in doubles, one must be at least 40 and the partner at least 45 (racketball).

Match: Two out of three games.

Off-Hand: The left hand if the player is righthanded, and vice versa.

Pass Shot: A shot that is hit out of reach of the opponent.

Place: To hit the ball accurately to a particular part of the court.

Power Serve: A ball that is hit low off the front wall and bounces towards a rear corner (handball).

Ready Position: The stance taken by a player to receive a serve.

Receiving Line: A line 5 feet in back of the short line. Players waiting for the serve must stand behind this line until the ball is served.

Roadrunner: Player whose speciality is retrieving (racketball).

Run-Around Shot: A shot that hits one side wall, the back wall, and a second side wall.

Screen: Ball that passes too close to a player's body for it to be seen clearly by the opponent.

Seamless 558: Ball used for racketball. Ball is 2 1/2 inches in diameter and weighs approximately 1.4 ounces.

(To) Serve: To put the ball in play.

Service Box: 18"-wide boxes at each end of the serving line. Nonserving partners must stand in one of these boxes while the other partner serves the ball.

Service Court: Area in which the ball must land after hitting the front wall.

Service Line: Line 5 feet in front of and parallel to the short line.

Service Zone: Where the server must stand when serving the ball.

Sharp Angle Serve: A shot that hits the front wall close to the floor and bounces at an angle to the right side wall and back towards the server.

Shooters: Players who rely on kill shots (racketball).

Short Line: Line in the middle of the floor from side to side halfway between the front and back walls. The serve must carry over this line from the front wall.

Side-by-Side: Doubles play in which partners stand side-by-side, as opposed to frontand-back.

Straddle Ball: Ball that moves between the legs of a player.

Straight Kill Shot: Ball that hits the front wall and returns on the same line.

Volley: Same as fly shot.

Wallpaper Ball: Ball that hugs the wall so closely that it is hard or impossible to return (racketball).

Winners: *Kill shots* (racketball).

HORSE RACING

Allowance: A race in which horses are matched by age, sex, or money won and in which poorer horses are allowed to carry less weight.

Bug Boy: An apprentice jockey, one who has not won 40 races.

Chalk: The odds-on favourite to win—as in "the chalk horse."

Claiming: A race requiring owners to state their horses' values before the race. The horses then can be bought, or "claimed," for that price before the race.

Colours: Also called "silks" these are the distinguishing jackets and caps worn by jockeys.

Daily Double: A wager in which the player attempts to pick the winners of two races on the day's card.

Exacta (also called Perfecta): A wager in which the player attempts to pick the winner and second-place finisher in order.

Field Horses: Two or more horses grouped together for betting purposes. A bet for one field horse is a bet for all in that group.

Furlong: Either 220 yards or 1/8 mile.

Futurity Race: A race for 2-year-olds scheduled far in advance, sometimes before the horse is born.

Handicap: Weight added to superior horses to make a race more even.

Handicapper: The person who assigns the amount of weight to be added to a horse. More commonly, the term refers to someone who rates horses and their chances of winning.

In the Money: Gamblers can win on three positions: win, place, and show. The horse owners, however, take a portion of the purse for running fourth, or "in the money."

Irons: The stirrups. A jockey is said to be "in the irons" when he races.

Inquiry: A review of a race by track officials, who look for violations of racing rules.

Maiden: A horse that has not won a race.

Morning Line: Odds set by a handicapper on the morning of race day before bets are taken. Generally not considered a good basis on which to place a bet, because ratings are based on past performance only.

Objection: A complaint filed by a jockey as soon as a race ends; leads to an inquiry.

Player: Anyone who bets on horses.

Paddock: The enclosure where horses are saddled immediately prior to a race.

Pari-Mutuel: A system of odds-making determined by the bettors, based on the amount of money wagered on each horse. Means "between ourselves" in French.

Photo Finish: A race so close at the finish that a final decision is withheld until a photograph taken at the wire can be developed.

Post Time: All horses are in the gates and ready to race. Signals the end of betting.

Purse: The prize money awarded in a race.

Quinella: Similar to the Exacta, but bettor wins no matter which of his two chosen horses finishes first and second.

Rail: The fence around the infield. A horse running the shortest route is said to be "on the rail."

Slow Track: Refers to a wet track, which slows down the horses.

Scratch: A horse that has been withdrawn from a race.

Sprint: A short race designed for fast horses with less endurance.

Stakes Race: A race for superior horses that have owners who must nominate them far in advance and must pay an assortment of high fees, assuring a big purse.

Steward: A race official, ususally on horseback, who monitors the race, horses, jockeys, and trainers for any improprieties.

Super Six: A wagering opportunity in which the player is asked to pick the winners of six consecutive races.

Tarmac: The paved outdoor viewing area near the finish line.

Thoroughbred: A specific breed of horse developed in England from the Arab, Turkish, and other breeds.

Tip Sheet: Any number of supposedly authoritative printed sheets bearing the names of horses given the best chances of winning.

Totalizator (or Tote Board): Big computer board that "totes" the odds on each horse and figures payoffs.

Trifecta: Wagering requiring player to pick first-, second-, and third-place finishers.

Win, Place, and Show: First, second, and third placers.

Wire: The finish line.

Wire-to-Wire: Refers to a horse that leads a race from start to finish.

Defensive Zone: Area of the team's own goal.

Dig: To fight for the puck; to take it away from an opponent.

Drop Pass: To stop the puck and allow a teammate to pick it up.

Face off: When the puck is dropped between two opposing players to start or restart play.

Feeding: To pass the puck to a teammate.

Forechecking: To check an opponent in his zone of the ice.

Goal: In hockey, the goal is 4 feet high and 6 feet wide and made of net. When the puck enters the net, one point is scored.

Hat Trick: Three goals in one game by the same player.

Major Penalty: Five minutes (or more) in the penalty box.

Minor Penalty: Two minutes in the penalty box.

Neutral Zone: Centre area of the ice from one blue line across the red line to the other blue line. Roughly similar to the area from the 25-yard line across the 50-yard line to the opposite 25-yard line in football.

Offside Lines: Same as blue lines.

Penalty Box: Seat off the ice that a player must sit in to serve time for a foul.

Penalty Time: Specified time that a player must spend in the penalty box.

Poke Check: To stab at the puck with the stick.

Red Line: Line that separates the ice into two halves. Similar to the 50-yard line in football.

Save: Defensive play by the goalie that prevents a score.

Uncovered: Offensive player left in front of opponent's goal without a defensive player blocking the goal.

Zamboni: Machine that rebuilds and smoothes the ice. To suggest that a player skates "like a Zamboni" would hardly be a compliment.

MOTOR SPORTS

Altered: Automobile or motorcycle that has been modified after it leaves the factory.

Apex: The point during a turn in which the car comes closest to inside edge of the corner. A tight apex usually means a good turn.

Back Off: To reduce speed.

Banking, Banked Turn: Turn that has a raised outer side to help driving control during the turn.

BHP (Brake Horse Power): Net power available at the output end of the engine. Brake refers to a dynamometer, a measuring mechanism, not the brakes of the car.

Bite: Tire traction on the road.

Block: Cylinder-containing unit of the engine.

Blower: Supercharged engine.

Blown: Two meanings: a blown engine may mean (a) an engine equipped with a supercharger, or (b) an engine that has a massive failure during a race.

Brick Yard: Common name for the Indianapolis 500.

Bucket Seat: Single seat contoured to body shape.

CC: Cubic centimeters. Engine displacement is usually referred to in CCs.

Camber: The angle at which the tires sit on the road.

Can-Am: The Canadian-American Championship for race car drivers.

Charger: Aggressive driver.

Chassis: Underside part of the car, usually consisting of frame and axles, brakes, wheels, engine, transmission, driveline, and exhaust components.

Chicane: Barriers added to an existing road to make the turns tighter or to add a turn or series of turns to an existing straight road.

Christmas Tree: Series of vertical lights that act as a "countdown" to the start of a drag race. There is a green "Go" light; a yellow "Warning" light, and a red "Foul" light, which means the driver jumped the start. The Christmas tress is positioned so that the driver can see it at the start of a drage race.

Circuit: Course used for racing in which drivers repeat the same route.

Closed Event: Race in which spectators or unauthorized drivers are not admitted.

Club Race: Race for members of a particular sports car club; usually refers to an amateur race.

Cool-Off Lap: Extra lap after a course that is driven at a slower speed than the race, to ensure that the engine parts cool slowly.

Cut-Off Point: A location before a turn at which point the driver takes his foot off the throttle and brakes the car for the turn.

Detroit Iron: Uncomplimentary term used by sports car elitists to describe most Detroit-made vehicles.

DNF: Did Not Finish. Started the race, but did not complete it.

DNS: Did Not Start. Entered the race, but did not start.

DOHC: Double Over-Head Camshaft cylinder head.

Dial In: To make adjustments to an engine. To "fine tune" it.

Differential: Gear-drive mechanism that transfers power from drive shaft to wheel. Differential refers to different speed of each wheel in a turn.

Displacement: Volume in cubic measure of a cylinder or engine.

Drafting: Same as slipstreaming.

Drift: Controlled slide, using engine power to keep the car on the road.

Driver's School: Special school for race drivers, using a closed race course to teach time trials, racing, and so on.

Esses: Winding curves on a race course.

ET: Elapsed Time. Drag racing term for a timed 1/4-mile straight run.

Fire Suit: Protective fire-resistant suit worn by drivers.

Flags: Flags used in motor racing carry the following meanings:

- *Black:* Return to pits.
- *Blue (motionless):* Another car is following you closely.
- *Blue (waved):* Another driver is trying to pass you—make room.
- *Checkered (black and white):* Driver has completed the race.
- *Green:* Starts the race.
- *Red:* Stop—clear the course.
- *White:* Emergency vehicle on the course.
- *Yellow (motionless):* No passing, caution.
- *Yellow with Red Stripes:* Caution—oil on the course.
- *Flagman*: Official responsible for displaying various flags to drivers.
- *Flat Four:* Horizontally opposed four-cylinder engine (old VWs had flat four engines).

- *Flat Out*: Racing at maximum speed.
- *Flat Six:* Horizontally opposed six-cylinder engine (the Corvair had a flat six engine).
- *Flip:* To turn over or to roll over. *Flying Start*: A "running start," passing the starting line at race speed, or nearly race speed.
- *FoMoCo:* Parts made by Ford Motor Company.
- *Formula:* Regulations governing a race car that involve engine displacement, length and width, weight, size of fuel tank, and type of fuel used. In general, these are common formulas for race cars:
- *Formula I:* Race car powered by a nonsupercharged V-8 or V-12 engine from 1,600 to 3,000 cc (up to 450 horsepower). Generally has a wedge shape, wide treadless tires, and 13-inch wheels. Has a self-starter and a transmission with four or five forward gears, plus reverse.
- *Formula II:* Slightly smaller version of Formula I car, has supercharged four-cylinder production engine of 1,300 to 1,600 cc. Generally more popular in Europe.
- *Formula III:* Racing car powered with a production engine up to 1,600 cc. Has specific limitations on air intake to the engine.
- *Formula A:* Similar to Formula 5000.
- *Formula Atlantic:* British car similar to
- American Formula B.
- *Formula B:* Formula car powered by a nonsupercharged production engine of 1,100 to 1,600 cc, powered by gasoline.
- Formula B is smaller and lighter than Formula 5000.
- *Formula C:* Formula car powered by an engine up to 1,100 cc.
- *Formula F (Formula Ford):* Formula car powered by a nonsupercharged 1,600 cc English Ford or Ford Pinto engine.

- *Formula 5000:* Formula car powered by an engine of 1,600 to 3,000 cc or a production V-8 engine of up to 5000 cc. No supercharging allowed. Must run on gasoline. Generally similar to the Formula I automobile.
- *Formula V:* Formula car that is powered by a Volkswagon 1,200 cc engine, gearbox, transmission, and wheels.

Formula Super V: Formula car that is powered by a Volkswagon 1,600 cc engine and gearbox, and runs on gasoline.

Four Wheel Drive: Mechanism that allows power to be distributed to all four wheels.

Fuel Cell: Special rubber-like container for gasoline, built so that it will not be split open during a crash. Might be called a "safety gas tank."

Full Bore: Driving at maximum throttle.

Funny Car: Drag race car that has had unorthodox modifications. Generally, a funny car has a one-piece body, is powered by a supercharged engine and has a driver's compartment behind the engine. The engine is completely exposed, rear wheels are wide, and front wheels are bicycle-type. Often contains a parachute-stopping device.

FWD: Four Wheel Drive.

Getting a Tow: Same as slipstreaming.

Grid: Position for cars at beginning of race. Also refers to markings on a track.

Gymkhana: Competition for best time on a Chicane-type course.

Hairpin: Ultratight turn on a race course.

Hairy: Frightening occurrence.

Hemi: Car with hemispherical combustion chambers.

Hill Climb: Race for the best clock time up a prescribed hill course.

History: Same as totalled.

IFS: Independent Front Suspension.

IRS: Independent Rear Suspension.

Impound Area: Area where cars may be required to be taken after a race so that officials can inspect them to make sure they have satisfied entrance requirements.

Jet Dragster: Drag racer powered by a jet engine.

Lap: One complete circuit of a race course.

La Mans Start: A start in which drivers run from a starting line, get into their cars and drive away.

Line: The best path through a race course.

MPG: Miles per gallon.

Mags: Wheel rims made of magnesium; used because magnesium is very light.

MoPar: Parts made by Chrysler Corporation.

Mule: Unattractive prototype automobile, made for testing or demonstration purposes only, usually without finishing touches, such as chrome.

NASCAR: National Association for Stock Car Racing.

OHV: Over Head Valve.

Oval: Oval-shaped track.

Pace Car: Vehicle used to pace racers at the start of a race.

Paddock: Area near the track where cars are worked on. Usually similar to pits.

Pit: An off-the-track area where a driver can get gas, minor repairs during the race, tire changes, and advice from crew members.

Pit Lane: Lane that drivers use to enter and exit the pit area to and from a race course.

Pit Stop: Stop made during race for fuel, minor repairs, and so on.

Prototype: Test model of a new car.

Pump Fuel: Fuel that is "consumer quality," that is, that can be obtained at any gas station.

Qualifying Times: Trials used to determine race position based on best time during trials.

Rally: Race organized to test navigational skills of driver and navigator. Contestants are given a route map and must check in at various predetermined points to obtain their time from point to point. Best time wins.

Roll Bar: Safety bar that protects the driver in the case of a roll-over accident. Sometimes called headache bar for obvious reasons.

SCCA: Sports Car Club of America.

SOHC: Single Over Head Cam engine.

Shut the Gate: To block a driver's path during a race.

Slipstreaming: To drive slightly behind another driver during a race to take advantage of reduced air resistance.

Slingshotting: To drive around the lead car after slipstreaming.

Sports Car: Racing automobile with high performance characteristics.

Sporty Car: Car that is promoted as a sports car but because of mediocre characteristics, is really not a sports car.

Stand On It: To hold the throttle pedal completely on the floor.

Standing Start: Race start with all cars motionless, with drivers ready and engines idling.

Starter: Official who controls the start of a race.

Stock: Automobile that has not been modified since being delivered from the factory.

Street Legal: Automobile that has been modified for race use, but has to be remodified for safety (street) purposes.

Supercharger: Engine that has been modified by a mechanism that blows exhaust air back into engine at a higher rate than air entering the engine from the outside. Gives a power boost to the engine.

Tach (Tachometer): Meter that measures engine speed in revolutions per minute.

Time Trials: Laps on a specific course for the fastest speed.

Totalled: Completely wrecked.

Torsion Bar: Rod in a suspension system attached to prevent side slipping of the automobile.

Transaxle: Transmission and rear axle mounted as a single unit.

SOCCER

Caution: Warning by the referee for unsportsmanlike conduct. Because of possible language differences between teams, the referee shows this caution by waving a yellow card.

Charging: Attempting to unbalance a player in possession of the ball.

Chip: A kick that rises above a player.

Clearance: Kicking or heading the ball away from the goal area. The goalkeeper may throw the ball to clear it.

Corner Kick: Kick made by the attacking team from a corner arc; this is awarded when the ball goes across the goal line without resulting in a score, and when the ball was last touched by a defensive player.

Direct Free Kick: Awarded after a severe personal foul. Similar to a free throw in basketball.

Dribbling: To control the ball with the player's feet.

Drop Ball: To put the ball in play by the referee by dropping it between two opponents. The ball is in play when it touches the ground.

Drop Kick: A ball that is put in play by being dropped on the ground; it is kicked on the bounce.

Goal: Is scored when the ball passes over the goal line, between the uprights and under the crossbar.

Goalkeeper: Player who guards the goal. In soccer, the goal keeper may carry the ball in the penalty area, or may throw it or kick it.

Goal Kick: Kick-in by a member of the defending team from the goal box. A goal kick results when the ball crosses the goal line without a score and when it was last touched by an offensive player.

Halfway Line: A line that runs across the field at mid-field. Similar to the 50-yard line in American football.

Hat Trick: Three goals in one game by one player. Same usage as ice hockey.

Heading: Method of directing the ball with the head. A skill that highly rated players have.

Indirect Free Kick: A free kick in which a score can result only after the ball has struck another player.

Instep Kick: Kick made with the instep or inside of the foot. Instep soccer kickers are now highly prized in American football because of their accuracy.

Kick-Off: A kick from the centre circle at the beginning of each quarter and after each score.

Live Ball: A ball in play after a free kick or throw-in or after it has been touched by a player, or has touched the ground after a drop. Match: A game.

Offside: Refers to the position of a player in relation to the opponents when a ball is put in play.

Off the Ball: Players who do not have possession of the ball.

Overhead Kick: A player who kicks the ball over his own head.

Penalty Kick: Direct free kick made from the penalty mark; this kick is awarded to the offensive team for a foul committed by the defence within its own penalty area.

Save: Play made by the goalkeeper to prevent a score.

Striker: An offensive player.

Tackling: An attempt to kick the ball away from an opponent. Players may not be held in tackling.

Touchlines: Side boundary lines in soccer.

Volley: To kick the ball while it is in the air.

SWIMMING & DIVING

Approach: The steps taken towards the end of the board (Diving).

Backstroke: To swim with alternate arm strokes while on the back.

Back Jackknife: Common name for the inward pike dive (diving).

Breaststroke: To swim by stroking under the water, with outward strokes beginning at the chest.

Butterfly Stroke: A stroke in which the arm motion begins with each arm stretched out sideways. The swimmer then brings both arms out of the water, swinging them together and into the water past the head; the arms are then brought sideways underwater.

Cast: Imperfect entry into the water (diving).

Crawl Stroke: Commonly known as *freestyle*. The swimmer's arms are brought forward one at a time over the shoulder and into the water; as one arm is pulling through the water, the other arm is entering the water, after being thrown over the swimmer's shoulder.

Cutaway: Common term for an inward dive.

Degree of Difficulty: Rate for a dive. Each dive has a rating from 1.2 to 2.9 depending on its difficulty.

Entry: How the diver enters the water.

Flutter Kick: Quick up-and-down kick of the feet, to accompany a swimming stroke.

Freestyle: Usually refers to the crawl stroke, but may be any stroke the swimmer wishes to use, during a freestyle (choice) event.

Groups: Categories for all various dives. Forward, backward, reverse, inward, twist, and arm stand groups.

High Board: The 3-meter board.

Hurdle: The jump at the end of the diver's approach to the end of the board.

Individual Medley: A four-course swimming competition in which a butterfly stroke is used in the first quarter; a backstroke used in the second quarter; a breaststroke in the third quarter; and freestyle in the last quarter.

Jackknife: Common name for the forward pike dive.

Kickboard: Board used to support a swimmer as he or she practices kicking style.

Lap: From one end of a swimming pool to the other end.

Layout: Diving position in which the body is extended without any flexing.

Low Board: The 1-meter board.

Medley: A swimming event in which the swimmer must use the butterfly, backstroke, breaststroke, and freestyle.

Pike: Diving position in which the body is bent at the hips and the legs are kept straight.

Pull: The part of a swimming stroke in which the arm motion is exerting the most power.

Push: The final part of a swimming stroke.

Reach: The lift of the arms and the legs during the take-off from the board.

Riding the Board: The act of riding the spring of the diving board for maximum upward thrust.

Scissors Kick: A kick used in swimming sidestroke. The cycle is begun with the legs together; one leg is then thrust forward and one backward, on a plane parallel with the surface of the water. The knees are bent during the return portion of the cycle. The scissors kick is somewhat like the opening and closing of a pair of scissors.

Six-Beat Crawl: A version of the crawl in which there are six beats of the legs in a flutter-style kick to one full arm cycle. Most common version of the crawl.

Stroke: The arm action during swimming.

Tuck: Position in which a diver is curled into a ball.

TABLE TENNIS

Note: Many of the terms in Table Tennis and Outdoor Tennis are similar.

Ace: A serve that is not returned by the opponent.

Ad: Abbreviation for Advantage. Advantage: First score after deuce (tie at 20-all).

All: Same as tie, that is, 20-all.

Backhand: Stroke used with the back of the hand facing the opponent.

Backspin: Stroke in which the ball spins towards the server.

Ball: Made of celluloid, approximately 4 ¼ inches in diameter, hollow, and weighing 37-41 grams.

Chop: Stroke hit with a downward stroke of the paddle, giving the ball backspin.

Dead Ball: Called when the ball bounces twice on the table, or after a point.

Deuce: When the score is tied 20-all. Winner must score two consecutive points.

Drop Shot: Shot played so that it dies before the opponent can return it.

Finger Spin: Spin imparted by the server's fingers during the serve. Illegal technique.

Forehand: Opposite of backhand. Stroke with the palm of the hand facing the opponent.

Game: The winner in table tennis is the player who first scores 21 points, or two consecutive points after deuce.

Let: Means "play the point over" and occurs if the ball touches the top of the net and falls into the opponent's court after a serve.

Mixed Doubles: Male and female player as a team.

Net: Table tennis net is mesh. The top of the net is 6 inches above the table.

Push Shot: Ball is stuck with a pushing motion of the paddle so there is no spin on the ball.

Slice: Stroke with the paddle so that the ball spins away from the server.

Slice: A late stroke so the ball spins away from the paddle.

Volley: Illegal stroke of the ball while it is in the air, and before it has touched the table.

TENNIS

Ace: Serve that is not returned by the opponent. Scores a point.

Ad: Abbreviation for Advantage. Advantage: The point scored immediately after deuce. If the same player scores the next point, that player wins. If the opponent scores the next point, the score returns to deuce.

Advantage Court: The left-hand service court.

Alley: The area between the singles and doubles sideline on each side of the court. The singles court is made 4½ feet wider for doubles play with the addition of the alley.

All-Court Game: Style of play that includes both net play and baseline play.

Approach Shot: Made when a player makes a shot and approaches the net.

Backcourt: The area of the court near the base lines, as opposed to the area near the net.

Backhand: Shot made with the back of the hand facing the net or opponent.

Backspin: A stroke that imparts spin on the ball in the direction of the server.

Baseline: End boundaries of the court, 39 feet from the net.

Break: To win a game served by the opponent.

Break Point: When the score is love-40, 15-40, or 30-40, the next point will win the game.

Bye: A term used to refer to a player who does not have to play in qualifying rounds of a tournament.

Centre Mark: Mark in the centre of the baseline, indicating the server's possible location. The server may stand to either side of the centre mark.

Changeover: A pause in a match when the players change sides of the court after odd-numbered games. They also have a chance to rest, cool off, and have something to drink. Choke: To hold the racket towards the face (strings); to shorten the grip.

Chop: A ground stroke that applies downspin to the ball.

Clay Court: Tennis court with a service of clay or that resembles clay.

Club Player: Tennis player who plays regularly at a tennis club, rather than a tournament professional.

Consolation: Rounds of a tournament in which first-time losers continue to play other losers.

Cross-Court: A shot made from one side of the court diagonally into the opposite court.

Cut Stroke: A shot in which the racket hits the ball at an angle to apply spin to the ball.

Deuce: When each player has won three points or when the score is tied after three points.

Dink: Soft shot that barely clears the net.

Double Elimination: Tournament in which no player is eliminated until he or she has lost twice.

Drop Shot: A shot that barely clears the net and that has more vertical bounce than bounce across the court.

Fault: An error, usually during the serve.

Fifteen: The first point won by a player.

Five: A scoring term used to indicate the number of games won or the number of the set. Used unofficially as an abbreviation for fifteen.

Flat Serve: A serve that has no spin.

Foot Fault: A serve declared illegal because of the placement of the feet during the serve.

Forecourt: Usually refers to the area of the court near the net.

Forty: The third point won by a player.

Game: A player has won a game in tennis when he or she has four points and is two points ahead of the opponent.

Groundstroke: A stroke that is made after the ball has bounced off the ground, as opposed to a volley, which is a stroke when the ball is in the air.

Gut: The stringing in a racket.

Handicap: A system of equalizing competition between players of unequal ability.

Kill: A powerful stroke, a ball hit so hard or placed so well that the opponent cannot possibly return it.

Let: Play in which the ball touches the top of the net and falls into the correct court. The point is replayed, as in table tennis.

Linesman: An official in tennis who observes the game and decides if the balls are in the court or not.

Lob: To hit a ball in a high arc.

Love: No score.

Love Game: Game in which a player or team fails to score a point.

Love Set: Set in which a player or team fails to score a point.

Match: Two out of three sets or three out of five.

Match Point: A point which, if won by the player, will make him or her the winner of the match.

Net Game: An individual's style of play near the net.

Out: A ball that lands out of bounds.

Overhead: Shot to return a lob, usually with an arm motion over the head. Also called "smash shot."

Poaching: To play in a partner's side of a doubles court.

Rally: Prolonged exchange of shots by both players or by members of a doubles play.

Ranking: Listing of players by their ability and records of past play.

Round Robin: Type of tournament in which all players play all other players.

Seeding: Placing top tournament players in a tournament in such a way that they will not compete against each other until the final rounds.

Service Line: The line drawn across the court 21 feet from the net and parallel to the net.

Set: The first player to win six games provided that the player is at least two games ahead of the opponent (6-3, 6-4, 7-5, etc).

Set Point: A point that, if won by the player, gives him or her the set.

Smash: A stroke used to return a lob, usually powerfully.

Slow Court: A court with a rough surface on which the ball bounces slowly or clumsily.

Stroke: The movement of hitting the ball with the racket.

Thirty: A scoring term; the second point scored by a player.

Topspin: To hit the ball to impart spin away from the server.

Unseeded: Player whose ability does not qualify him or her for special placement in a tournament.

Volley: To return a ball to the opponent by hitting it before it bounces on the ground.

Wightman Cup: Trophy awarded to the winner of the annual tournament between the top women's team from the U.S. and the top women's team from England. Held alternately in the U.S. and England.

Wimbledon: The All England Lawn Tennis Championship played annually in the summer at the All England Tennis and Croquet, Wimbledon, London. Begun in 1877, it became an open event in 1968. The tennis equivalent of the Super Bowl in professional football.

TRACK & FIELD

Anchor: Last runner in a relay team.

Baton: Metal, cardboard, wood, or plastic cylinder that is passed from runner to runner in a relay race.

Crossbar: Metal or wood bar about 16 feet long that serves as an obstacle that the high jumper or pole vaulter must cross without knocking down.

Dead Heat: Tie finish between two or more runners.

Exchange Zone: Area of race track approximately 20-22 yards long where a baton pass must be made.

Flight: One lane of hurdles.

Get Set: To hold the starting position in a running race; the command just before "Go."

Go: The command to begin a running race.

Heat: Preliminary set of races in which the winners qualify for semifinal or final races.

Hurdle: Wooden or metal obstacle that a runner must leap over in a steeplechase or hurdles competition.

Lane: Path marked on a track. A runner must stay in his own lane during a specified part of a race or a complete race.

L-type Hurdle: Hurdle and base that resemble the letter L.

Mark: The spot where the broad jumper, discus, hammer, javelin, or shot lands.

On the Mark: Command to take a starting position behind the scratch line, prior to a running race.

Pace: A runner's speed, as in slow pace, fast pace.

Planting Box: Slot at the immediate front of the pole vaulting pit, where the vaulter places or plants the pole for a vault.

Pole: The inside lane of a running track; or the vaulting pole used in pole vaulting.

Preliminaries: Same as *heats*.

Qualify: To survive the heats and enter final races.

Rabbit: Runner who may lead the field during the early stages of a long race, but who may set a pace too fast to continue the lead to the finish.

Relay Leg: One runner's part of a relay race.

Scratch Line: A line that runners or jumpers must not cross before the race begins. Similar to the *line of scrimmage* in football.

Seeded: To place the fastest runners in separate heats so they do not meet until the final races.

Slipstreaming: To run slightly behind another runner so the second runner does not have to fight the wind. Also appropriate in motor sports, where one car will slipstream another.

Starting Blocks: Objects that a runner uses to keep correct foot position before a race begins.

Stride: One step in a running race.

Take-Off Board: Board that a broad jumper uses to begin his jump from.

Throwing Section: Area in which a thrown object (javelin, discus, etc.) must land.

Toeboard: Board that a shot-putter must not step on or across during the act of putting the shot.

Trail: One attempt in field events; one javelin throw, and so on.

Trial Heat: Same as *heat*.

VOLLEYBALL

Antenna: 2½- to 3-foot high vertical rod attached to each side of the net. If a ball hits the antenna, it is out of play.

Attack Block: An attempt to block the ball before it crosses the net.

Block: A defensive move to intercept the ball near the net.

Bump Pass: An underhand pass using the forearms to strike the ball.

Contacted Ball: A ball that has been touched by any part of a player's body.

Court: Playing court should be 59 feet by 29 feet, 6 inches, with a centre line under the net.

Dig: Underhand pass made near the floor level.

Dive: A low attempt to block a ball from hitting the floor.

Double Block: A block at the net by two team members.

Floater Serve: A serve that travels erratically. Foul: Illegal play.

Game: Volleyball games are won when a team first reaches 15 points with a 2-point advantage.

Net: Top of net should be 7 feet, 11¾ inches for men; 7 feet, 4½ inches for women.

Netting: Making contact with the net while the ball is in play. Offending team loses possession of the ball or the loss of one point.

Off-Speed Spike: A slow spike.

Out of Bounds: Ball is out of bounds if it strikes any object out of the court, or if it strikes the antenna.

Overhand Pass: Pass made with both hands held head-high.

Scoring: One point is awarded for each score. Only a serving team may score a point.

Serving: The act of putting the ball into play by propelling it over the net and into the opponent's court.

Set: An overhead pass designed to allow a teammate to spike the ball.

Spike: A ball hit hard into the opponent's court.

Spiker: Player who performs a spike.

Spin Serve: Serve that has spin imparted by wrist action.

Side Out: Exchange of serve after a previous serving team fails to score.

Thrown Ball: Judgment by an official that the ball was momentarily caught or came to rest. Penalty results.

Underhand Serve: Basic serve in which the ball is struck with the heel of the server's hand.

WEIGHTLIFTING

Barbell: A steel bar approximately 5-6 feet long, with wheel-shaped or disc-shaped weights attached to each end for weightlifting.

Cheating: To lift weights by using muscle groups not appropriate to that event, or to use a body position not appropriate to that event.

Class: Group of contestants as determined by weight. In U.S. powerlifting, the classes are:

Bantam Weight	123½ lbs.
Featherweight	132¼ lbs.
Lightweight	148¾ lbs.
Middleweight	165¼ lbs.
Light Heavyweight	181¾ lbs.

Middle Heavyweight	198¼ lbs.
Heavyweight	220¼ lbs.
Light Super Heavyweight	242½ lbs.
Super Heavyweight	Unlimited

These divisions are the same for International Powerlifting, except that there is no Light Super Heavyweight division. These are also the same for Olympic weightlifting, except that there is no Light Super Heavyweight division.

Clean: First action in a Clean & Jerk competition. To lift the barbell to shoulder height before it is jerked overhead.

Disqualification: To void a lift or other action because of a rules violation.

Dumbbell: Short barbell, 10-20 inches long, used for hand and arm lifts.

Repetition: To repeat a lift or action.

Reverse Grip: A grip in which the knuckles of one hand are under the bar and the knuckles of the other hand are over the bar.

Set: A predetermined number of repetitions.

Steroids: Drugs used by some weightlifters, football players, and other athletes to build muscle bulk. The use of steroids is certainly controversial and potentially harmful.

Supine Position: Lifting position lying down.

BIBLIOGRAPHY

"Aikman keeps fortunes in perspective". (January 29). *The Dallas Morning News*, 1994

"Aikman recalls little of NFC title game". (January 25). *The Dallas Morning News*, p. B17, 1994

"Aikman to skip Pro Bowl". (January 29). *The Dallas Morning News*, 1994

"Air service plentiful to Atlanta". (January 25). *The Dallas Morning News*, p. B23, 1994

"All things considered, Cowboys will beat Bills". (January 30). *The Dallas Morning News*, 1994

"Apple spot at core of Super ads". (January 27). *The Dallas Morning News*, p. 24B, 1994

"Artificial turf gives groundskeeper a new set of worries". (January 30). *The Dallas Morning News*, 1994

"Atlanta develops habit of drawing big events". (January 28). *The Dallas Morning News*, 1994

"Atlanta hotel manager compares city to Dallas". (January 26). *The Dallas Morning News*, B14, 1994

"Atlanta's top tables are taken". (January 25). *The Dallas Morning News*, p. B23, 1994

Albom M. (September). "Fontes losing hearts of QBs". *The Detroit Free Press*, 1993

Albom M. "A tragedy too easy to ignore". In F. Deford (Ed.), *The best American sports writing,* 1993 (pp. 409-415). Boston: Houghton Mifflin, 1994

Andersen, Mark B. *Doing Sports Psychology*. Human Kinetics, 2000

Anderson D. (February 20). "Keney M. applies for commissioner". *The New York Times*, 1994

Aschburner S. (March). [Article about the San Antonio Spurs basketball team]. *Minneapolis Star and Tribune*, 1994

Asimov, Isaac. *The Brain*. Boston, MA: Houghton Mifflin, 1963.

Associated Press. (December). [Article about Indiana University basketball coach Bobby Knight], 1993

Associated Press. (February). [Profile of Olympic ski star Picabo Street], 1994

"Bills don't qualify as lovable losers". (January 27). *The Dallas Morning News*, p. 22B, 1994

"Bills enter Atlanta prepared for questions about futility". (January 25). *The Dallas Morning News*, p. B20, 1994

"Bills still Buffaloed by Super Circus: Bet Cowboys". (1994, January 29). *The Dallas Morning News.*

Baker, William J. *Sports in the Western World.* Rev. ed. Urbana: University of Illinois Press, 1988.

Bandler, Richard. *Using Your Brain for a Change.* Moab, UT: Real People Press, 1985.

Barreiro D. (May). "Rough play in NBA not new or outrageous". *The Minneapolis-St. Paul Star Tribune*, 1994

Barry D. "The old ball game". In F. Deford (Ed.), *The best American sports stories* (pp. 304-321), 1994

Baum, Ken; Trubo, Richard. *The Mental Edge : Maximize Your Sports Potential With the Mind/Body Connection.* Perigee, 1999.

Bedard P. (April). "Dodge Neon". *Car and Driver*, p. 57, 1994

Bedell D. (May 1). "A & M bowl funds go to purchase gifts". *The Dallas Morning News*, pp. 1, 1994

Benson, Herbert, M.D. et al. "Historical and Clinical Considerations of the Relaxation Response." In *American Scientist*, July-August, 1977

Best N. (November). [Article about runner Keith Brantly]. Newsday, 1993

Blanchard, Ken; Shula, Don. The Little Book of Coaching : Motivating People to Be Winners. Harperbusiness, 2001

Brockopp, Gene W. "Review of Research on Multi-Modal Sensory Stimulation with Clinical Considerations and Research Proposals. 1984

Burke, Ed; Burke, Edmund R. *Cycling Health and Physiology : Using Sports Science to Improve Your Riding and Racing.* Vitesse Pr., 1999

Cade, C. Maxwell. *The Awakened Mind: Biofeedback and the Development of Higher States of Awareness*. New York: New American Library, 1980

Cahn, Susan K. *Coming on Strong: Gender and Sexuality in Twentieth-Century Women's* Sports. New York: Free Press, 1994

Chernow, Fred B. *The Sharper Mind. Mental Games for a Keen Mind and Foolproof Memory*. New Jersey: Prentice Hall, Inc., 1997

Cohn, Patrick J. *Peak Performance Golf: How Good Golfers Become Great Ones*. Contemporary Books, 2000

Cooper, Andrew. *Playing in the Zone : Exploring the Spiritual Dimensions of Sports* Shambhala, 1992

Counsilman, James, E. *The Science of Swimming*. Englewood Cliffs, NJ: Prentice Hall, Inc., 1994

Csikszentmihalyi, Mihalyi. *Beyond Boredom and Anxiety: The Experience of Play in Work and Games*. San Francisco, CA: Jossey-Bass, 1975

Cypert, Samuel A. *Believe And Achieve: W. Clement Stone's 17 Principles Of Success*. Avon, 1991

Davies, Philippa. *Total Confidence*. London, England: Piatkus Publishing, 1994

Dawson, Roger. *The 13 Secrets of Power Performance*. New Jersey: Prentice Hall, Inc., 1994

Douillard, John; King, Billie Jean; Navratilova, Martina. *Body, Mind and Sports: The Mind-Body Guide to Lifelong Health, Fitness, and Your Personal Best*. Three Rivers Press, 2001

Dyreson, Mark. *Making the American Team: Sports, Culture, and the Olympic Experience*. Urbana: University of Illinois Press, 1998

Ehret, Charles and Lyn Scanlon. *Overcoming Jet Lag*. New York, NY: Berkeley Publishing, 1983

Enhanger, Kjell. *Quantum Golf: The Path to Golf Mastery*. Warner Books, 1992

Enos, Brian. *Practical Shooting*. Clifton, CA: Zediker Publishing, 1990

Evers, Anne Marie; Pulos, Lee. *Affirmations—Your Passport to Happiness*. Berkana Books, 1999

Fehmi, Lester F. and George Fritz. "Openfocus! The Attentional Foundation of Health and Well-Being". *Somatics*, Spring, 1980

Flow: The Psychology of Optimal Experience. HarperCollins, 1991

Gardner, Howard. *Frames of Mind.* New York, NY: Basic Books, 1983

Gawain,Shakti. *Creative Visualization : Use the Power of Your Imagination to Create What You Want in Your Life*. New World Library, 1995

Gaynor, Mitchell L.,M.D. *Sounds of Healing: A Physician Reveals the Therapeutic Power of Sound, Voice, and Music.* Broadway Books, 1999

Graham, Deborah; Stabler, Jon. *The 8 Traits of Champion Golfers: How to Develop the Mental Game of a Pro.* Simon & Schuster, 2000

Greene, Don, Ph.D. *Fight Your Fear and Win : Seven Skills for Performing Your Best Under Pressure—At Work, in Sports, on Stage* Broadway Books, 2001

Games and Empires: Modern Sports and Cultural Imperialism. New York: Columbia University Press, 1994.

Gross, Ronald. *Peak Learning.* New York, NY: Tarcher, 1991

Guttmann, Allen. *From Ritual to Record: The Nature of Modern Sports.* New York: Columbia University Press, 1978

Hannaford, Carla, Ph.D. *Smart Moves.* Arlington, VA: Great Ocean Publishers, 1995

Hill, Napoleon and Stone, W. Clement. *Success Through A Positive Mental Attitude.* Simon & Schuster, reissue 1992

Holt, Richard. *Sports and the British: A Modern History.* New York: Oxford University Press, 1989

Holtz, Lou; MacKay, Harvey. *Winning Everyday.* HarperBusiness, 1998

Howell, Colin. *Blood, Sweat and Cheers: Sports and the Making of Modern Canada.* Toronto: Toronto University Press, 2001

Hughes, Thomas. *Tom Brown's Schooldays.* Edited with an introduction by Andrew Sanders. New York: Oxford University Press, 1989. First published in 1857

Hutchison, Michael. *MegaBrain: New Tools and Techniques for Brain Growth and Mind Expansion.* New York, NY: Ballantine, 1991

Inlander, Charles and Cynthia Moran. *62 Natural Ways to Beat Jet Lag.* New York, NY: St. Martin Paperbacks, 1997

James, C. L. R. *Beyond a Boundary.* Durham, N.C.: Duke University Press, 1993. Originally published in 1963

Johnson, Rebecca and Bill Tulin. *Travel Fitness.* Champaign, IL: Human Kinetics Publishing, 1958

Jackson, Susan A. Flow in Sports: *The Keys To Optimal Experiences And Performances.* Human Kinetics, 1999

Jones, Charlie; Deford, Frank. *What Makes Winners Win: Over 100 Athletes, Coaches, and Managers Tell You the Secrets of Success.* Bantam Books, 1998

Kyle, Donald G. *Spectacles of Death in Ancient Rome.* London: Routledge, 1998

Klipper, Miriam Z. *The Relaxation Response.* Wholecare, 2000.

LaFeber, Walter. *Michael Jordan and the New Global Capitalism.* New York: W. W. Norton, 1999

Leverte Farley, Kara; Curry, Sheila M. *Get Motivated!: Daily Psyche-Ups.* Fireside, 1994

Lewis, David and James Greene. *Thinking Better.* New York, NY: Holt, 1982

Liggett, Donald. *Sports Hypnosis.* Human Kinetics, 2000

Lilly, John C. *Programming and Meta-Programming in The Human Bio-Computer.* New York, NY: Julian Press, 1972

Lombardi, Vince, Jr. *What It Takes To Be Number #1: Vince Lombardi on Leadership.* McGraw-Hill, 2000

Mack, Gary; Casstevens, David and Rodriguez, Alex. *Mind Gym: An Athlete's Guide to Inner Excellence.* NTC Publishing, 2001

Mackenzie, Marlin. *Golf: The Mind Game.* New York, NY: Dell Paperbacks, 1990

Maglischo, Ernest. *Swimming Faster.* Human Kinetics, 2001

Miller, Saul; Hill, Peggy Maass. *Sports Psychology for Cyclists.* Velo Press, 1999

Millman, Dan. Body Mind Mastery: *Creating Success In Sports And Life*. New World Library, 1999

Murphy, Joseph, Ph.D. *The Power of Your Subconscious Mind*. Englewood Cliffs: Prentice Hall, Inc., 1963

Murray, Bill. *The World's Game: A History of Soccer*. Urbana: University of Illinois Press, 1996

Nideffer, Robert M. *Psyched to Win*. Human Kinetics, 1992

Oriard, Michael. *King Football: Sports and Spectacle in the Golden Age of Radio and Newsreels, Movies and Magazines, the Weekly and the Daily Press*. Chapel Hill: University of North Carolina Press, 2001

Orlick, Terry. *In Pursuit of Excellence : How to Win in Sports and Life Through Mental Training*. Human Kinetics, 2000

Ornstein, Robert, and Richard F. Thompson. *The Amazing Brain*. Boston: Houghton Mifflin Company, 1984

Packer, Billy. *Why We Win : Great American Coaches Offer Their Strategies for Success in Sports and Life*. NTC Publishing, 1999

Riley, Pat. *The Winner Within: A Life Plan For Team Players*. Berkeley Publishing Group, 1994

Robbins, Jim. *A Symphony in the Brain: The Evolution of the New Brain Wave Biofeedback*. New York: Atlantic Monthly Press. Inc., 2000

Sandoz, Joli; Winans, Joby. *Whatever It Takes: Women on Women's Sports*. Farrar Straus & Giroux, 1999

Silby, Caroline, Ph.D., Smith, Shelley. *Games Girls Play : Understanding and Guiding Young Female Athletes*. St. Martin's Press, 2000

Skiing: The Mind Game. New York, NY: Dell Paperbacks, 1993

Singer, Robert N. *Handbook of Sports Psychology*. John Wiley & Sons, 2001

Thompson, Jim. *Shooting in the Dark: Tales of Coaching and Leadership*. Warde Publishing, 1998

Tracy, Brian; Wood, Andrew. The Traits of Champions: The Secrets to Championship Performance in Business, Golf, and Life. Executive Excellence, 2000

Tennis: The Mind Game. New York, NY: Dell Paperbacks, 1993

"The Mental Edge." Outside Magazine. April, p. 131-134, 2001

Ungerleider, Steven *Mental Training for Peak Performance : Top Athletes Reveal the Mind Exercises They Use to Excel.* Rodale Press, 1994

Van Raalte, Judy L.; Brewer, Britton W. *Exploring Sports and Exercise Psychology.* American Psychological Association, 1996

Vernacchia, Ralph; McGuire, Rick T., et. al. *Coaching Mental Excellence : It Does Matter Whether You Win or Lose.* Warde Publishers, 1996

Waitley, Dennis. *Being The Best.* Pocket Books, 1988

Warren, William E. *Coaching and Motivation: A Practical Guide to Maximum Athletic Performance,* Prentice Hall, 1991

Whitten, Phillip. Ph.D. *The Complete Book of Swimming.* New York, NY: Random House, 1994

Wilson, Susan M. *Sports Her Way: Motivating Girls to Start and Stay With Sports.* Simon & Schuster, 2000

Winter, Arthur, M.D. and Ruth Winters, M.S, *Brain Workout: Easy Ways to Power Up Your Memory, Sensory Perception, and Intelligence.* New York: St. Martin Press, Inc., 1997

Wise, Anna The High-Performance Mind : Mastering Brainwaves for Insight, Healing, and Creativity. JP Tarcher, 1997

Wooden, John R.; Jamison, Steve. *Wooden: A Lifetime of Observations and Reflections on and Off the Court.* NTC Publishing, 1997

Yates, Brad. *Fuel The Fire, Perform With Passion.* HiLevel Productions, 1998

Young, David C. *The Olympic Myth of Greek Amateur Athletics.* Chicago: Ares, 1984

Zimmerman, Jean; Reavill, Gil. *Raising Our Athletic Daughters: How Sports Can Build Self-Esteem and Save Girl's Lives.* Main Steet Books, 1999